Community schooling and the nature of power

In 1981 Liverpool Council ordered the closure of Croxteth Comprehensive because of falling rolls. The local residents protested and, when this failed, occupied the school and for a year ran it themselves with the help of volunteer teachers. Phil Carspecken was one of those volunteers, and this book tells the story of that year of community schooling. The period was marked by intense conflict among the members of the militant action committee running the school, and attempts by far left political organisations to take over the movement. At the same time, within the school, traditional teaching methods were gradually modified to reflect the culture and aspirations of the working-class community which used it. Carspecken places all these events within a framework of sociological interpretation, developing throughout the book a new theory of intersubjectivity and its relation to power, and he concludes with an assessment of the lessons of Croxteth for schooling in other deprived urban communities, not only in the UK, but also in the rest of Europe and in the United States.

Phil Francis Carspecken is currently Assistant Professor of The Sociology of Education at the University of Houston. He is engaged in research on community–school relations in urban settings and the development of theory on social movements.

Activists in the Croxteth occupation, July 1983
Source: Open Eye Gallery, Liverpool

Community schooling and the nature of power
The battle for Croxteth Comprehensive

Phil Francis Carspecken

London and New York

First published 1991
by Routledge
11 New Fetter Lane, London EC4P 4EE

Simultaneously published in the USA and Canada
by Routledge
a division of Routledge, Chapman and Hall, Inc.
29 West 35th Street, New York, NY 10001

© 1991 Phil Francis Carspecken

Typeset from the author's wordprocessor disks by
Michael Mepham, Frome, Somerset, BA11 2HH
Printed and bound in Great Britain by
Biddles Ltd, Guildford and King's Lynn

British Library Cataloguing in Publication Data
Carspecken, Phil Francis
  Community schooling and the nature of power : the battle
  for Croxteth Comprehensive.
  1. Merseyside. Liverpool. Croxteth. Comprehensive schools
  I. Title
  373.42953
  ISBN 0-415-03560-0

Library of Congress Cataloging in Publication Data
Carspecken, Phil Francis, 1951–
  Community schooling and the nature of power : an analysis
  of the battle for Croxteth Comprehensive / Phil Francis
  Carspecken.
     p.   cm.
  Includes bibliographical references (p. 204) and index.
  ISBN 0-415-03560-0
  1. Community and school—England—Liverpool.
  2. Community education—England—Liverpool. 3. Croxteth
  Comprehensive School.
  I. Title.
  LC221.4.G7C37   1990
  370.19'4'0942753—dc20   90–38746
                                                           CIP

Contents

For my parents,
Margaret and Phil Carspecken

Foreword

In a time of Rightist resurgence, there are few questions more important than the following ones. How can communities be mobilized to support educational change? How can they be mobilized to defend the gains that have been made? Is it possible to build alliances, even across class boundaries, among different groups within that community that last, that can actually succeed in fundamentally altering the ways decisions are often made and who benefits from them?

A key word here is community, and the idea (and ideal) of community is essential to this volume. Phil Carspecken grounds his analysis in the literature and history of community education. His book concerns one instance in which the residents of a working-class community took over a local school that was to be closed and ran it with sympathetic teachers, activists, and others for two years. Yet *Community Schooling and the Nature of Power* is ultimately about power, about how it works, who has it, and what can and cannot be done about it in education.

Education, as we know, is inherently a political process. By its very nature as an act of influence, it embodies concepts of justice and power. Perhaps this can be made clearer when we consider the fact that even though schooling has been the result of historic struggles between and among dominating and dominated groups – a number of which struggles have resulted in democratic gains – it is still the case that our educational institutions roughly reproduce the social, sexual, and racial divisions of the larger society. They do not do this alone, of course, but it is clear that schooling is deeply implicated in the production of differential power.

Just as important are the politics of curriculum and teaching. Certain groups' knowledge is legitimate knowledge. Other groups' knowledge is simply never found within the official corpus of school knowledge. Teaching – an act done so often by women – is subject to greater centralized control and deskilling, thereby demonstrating the historical relationship between patriarchal relations and the politics of education as well.[1]

Finally, to do anything different in schools as we know them – with their increasingly bureaucratized styles that stress efficiency, the accountant's 'bottom line', industrial models of accountability, and so on – requires that we take politics very seriously. Unless we can deal effectively with internal power relations within the school, the local county, or at a national level, we will simply fail in the end to make a difference.

These are not abstract issues. They are played out every day as so many committed groups attempt to withstand the right as it strives to create the conditions for a new hegemonic accord under its leadership.

What the right has attempted to do has been to convince the citizenry that what is public is bad and what is private is good. This has, of course, required a good deal of hard ideological work. In its most abstract sense, what we are witnessing today is nothing less than the recurrent conflict between property rights and person rights that has been a central tension in our economy. On a less abstract level, Hugh Stetton evokes a sense of what is going on when he says that:

> The commonest trick is this: of people's individual spending, mention *only the prices they pay*. When they buy a private car and a public road to drive it on, present the car as a benefit and the road as a tax or a cost. Tell how the private sector is the productive sector which gives us food, clothing, houses, cars, holidays and all good things, while the public sector gives us nothing but red tape and tax demands.[2]

In the process of doing this, the right in the United States and Britain has thoroughly renovated and reformed itself. It has developed strategies based upon what Hall has so nicely called an 'authoritarian populism'.[3] Such a policy is rooted in an increasingly close relationship between government and the capitalist economy, a radical decline in the institutions and power of political democracy, and attempts at curtailing 'liberties' that have been gained in the past. The strategy entails the attempted dismantling of the welfare state and of the benefits that working people, people of colour, and women (these categories are obviously not mutually exclusive) have won over decades of hard work. This has been done under the guise of anti-statism, of keeping government 'off the backs of the people', and of 'free enterprise'. Yet, as is immediately clear to anyone who is living through this period, in many cultural, political, and economic areas the current government is extremely state-centrist both in its outlook and very importantly in its day-to-day operations.[4]

Education has been one of the hardest hit areas during the current conservative restoration. It has been placed under severe ideological scrutiny in terms of the attacks on the curriculum, on the rights of teachers, and on the power of 'minority' groups to gain an education that is culturally responsive. At the same time, education has been subject to immense fiscal pressures. Schools have been closed and consolidated, and have had their budgets squeezed mercilessly by a rapidly centralizing authority that cares more for the bottom line and the use of the school in meeting only the needs established by business and industry than it does about the lives, hopes, and dreams of the communities, students, and teachers who now inhabit these schools.

What happens when these ideological and fiscal pressures actually intervene at the level of the daily lives of schools? When a school is about to be closed, does the community sit back and passively acquiesce, knowing that 'nothing can be done'? Enter Phil Carspecken. He has presented us with a fascinating account of the internal workings of just such a school. It has much to offer any of us who are committed to expanding democracy in all our institutions, and especially to those readers who wish to explore the possibilities and contradictions of doing this in educational institutions.

Carspecken has written this book in a way that is more than a little unique. He tells the story of the battle for Croxteth Comprehensive without losing the complexities involved in situations such as this. Class and age relations, the partly hidden gender dynamics at work in this case, the internal conflicts within movements for more democratic educational practices, the political alliances and shifts that are ever present when power is being contested, all of these are present in his account. Yet, so much more is there as well. He has been able to integrate throughout his narrative some of the most recent theory on how ideologies actually work both to give meaning to people's lives and as contradictory representations of differential power relations. *Community Schooling and the Nature of Power*, however, doesn't treat these issues – as is the case in so much of the current literature – as abstractions to be added on to one's account. Rather, these theories are blended so nicely into the story Carspecken tells that they become part of the story itself. In this way Carspecken is employing 'critical theory' in exactly the manner Stuart Hall urges us to do. As Hall says, 'The purpose of theorizing is ... to enable us to grasp, understand, and explain – to produce a more adequate knowledge of – the historical world and its processes; and thereby to inform our practice so that we may transform it.'[5]

Finally, Phil Carspecken has chosen to write in a very personal manner. This is entirely correct since he was deeply involved in the actual day-to-day struggle to keep Croxteth Comprehensive open and functioning as a community school. Yet, it is correct in another way, for it portrays real people, himself included, in the forefront of social transformation. Rather than abstract movements, laws of history, and the like, we hear and see the victories and compromises, the possibilities and limitations, of educational struggles from the ground up. These struggles may be filled with elements

---

of what that great analyst of social change, Antonio Gramsci, called 'good' and 'bad' sense, they may be filled with contradictory beliefs, but *these are people like ourselves.* They have organized and taken action to defend and extend the substance of democracy.

This is a critically important point. Only by keeping alive the collective memory of the very possibility of such action, and of the gains and losses attached to it, can we specify the material and institutional conditions necessary for full democratic participation. *Community Schooling and the Nature of Power*, when read as carefully as its treatment deserves, will undoubtedly prove to be a very real contribution to that task.

Michael W. Apple
The University of Wisconsin, Madison

Notes

1. I have discussed these issues in considerably greater depth in a series of volumes. See Michael W. Apple, *Ideology and Curriculum* (New York and London: Routledge, revised edition, 1989), *Education and Power* (New York and London: Routledge, ARK Edition, 1985), and *Teachers and Texts: A Political Economy of Class and Gender Relations in Education* (New York and London: Routledge, 1986).
2. Hugh Stetten quoted in David Horne, *The Public Culture* (London: Pluto Press, 1986), pp. 172–3.
3. Stuart Hall, 'Popular democratic vs. authoritarian populism: two ways of taking democracy seriously', in Alan Hunt, ed. *Marxism and Democracy* (London: Lawrence & Wishart, 1980), pp. 160–1.
4. Stuart Hall, 'Authoritarian populism: a reply', *New Left Review* 151 (1985), 115–24.
5. Stuart Hall, 'The toad in the garden: Thatcherism among the theorists', in Cary Nelson and Lawrence Grossberg (eds), *Marxism and the Interpretation of Culture* (Chicago: University of Illinois Press, 1988), p. 36.

Author's preface and acknowledgements

This book tells a story – the story of Croxteth Comprehensive School which was illegally occupied and run for an entire year by working class residents of Croxteth, Liverpool. On the surface it reads primarily as an historical account, narrated by one of the participants in the events described (myself), and analysed according to a number of issues within the sociology of education. Indeed, the explicit theoretical concerns of the book are introduced in Chapter 1. They include the idea of community education and the nature of power as it applies to community–school relations. As the story proceeds, new theoretical terms are introduced, particularly in Chapter 5 where I dwell upon the intersubjective structures constructed within the school and define a number of new terms in order to do so. This expanded vocabulary is then integrated into the further narrative as it develops, becoming part of the story I wish to tell.

The reader will get more from this book, however, if something is said of the considerable body of theory I have very consciously built into it, but left largely unstated, and something of the methods I used to collect the information I present. In a very condensed manner, I have acknowledged my theoretical sources and the contributions this book implicitly makes with respect to them in the book's Appendix. As explained there, this book is constructed about an integration of social-theoretical perspectives drawn from Giddens' theory of structuration (Giddens 1976, 1979, 1984), Habermas' theory of communicative action (Habermas 1981; McCarthy 1982), and the Birmingham school of cultural studies (Johnson 1983, 1979; Willis 1976, 1981, 1983). Additionally, this book was written with the vast body of literature on social movements in mind. I explain in the Appendix that three main schools of thought on social movements are incorporated in my study though I never refer to them, for want of space, in the narrative itself. These include neo-Marxist work on urban social movements developed during the 1970s by various European sociologists; the resource mobilization school developed during this same period and extended into the 1980s by primarily

American authors; and the so-called identity school of social movements (see Appendix for references). Once again I have integrated perspectives, this time by progressively dropping my principle objects of analysis – from broad structural conditions of national and even international scope (Chapter 2) through the local government of Liverpool and the specific protest group which formed in Croxteth (Chapters 3 and 4), and finally to the individuals who participated in the struggle and their interactions (Chapters 5–9). As the Appendix explains, I found work from the different schools appropriate to the different levels of analysis highly general and abstract to highly particular and empirically concrete. Implicitly, I make use of an integrated theoretical framework for the study of social movements, applying insights from conflicting schools to the levels of abstraction for which I believe each is appropriate. Theoretical linkages between the three schools of thought are thus implied, integrated through my use of a number of key social-theoretical concepts – power being one of them (see Carspecken 1989b for an explicit discussion).

Readers who are primarily interested in sociological theory may wish to read the Appendix first, before reading the rest of the book, and then return to the Appendix after finishing the story of Croxteth. Readers who are mainly interested in the history of the Croxteth campaign, or in more surface features of educational sociology, are advised to consider the Appendix only after reading the book.

I wrote *Community Schooling and the Nature of Power* with both British and American audiences in mind. The spelling is British, as is the social context in which the events described took place. Where certain educational practices and policies come into the story which may be mysterious to the American reader, I have provided brief explanations that are sure to seem over-statements of the obvious to British readers. Although much of the literature on community education I cite is primarily British, I do occasionally reference relevant American works and will insist at the outset that this analysis of the Croxteth occupation has much to say to American educators. The approach I've developed to examine community education is essentially context-free, applicable to community–school relations in any society.

I should say something as well about two other publications which develop material presented in this book in different directions or with different emphases. Portions of Chapter 2 develop material present in a chapter I contributed to Geoff Walford's 1985 book *Schools in Turmoil* (Croom Helm – see Carspecken 1985). I have expanded portions of this material for the present book and dropped other portions. Chapters 5 and 6 develop material also present in a chapter I've written for a recent publication of the Centre for Contemporary Cultural Studies (CCCS 1990). However, the analysis in this book is far more detailed than that in the CCCS publication and linkages between political and educational themes are made explicit here where they are left implicit there. Moreover, the purposes of the analysis in the two works are different. In the CCCS chapter I address aspects of Kenneth Baker's educational reform bill, in this book I am mainly concerned with the relationship between power and intersubjective structures, with the ways in which articulations of such structures alter action, and with connections between political and educational interpretative frameworks.

Finally, I wish to acknowledge the contributions made by others to this study. First and foremost I wish to thank Henry Miller of Aston University for his immense support during my years of work in Croxteth. Henry actually taught one day a week at Croxteth during the final months of the occupation. He discussed all aspects of my study with me and commented on early drafts of what follows. Henry also conducted some of the interviews from which quotations have been taken in this book and he wrote a related study on Liverpool teachers during the period in which Croxteth Comprehensive was occupied.

Next, I learned a great deal from Richard Johnson, director of the Centre for Contemporary Cultural Studies at the University of Birmingham during two years of study there. Richard read my larger study of Croxteth (Carspecken 1987), discussed the study with me on several occasions, and directed my general studies of social theory in important ways.

Geoff Walford at Aston University discussed many early drafts of the chapters which follow and went out of his way to put me in touch with materials I have used. Henry Stewart collaborated with me on a follow-up study of Croxteth in 1984. Henry also helped with a number of tape transcriptions and co-authored a paper on the Croxteth campaign which we presented at a conference in 1984.

I also wish to thank the people of Croxteth who cooperated in every way during my study. Phil Knibb, Cyril D'Arcy, Pat Rigby, Margaret Gaskell, and Pat Brennen are all extremely astute social theoreticians in their own right and were always willing to supply me with needed information. Phil, Cyril, and Margaret have all commented on earlier drafts of portions of this study. The list of other Croxteth residents who contributed to my book is vast but unfolds throughout the story to follow. I thank every one of them both for their help and for the camaraderie we shared during the two years I spent on their estate.

Many thanks to Tracy Lilly for her excellent work on typing, format and layout of the text. Last, but not least, I thank my wife Lucinda and son Gabriel (Sunil) for their support at home during the many hours I put in on this project.

1
Power, community schools, and Croxteth

Early in the autumn of 1982 I visited a community reputed to be amongst the most deprived in all of Great Britain. Its name was Croxteth, one of Liverpool's council housing estates. I went there because I had heard that a secondary school on that estate was occupied illegally by angry parents who were protesting its closure. I intended to write an article on the school, which was named Croxteth Comprehensive. When I arrived I was invited to work long hours without pay to help the parents run a full educational programme. I immediately agreed to do it. I thought that not to volunteer would be to miss an opportunity to be part of an exciting, unique, and enlightening event unlikely to be repeated again in my lifetime. I was right. As the school months unfolded I had about as much excitement and unique teaching experience as I could take. The work was hard, the material rewards were nil, and the environment was rife with conflicts between teachers, local residents, and pupils. But in all my teaching before and since, I have never learned as much or felt as gratified as I did during the occupation of Croxteth Comprehensive. Against the odds, those of us who came and stayed to work in the school accomplished something unique and important.

Exactly what we accomplished can not be expressed in a sentence or two it took me some 300,000 words to try to capture what it was in my doctoral thesis. This book is an effort to share some of the lessons and some of the excitement of that year in Croxteth. It is both a condensation and a reanalysis of my earlier study. In writing it I had to make many difficult decisions on what to leave out. I decided to focus on only one of several theoretical areas illuminated by the battle for Croxteth Comprehensive: the power relationships which exist between working-class communities and their schools. In the course of developing my analysis I will delineate several dimensions of these power relationships, from the position of a community like Croxteth with respect to its local government, to the intersubjective frameworks through which working-class residents perceive the purposes of schooling and construct their interactions with teachers and pupils.

I have organized the book with two purposes in mind: to provide both a chronological narrative of the exciting story of Croxteth Comprehensive and a theoretical analysis of power as mediated through community–school relations, pedagogic practice, national policies on education, and intersubjective structures. This first chapter begins both: it introduces the reader to Croxteth through an account of my own discovery of the community and it sets out the central theoretical problems to be addressed throughout the rest of the book.

DISCOVERING CROXTETH

By September 1982 I had lived in England for just over one year. My wife and I had moved from London to Liverpool seven months earlier to be near friends for the birth of our son. Gabriel was two months old in September and a friend was up from London to get acquainted with him. She was the first person to draw our attention to a topic which, we learned, had frequently been in the local news during recent weeks: a Liverpool community called Croxteth had taken over its comprehensive school in protest of its closure. Lucinda and I had missed news of the event by ignoring Liverpool's daily papers in favour of the national ones. Jo showed us the articles and we learned that residents of Croxteth had just finished teaching their own summer school programme. Now they were announcing their intention to provide a full educational programme for the autumn term.

I was instantly interested in the occupation for I had taught secondary mathematics for two years in the inner city of Los Angeles just prior to my move to England in 1981. Like many urban school teachers, I had come to believe that my classroom activities were doing little to benefit the pupils who participated in them day after day. Their lives were difficult. Theft and violence were constant daily problems, as were unmet needs for economic security and a sense of dignity. Many of my students were frequently robbed and beaten by classmates, others did the robbing and beating themselves, and all had to negotiate in some way with the ghetto gangs outside who had little to do with schools, other than an occasional weekend raid on our buildings to destroy equipment and leave their gang's distinctive graffiti painted on our blackboards and walls.

I was frustrated by the cultural gap between us. I couldn't speak their language, could only make crude penetrations into their cultural system, their set of rules for winning respect and dignity, their culturally formed orientation towards the future. I was powerless, or felt powerless, locked into a complex situation in which schools seemed to be offering ways out of the ghetto at the same time that they helped to keep most pupils in. They kept them in by being a foreign institution, with a foreign culture, into which pupils were forced to go and in reaction to which most formed their identities – identities of not belonging, of rebelling in many cases, of affirming values of the outside against those we tried to offer within.

Croxteth interested me immediately because it reversed several key conditions which had constrained my work as a teacher. Instead of a state-controlled institution, it had become occupied territory in a battle between a deprived community and the local government. Instead of the usual social distance between teachers and parents, I read that both were working along-side each other to teach pupils. I wondered if the resulting educational activities were better tied to the needs of the students, and if the pedagogy was more in line with local culture and so acceptable, understandable, and ultimately beneficial to Croxteth youth.

Soon after hearing of the occupation I watched a television programme on BBC Open Door which was entirely on the Croxteth housing estate and the long battle to win back its closed school. The programme, entitled 'Who's Killing Croxteth?', displayed vivid scenes of decrepit government housing in which people lived without water or electricity for months before getting repairs. It filmed interviews with doctors who testified to serious health problems on the estate, and presented shots of a mathematics class being taught by a future friend of mine, Henry Stewart. The impression was of a school which the parents had under control, certainly with enough teachers, valiantly fighting against a great injustice which the sordid politics of the Liverpool Liberal Party had perpetrated upon them. The programme ended with shots of a public meeting held at the Croxteth Labour Club. A stocky local resident named Charles Wallace stood up and posed the rhetorical question taken for the programme's title: 'Who's killing Croxteth?' he asked in a booming voice. And then, to answer the question himself: 'The Liberal Party!'

'Where's Croxteth then, Albert?' I asked my friend Albert Perkins, a lifelong Liverpool resident and veteran of the Liverpool 'Dingle' which had also housed Ringo Star in his formative years. 'I'd like to go over there and see if they need any help.' I had decided to visit Croxteth for two reasons. I wanted to write a short article on the school for a newsletter based in London and I decided to offer my help as a youth worker, someone to set up a programme based in the occupied buildings for school-leavers. Lots of interesting things could be done, I thought. The television programme had convinced me that Croxteth didn't require any more teachers, but a youth worker might expand the scope of the occupation. 'Croxteth's just down the road, I think,' said Albert. We were living on the edge of Liverpool 8 or 'Toxteth', site of fierce riots only a year before. 'Come on,' he said, 'let's look for it in the car.'

The car ride extended as we discovered that Croxteth wasn't just 'down the road' nor just down the next road or the next. We stopped at a newsagent and got some directions, drove for another twenty minutes and stopped for more directions. Croxteth turned out to be on the very northeastern edge of Liverpool, at the borders of the city.

I retain many images of that first journey to Croxteth. Winding city streets full of trees ('Liverpool has more trees per block than any other European city,' Albert proudly told me), full of brick rowhouses, little sections of shops suddenly breaking into view around a turn and then, two or three blocks later, falling out of sight again. After a long stretch of driving, several wrong turns, and the two stops for directions, the buildings ended and a huge field opened up before us on our left, trees bordering the right. A parallel road several blocks to the left was outlined by a series of enormous white tower blocks, which I later learned were the Storrington Hays high-rises on the inner edge of Croxteth. Immediately on our left were the long playing fields of a Catholic comprehensive school, some way still ahead of us was a T-junction with thick forest facing our direction. 'That's Croxteth Hall through there, I think,' said Albert, pointing straight ahead into the trees. Croxteth Hall is the former manor home of the Earl of Sefton whose lands had extended through forested areas and fields. The expansion of Liverpool in all directions during the mid-twentieth century eventually led to the sale of the earl's lands to the city. The hall was now a museum with beautiful woods and gardens surrounding it. The Croxteth council housing estate had been built on former hunting grounds. 'This is lovely!' I said, 'So much open space and an actual wood!'

We turned left at the T-junction onto Stonebridge Lane and followed it towards the line of high-rises, Storrington Hays. After one block yet more playing fields and another Catholic comprehensive school opened on our right. 'They've got a lot of schools around here!' I said, wondering why one in particular had caused so much commotion. The buildings looked good too, a modern style, clean with many windows and coloured beige with turquoise sections about the windows and doors. I noticed that it was in the same style, right down to the colour, of most schools in Liverpool, which somewhat subtracted from the impression of freshness it gave me.

We drove past this school on our right, which I later learned was St. Swithin's, past a pub called the Dog and Gun on the left, then a boarded up old supermarket which had the word 'Co-operative' written on its ageing and battered sign. At a five-way junction I again noticed the huge tower blocks, now immediately on our left and spreading back towards Liverpool. Storrington Road intersected Stonebridge Lane here, at one corner of the Croxteth Housing Estate. The bulk of the estate lay on our right and consisted mainly of two-storey council homes linked together in great rows. Many houses in terrible condition could be seen near this junction. I later learned that this group of homes was called the 'Croxteth Triangle' and was one of two sections of the estate which had greatly deteriorated. Some had roofs which appeared burned and shredded. The area was full of broken glass and graffiti. A few windows in the devastated buildings looked outwards from obviously inhabited flats, sandwiched between the completely empty and ruined ones. In the other direction, opposite the tower blocks on our left and stretching back along the other side of Storrington Road towards Liverpool centre, were similarly devastated buildings, though older and single-storey, completely uninhabited and uninhabitable.

With the change of light we drove ahead and immediately up to another school on our left. Albert drove over and stopped so that we could read the school sign. The school had exactly the same architecture and paint as the other two schools and I could see another large playing field behind it with yet another school at the playing field's end. That made four schools within a small area, each boasting large fields. This particular playing field lay just behind the row of white tower blocks on Storrington Hays, extending from our current position back towards Liverpool centre. To our right, and across Stonebridge Lane, extended yet another large playing field just behind an infants' school, this school having an older architectural style and no paint to brighten its aged brown and red bricks. It was almost dismal. It was the fifth school I'd seen. Behind the long playing field on the right were rows of council houses extending as far as one could see from this point the Croxteth housing estate proper, a sea of brick row houses linked together and sharing this far outpost, the cleared lands of the Earl of Sefton, the very northeastern edge of Liverpool.

'Let's see,' said Albert, who had stopped just before a sign in front of the school on our left. 'St Mary's Help ... no that's not the school.' 'Another Catholic school! Keep driving then!' I said. Going slowly past St Mary's we noticed another school building on our right just past the junior school. Counting the infants' school, this was the sixth school we'd seen. A row of hedges had blocked it from our view while parked beside St Mary's. The new school, 'school number six', I thought, had a man in his late middle age standing guard at its front door. Some chairs placed in a semi-circle of large diameter on the ground near him indicated that a number of other people must have been sitting out there at some time. We pulled up into a parking lot near the school. A huge banner hung from the roof, two stories above the ground level: 'We Won by Thirty-One Votes!' it read. Windows bore various slogans painted in red and blue: 'This is YOUR school', 'Occupied'.

The building itself looked old: brick without paint, and an architectural style of the late 1930s or early 1940s. It was not a cheerful building: not many windows, each not very large, the colour being a mixture of red and grey brick of the sort which collects dew in damp climates like Liverpool. Wings extended from either side of a central area in which two main doors were located symmetrically at some distance from each other. A round quasi-tower or turret lay at the side of each door, making the building look something like a crude fortification.

'Hello,' I greeted the man standing guard, 'we came to see if you need any help.' The man looked very friendly and shook our hands. He had an unhealthy appearance, a bit too bulgy and pale, possibly in his 60s. He knocked on the door behind him, which was locked, and another man stuck his head out. This man was short and thin with the look of years of work on him, small but tough and prominent muscles with their tendons showing up through wrinkled skin. 'They've come to help – teachers,' the guard explained, pointing to us. The new man let us in with a friendly and respectful greeting and asked if we'd like some tea. He introduced himself as Dennis. Inside the front door was a long corridor running horizontally. A number of women, maybe five or six, sat there with tea cups and a couple of babies, talking amongst themselves. 'Teachers,' said Dennis. They smiled at us respectfully, but said nothing.

Dennis took us to an office just around the corner and introduced us to a slightly harassed-looking man in his middle age: 'This is Cyril – he can tell you all about it.' It was Cyril D'Arcy, the secretary of the Croxteth Community Action Committee. Cyril smiled and asked what we wanted. I then went into a rehearsed presentation of my interests and intentions. I told him we had seen the television programme and were sympathetic and that I thought we could run a youth programme for them if they wanted. 'What we really need is teachers!' said Cyril. 'We're supposed to be running this as a school next Monday and so far we only have a few teachers.' 'Really! It looked on the television like you had enough,' I said. Cyril just smiled, a bit slyly, and I got his meaning – the programme had been a PR stunt, at least in part. He explained that he couldn't talk to us long as he had a meeting to attend about the school. 'A lot of it has been on me lately because our chair's not here, Phil Knibb. He's off the estate working a job. But he should be back soon. It'll be better when he's back.' Cyril moved us out of the office as he talked, beckoned to Dennis and asked him to show us around. 'Remember that we need teachers!' were his departing words.

Albert and I had a cup of tea and talked a bit with the women sitting in the corridor. They looked relaxed compared with Cyril. I asked them a few questions, intending to quote them for my article. 'If this school goes, the whole community will go,' said one. 'We don't have anything in this community. If it goes, I'll go.' I quickly scribbled it all down in a notebook, though it sounded like lines used before for the newspaper, television, and radio people. Dennis gave us a tour of the school and then asked a young person named Jimmy to show us the staffroom upstairs. Jimmy had been sitting on the stairs when Albert and I talked to the women. As we walked up I said, 'You've really got something impressive going here!' 'Oh, if it weren't for some of the left-wingers it'd be all right,' he answered. 'Who?' Albert asked. 'We've had a couple from the WRP who've just about wrecked it.' 'Who's in the WRP?' Albert asked. 'Two of the teachers.' We didn't see any teachers but Jimmy didn't elaborate. The WRP, Albert explained on the way home, stood for Workers' Revolutionary Party – a Trotskyist organization, small but well-financed through the support of such wealthy notables as Vanessa Redgrave, the actress.

After seeing the staffroom Dennis asked the guard, whose name was Joe, to take us over to the other building. Croxteth Comprehensive, we learned, had two buildings, this one called Stonebridge and another across the long playing field behind it called Parkstile. It was a long walk along the edge of the playing fields. Ahead was an extremely narrow, polluted-looking river which cut the playing fields in two. 'That's the River Alt,' said Joe. Across a narrow bridge the playing fields sloped up towards the back of a much newer building, much in the style of the Catholic school buildings we'd noticed during the drive. Compared with Stonebridge, this one looked cheerful and light. We walked around to its front and Joe again had to bang on the door as it was locked. A woman looked through the window. 'Teachers,' explained Joe, 'give 'em a look.' She let us in and Joe left us to return to his post outside Stonebridge.

We were taken to a classroom just around the corner from the main doors which was full of blankets, mattresses, and a number of placards obviously used for demonstrations. Introductions, chatting over the obligatory tea, a short tour through the much nicer, it seemed to me, rooms of the Parkstile building, and then an invitation to see some of Croxteth. 'OK,' I said, and Pat Irving, treasurer of the Croxteth Community Action Committee, led me through the school gates and onto one of the more central roads of the Croxteth Housing Estate. After a short block of housing we entered a single block of shops. The Croxteth-Gillmoss Federation office lay on the corner to our left. To the right was the Lobster Pub, and all along the left were small shops: a chippy, a newsagent, butcher, fruit and vegetable shop, and at the end a very small library. Pat pointed out the last: 'They're trying to close that too.' Pat was reserved and seemed to have a number of emotions under tight control as she pointed out buildings and explained the wrongs of Croxteth to me. There was anger there, or something akin to it.

Back at the school Albert and I were told of a public meeting which was to be held the next Friday night, a few days away, for people wanting to know about the autumn term. We agreed to come to the meeting and drove off, this time taking Storrington Road, bordering the tall white tower blocks we'd noticed before. As we drove up the road a bus coming from the opposite direction approached and passed us. I looked at the number and name: '14 Croxteth', the bus I'd take nearly every day for the next two years.

POWER AND COMMUNITY EDUCATION

What is a community?

In Los Angeles I had felt isolated from the community of my pupils; in Liverpool I became drawn to Croxteth because the community had taken its school over. 'Community' was obviously an important term for me, as it is for many people. Yet what does it mean exactly? Within sociological circles the term has gained notoriety for its vague and misleading qualities (Bell and Newby 1976). Since this book is essentially about community–school relations analysed partly through the theory of community education, some initial comments on its meaning are in order.

I will distinguish between a strong and a weak sense of the term 'community'. There are many schools which draw their pupils from a fairly homogeneous socio-economic and/or ethnic population surrounding them. The schools in which I taught during my Los Angeles years were of this type as was (and still is) Croxteth Comprehensive. Class relations and ethnic relations are broad features of society as a whole which structure the most general conditions of our lives. Class and ethnic cultures thus bear similarities across society, for they are produced and transmitted through the generations in response to the common living conditions of their members. Where such broadly drawn groupings coincide with geographic locality, the makings for a community in the strong sense exist. Residents will share certain cultural outlooks and values and will have similar interests to protect. Cultural resources will thus exist by which to integrate social routines with neighbours and construct a group identity based on geographical residence. The strong sense of the term community, then, refers to a cultural product the development of a common identity based on a common residential area. This cultural product will be affected by non-cultural conditions: the degree to which residents share a class or ethnic position in society, the extent to which residents remain in the area for significant periods of time, the existence of common interests shared by neighbours.

However, there are many other schools which draw students from a large variety of social and ethnic groupings, and even from a variety of geographic areas as some schools bus significant proportions of their student bodies in each day. This is especially common in the United States, where government policy has attempted to integrate schools along both class and ethnic lines. There are also school neighbourhoods with high turnover rates. There is little opportunity for processes of social integration to take place amongst the parents at schools like these, and therefore it may be misleading to speak of 'school–community relations' for such schools. 'Community' becomes a weak term, applied to the aggregate of families sending their children to the school or living within its proximity. There may be few structural features linking the interests of such groups of families in a way to facilitate a common identity. Indeed, in most cases the only set of interests held in common by such families would be certain gross features of the school itself – its budget, its teacher–pupil ratio, and so on. Because of cultural differences between the groups sending children to such schools, many issues pertaining to the school could be areas of conflict: the use of ability grouping, pedagogic styles, assessment procedures, and curricular policies will affect diverse populations attending a school in diverse ways.

Advocates of community education, whose theories will be reviewed and critiqued below, have generally sought one of two quite distinct objectives. Some have sought to use existing communities (in the strong sense of the term) as a resource to alter educational practices for the benefit of the pupils. Others have proposed to 'create' communities through a supposedly common interest shared by all parents with children in a single school, regardless of their divisions along class and ethnic lines (Williams, M. 1989). I won't spend any time comparing these two approaches but will simply state at the outset that my interest in this study is in the former approach rather than the latter. Croxteth was already a community before its school takeover. Residents were very homogeneous with respect to their class and ethnic status. Moreover, in both Britain and the United States many schools continue to serve communities like the one in Croxteth. Although this study of the Croxteth occupation throws much light on the experiences of working-class children in schools generally, and on the attitudes of their parents towards education, it is also capable of addressing the specific concerns of those schools serving homogeneous populations. The extent to which such communities may be mobilized to alter educational practices in their favour will consequently be a central focus in what follows. Applications of my findings to the weaker sense of community–school relations exist, but will be left for future studies.

Power and education

Theorizing the relationship of disadvantaged communities (in the strong sense discussed above) to their schools requires a theory of power. The power relations existing between schools and communities involve a number of levels or dimensions. On the most obvious level there is the question of what formal access members of such communities have to the government decision-making procedures which determine school budgets and general school policies such as assessment procedures, teaching styles, and educational goals. Similarly, the formal access allowed residents to the decision-making processes of their school itself will partly determine the power they have over the educational experiences of their children.

Formal access, however, lies only at the surface of power relations between communities and schools. Sociologists have long been aware that informal processes play a crucial role in the politics of government and institutions (Bachrach and Baratz 1970). Formal access to schools and local government may be equal for all citizens but middle- and upper-class families are frequently better able to influence teachers over their treatment of children and pressure politicians over such things as school closures and budget allocations. This is partly due to the familiarity of middle- and upper-class individuals with the culture of politicians and teachers, who are often their class peers or subordinates. They know how to approach and influence such individuals. There are thus informal as well as formal 'rules' of access to decision-making procedures which systematically offer an advantage to some groups over others (see Saunders 1983 for a detailed analysis).

Power, however, is expressed on deeper levels than those of formal or informal access to decision-making procedures. If people are fully aware of their needs and of what institutional policies will help them meet their needs, then they will be able to act in favour of their interests according to the formal and informal channels available. However, people become aware of both their needs and their ability to act in order to meet their needs only through culturally available interpretative schemes. Personal interests and the world at large are perceived through the lens of culture, and sometimes culture systematically distorts the view (see Johnson 1983). To illustrate this point, let us take some examples from the field of education. If a working-class family, in which the parent(s) work, depends upon a local school to look after its children during working hours and one day hears that this school has been proposed for closure, it will likely believe that the closure would not be in its best interest. It may, however, be accustomed to think that the 'ordinary person' can do nothing about such events which are dictated by powerful, unknown, and distant others and therefore do nothing about the situation other than plan to add more time and worry to an already crowded and stressful daily schedule in order to arrange for the transportation of its children. Its accustomed manner of perceiving such events as dictations from the powerful to the powerless rules out the possibility of seeking either formal or informal means to resist the closure. This perception, moreover, will likely be tied to past experiences and reinforced by the attitudes of friends and associates. In other words, it will be partially a culturally determined perception which effectively reduces the power of the family over important conditions of life.

On a deeper level, take the case of working-class parents whose child is doing poorly in school and intends to drop out as soon as compulsory attendance requirements allow. Their perception of their child's educational experiences and future could take a number of culturally shaped forms. They could blame their child for being lazy or 'thick' and resign themselves to her future. They could see the situation as of little significance because it corresponds to their own past experiences with school and that of their neighbour's children. The real reasons for their child's negative experience, however, would likely be related to the difference between the culture of the school and the culture the child is growing up within. Sociologists know that middle- and upper-middle-class homes have a more 'organic' relationship to the culture of schools than do working-class homes (Connell et al., 1982). The organization of knowledge (Whitty 1985), the pedagogic style (Bernstein 1977), the language dialect and system of values (Bourdieu and Passeron 1977) all better correspond to middle- and upper-middle-class groups than to lower. Yet there are few resources within working-class cultures to articulate these facts and bring them to critical awareness. Working-class families are more apt to interpret poor educational results in terms of personal faults or as being of little importance than to view them as the product of cultural disjunctions between home and school. Power, the power which maintains the dominant relation of some groups in society over others from generation to generation, is in this case expressed through cultural frameworks limiting critical awareness. Both formal and informal means to alter educational practice in the direction of the culture of the community could exist in this case and yet never come into play, for the advantages of such an alteration would not be apparent to those most affected.

Hence power enters into school–community relations in a number of ways. It involves the access communities have to the decision-making procedures affecting schooling practices, the familiarity of residents with the informal rules which determine effective use of the formal channels, and it includes the interpretative frameworks carried by culture through which residents assess their needs and their possible courses of action. Power is both a function of the resources available to various populations for pursuing conscious goals and of the cultural resources available for putting institutional practices into question, that is, for formulating appropriate goals in the first place (see Apple 1979, 1983 for an extensive analysis of power, culture, and education).

The theory of community education

Educationalists who have noted the disjunction between school culture and the culture of working-class and ethnic minority groups have made different suggestions for alleviating the difficulties it causes. I have chosen to examine one such suggestion, the theory of community education. While some theorists and policy-makers have stressed programmes to bring the culture of the school to those groups most devoid of it with compensatory pro-grammes like Head Start, advocates of community education have pushed for the opposite: to bring the culture of the school more in line with that of the pupils being taught (Boyd 1977; Williams, M. 1989). While the propo-nents of critical pedagogy have sought alterations in schooling practice by encouraging teachers to draw forth and utilize the implicit critical conscious-ness of their pupils (Giroux 1983; McLaren 1989), the architects of community education have sought such alterations through involving adults intimately in the educational activities of the school. It is because the occupation of Croxteth Comprehensive provides an excellent test case of the community education perspective that I have chosen it for my attention. The reader must bear in mind, however, that community education theory is not in competition with all other approaches. It has simply focused upon one of several variables in the same equation addressed by theories like critical pedagogy. It has focused upon adult involvement in schools instead of teaching practice *per se*. My decision to focus upon theories of community education in the analysis of the Croxteth Comprehensive occupation is simply a choice of one of many doors leading to the same cluster of concepts, the same nest of conditions, which others have studied from different perspectives.

Moderate and radical approaches

In England the idea of community education goes back at least as far as Henry Morris, who implemented a rural-based programme in Cambridgeshire dur-ing the post-World War I period (see Fletcher 1980). It was during the 1960s, however, that the concept began to be considered as a possible solution to urban school problems. Between 1968 and 1971 the Educational Priority Area (EPA) projects, run under the direction of A.H. Halsey, were carried out as experiments on the community school concept. Community schools were developed in the inner-city districts of four British cities with the goals of increasing parental awareness and involvement and adapting curricular practice to better meet community needs (Halsey 1972). The EPA projects were consciously planned as alternatives to the compensatory approach, rejecting the goal of bringing middle-class culture to the working class in favour of altering middle-class curriculum and school authority relationships to meet working-class needs. The Liverpool project, directed by Eric Midwinter, went the furthest in designing an alternative curriculum to achieve these ends. The results of the Liverpool community school looked positive (Midwinter 1972) and inspired a number of existing comprehensive schools throughout Britain to modify their programmes in the direction of community education. (For an historical review of community education in the United States see Williams, M. 1989 Chapters 5–6).

In their survey of a variety of community schools during their early stages, Hatch and Moyland (1972) found the attempt to blur community–school distinctions to be the essence of the community–schooling principle. They specified two approaches to it: a 'moderate' approach and a 'radical' one. Schools taking the moderate approach simply make their facilities available to the community after school hours and offer adult education courses. Some moderate approaches offer classes which adults and pupils attend together, and all attempt to get adult input through their governing board.

The radical approach aims at introducing a 'community curriculum' for all pupils. Learning activities based on the sorts of suggestions made by Midwinter (and David Hargreaves in more recent times, see Hargreaves 1982), and which aim at maximizing the presence of the community in the school, are key aspects of the radical version. At the same time, the radical version advocates putting schools under community control. Williams and Robins (1980) make a similar distinction to that made by Hatch and Moyland in their study of California community schools by aligning the schools they studied along a 'community education continuum' having 'programme-oriented' activities at one end and 'process-oriented' activities at the other. The process-oriented end of the pole includes aims of community action, grassroots democracy, and self-actualization, implying a combination of progressive pedagogy with local power similar to Hatch and Moyland's radical approach. It is this sense of community education, the 'radical' or 'process' sense, that will be considered in the rest of this discussion.

Problems with community education

As the 1970s proceeded, results of long-term efforts to apply the ideals of community education in various comprehensive schools became available for study and for a re-evaluation of the policy. Bob Moon (1983), in a summary of six community school case studies, concludes that a problem common to nearly all such attempts resides between the 'progressive ideas' of the educationalists and the 'conservative' attitudes of parents (p.133):

This discrepancy between the ambitions of those in the schools and the unfamiliarity of the community, represents a central dilemma in the efforts to reform comprehensive education. How is it possible to reconcile a commitment to changing what, for many young people, is clearly an unsatisfying experience with an equal commitment to acknowledging the significance and importance of community opinion on the directions the school should take?

Other writers have agreed that the objectives of community education for changing the content and style of teaching ironically run into serious obstacles from adults in the community. Bernstein, in 'Pedagogies: visible and invisible' (1977), argues that the progression of roles based on age and gender in working-class communities are in opposition to age and gender roles accompanying the progressive approach of most community schools. He thus predicts that parental understanding of the pedagogical objectives of progressive schools is nearly impossible in the case of the working class. David Hargreaves (1982) believes for similar reasons that one of the key components of the radical version of community education, the devolution of power to parents, may have to be dropped:

> At the present time it is very unlikely that parents would be strongly in favour of a community centred curriculum in a comprehensive school; it is much more likely that they would show a strong preference for the traditional curriculum.... A community centred curriculum is much more likely to be developed in a school where the head teacher and staff are committed to the notion but are highly insulated from relatively powerless and non-participating parents.
>
> (Hargreaves 1982: 124)

Yet insulation can lead to disastrous consequences, as the case of William Tyndale Primary School (where enraged parents helped to close down a school which employed 'progressive' methods without any prior communication or consultation with them; see Dale 1979) and the case of Rising Hill Comprehensive (see Berg 1968) show. More importantly, removing the components of participation and grassroots power from the notion of community education reduces the concept to a version of progressivism, an imposition of the ideas of educators upon populations they don't belong to and little understand. Thus it is not surprising that efforts at creating community schools have tended to involve changes in curriculum and school social relationships with only slight involvement of adults from the neighbourhood (Moon 1983). Power, in other words, has not devolved.

The problems encountered by community education programmes designed from above have rested partially with their limited theory of power. Power has been conceived primarily in terms of formal access to decision-making procedures within schools. Such schools usually invite local adults to attend regular meetings and to give suggestions, but this feature of the programme is the one which consistently fails in lower-income areas. While many educationalists put the blame on 'apathetic parents', the real processes involved are not captured with a term like apathy. They are rather aspects of power itself. As discussed above, power resides in levels deeper than those associated with formal decision-making. In this study of the occupation of Croxteth Comprehensive, for example, it will become clear that local attitudes to schooling in Croxteth were initially prohibitive of adult participation in educational decision-making. Croxteth residents were far from being apathetic, but felt themselves incapable of making competent contributions for reasons analysed in chapters ahead. Where they did put forth their views, their opinions took traditional and repetitive forms, arguably not in the long-term best interests of their children.

It is thus impossible to advocate the devolution of educational power to parents without taking into account cultural factors which will influence their perceptions and choices. If these cultural factors are hegemonic, that is, if they exist at tacit levels of awareness and are in reinforcing relationships with broad patterns of social inequality, simply devolving educational decision-making power may not have desirable effects on curriculum and pedagogy.

Boyd (1977) criticizes community education through an analysis of power, not by reference to cultural attitudes but rather by noting the futility of trying to empower residents with respect to their schools alone, when they have so little power over the many other conditions of their lives. Since the goal of community education is to unify 'community action' with learning, residents would have to possess the means to carry out community actions as well as the means of making educational decisions. Their relatively powerless position with respect to housing, employment, and health care means that unifying school curriculum with meaningful community action would be a mere dream without a fundamental alteration in all power relationships:

> Involvement of those living in the neighbourhood so that they cease to perceive themselves as recipients, and see themselves as agents bringing about change would seem to be a necessary condition.... Yet, paradoxically, it would seem that people in the inner city are powerless to bring about change of and by themselves.
>
> (Boyd 1977: 16–17)

Thus the radical version of community education implies the devolution of more than just educational power; it must involve the devolution of command over a score of resources which are in the hands of the local government and landowners living outside the community. There is no way in which a purely educational policy could bring this about.

In Croxteth, however, as succeeding chapters will reveal, we find a unique situation. Residents took over their school and for two years had total formal control over it. At the same time, residents had gained a significant degree of power over other local resources such as housing and health facilities, through effective organizing and campaigning. Moreover, the Croxteth Community Action Committee, the group which controlled the school occupation, made linkages to the trade union movement in both Liverpool and England as a whole and received thousands of pounds of donations to run their school and maintain their organization. Thus the disadvantaged urban community need not remain powerless, though the case of Croxteth provides no set recipe for community empowerment. A key question I will be exploring in this book is whether or not such power would have effects on educational practice in Croxteth, or, even more significantly, what effects such power could have had.

Another objection to community education has been the argument that it seeks to create a different type of education for working-class children which would undoubtedly be regarded as 'second class' in society as a whole and which would thus simply exacerbate the disadvantages facing the working class on the job market. Halsey (1972) was not unaware of this problem, but he argued that traditional curricula in comprehensive schools would enable only a small minority of the working class to move upwards in society. Since the bulk of working-class children have to face futures within deprived communities, a different type of education, geared to making empowered adults capable of changing their environment, seems justified to him.

A more realistic recognition of this problem can be found in the work of David Hargreaves (1982), who argues that unless the British standard examinations are eliminated, there is little chance of developing genuine community curricula which are not regarded as inferior in comparison with the traditional curriculum. This being so, standardized national examinations greatly reduce the probability that parents and teachers would choose to develop a full community curriculum along the radical lines specified above. It is clear that as long as examinations remain the key link between schooling and jobs, all schools will have to offer them. Offering examinations means that classes will effectively be streamed into examination and non-examination groups. While alternative curricula could be developed for the latter (and have been in many schools), their effectiveness would be enormously reduced through their low position in a status ranking of subjects determined by examinations. Hargreaves accordingly recommends doing away with standardized national examinations, at least for 15-year-olds completing secondary school (1982: 128).

It has yet to be seen what the full effect of the new British GCSE examinations instituted by Kenneth Baker will be. However, it would seem that any interpretation of the radical version of community education would lead logically to the decision to abolish or greatly modify the use of standard examinations taken by students of all secondary schools. A flexible curriculum cannot be created without flexible assessment procedures. Examinations played a key role in the Croxteth occupation in all the ways specified by Hargreaves (and in additional ways as well, shown below). They stifled the creativity of parents and teachers in curricular planning, constrained the organization of the school into streamed classes with the allocation of a limited number of teacher volunteers to favour the higher streams, and bolstered traditional authority relationships between teachers, parents and pupils, all in highly tacit ways.

Pupil resistance has been yet another problem with experiments in community education. Reports from Neil Thompson on the Abraham Moss Centre, from Bob Evans on Countesthorpe College, Mervyn Flecknoe on the Sutton Centre, and Bob Moon on Stantonbury Campus (all in Moon 1983) all refer to initial periods of pupil disruption in their experimental schools. As Moon explains in the representative case of his own school, pupils came to the new institution with deeply ingrained attitudes: 'Ideas about school and what school stood for had been established both by personal experience elsewhere as well as by the expectations of family, friends and the world at large' (1983: 68). These ideas included patterns of resisting school authority which were capable of even greater expression in the 'pupil-centred' atmospheres of these schools. Yet all the contributors to Moon's book argued that pupil disruption decreased over time (two to three years) and that they expected the problem to continue to decrease as yet more time goes by (see Moon's summary, p. 148). It will be seen that pupil resistance was a major feature of the Croxteth occupation which had an effect on the development of school organization and authority relationships. I found the reasons for pupil disruptions to be complex and will analyse them in future chapters.

Finally, another problem which has faced practitioners of community education has been the lack of practical ideas and appropriate materials available. Neil Thompson (1983: 38), for example, reports that at the Abraham Moss Centre in Manchester, an alternative curriculum was first attempted but later dropped because no materials and thought-out programmes existed upon which teachers could draw. Teachers tried to make their own materials at first and to plan projects, but found that constraints of time soon greatly curtailed their efforts: If the ground had been better understood, if the ideas had been previously rehearsed, there would have been fewer difficulties (p. 39).

This problem proved insurmountable even though the staff at the Abraham Moss Centre had been carefully selected for their enthusiasm. The problem of few formulated alternatives is, of course, lessened by the pioneering efforts of schools like Countesthorpe, the Sutton Centre, and the Abraham Moss Centre themselves. But it is rooted in a more general problem: the lack of what can be called a 'counter-hegemony' in educational ideology and practice. As Broadfoot (1979) points out, traditional educational practice and ideology are so deeply embedded within a narrow framework of assumptions held by policy-makers, teachers, and parents, that even when clear alternatives are formulated in theory they aren't taken very seriously.

Summary

To summarize, theoretical objections and practical problems found with community education fall into five areas:

1. Parental attitudes which originate in local cultures and which, I've argued, may exist in reinforcing relationships to society-wide patterns of inequality;

2. general lack of power on the part of residents over many features of their lives outside of schooling itself;

3. examinations which back up traditional forms of teacher authority and constrain curricular and organizational innovation;

4. pupil resistance which is conditioned by a variety of factors to be explored in future chapters;

5. lack of available alternatives to traditional educational practice upon which teachers (and parents) can draw.

I suggested above that many of these problems stem from limitations in the implicit theory of power used by advocates of community education. The key hypothesis of community education theory is that formal decision-making power is the major variable to be changed. The devolution of formal educational power to community adults is then proposed as a solution to the undesirable educational consequences of urban schooling focused upon in this approach: poor examination results, low rates of pupils continuing into higher education, and the movement of most lower-class pupils into lower-class jobs after completing school.

This, however, is a limited theory of power. Power relations are maintained in ways other than the formal access allowed to working-class residents over school decision-making procedures. The interpretative schemes prevalent·within the cultures of community residents transmit general relations of domination in often unnoticed ways. For community education to work, participants would have to gain an increased awareness of the conditions that influence the ways they perceive schools and make decisions about them. Moreover, in addition to gaining an awareness of hegemonic and ideological elements framing the ways in which they think and act, they would have to have two other things: the cultural means to construct alternatives in theory and the power to implement these alternatives in practice.

The previous discussion suggests that a combination of all three of these needs: critical awareness, alternative perspectives, and power over many features of community life, is unlikely to occur, especially if community education remains a state policy conceived and implemented from above. Since the radical version of community education challenges the client-administrator relationship of the welfare state, it is certainly problematical to make radical community education an official policy. This doesn't mean that a state policy of community schooling is totally self-contradictory, but simply that such policies are difficult to achieve because there is a tension built into the situation between the form (a state policy) and the ideal content (an alteration of the client-administrator relationship). As Boyd many times stresses in his critique, the idea of the community school did not come from the grass roots but has been developed by researchers concerned with the regeneration of inner-city neighbourhoods (see Boyd 1977: 12). Thus what usually results is a moderate rather than a radical version of the ideal.

However, the case of Croxteth Comprehensive is different from the experiments made so far with community education. Unlike them, it was never consciously intended to be a community school with an alternative curriculum and pedagogy. Yet it actually succeeded in placing a secondary school under formal community control for an entire year with up to 30 local parents participating in its daily operations. These parents and residents had gained access to financial resources through their connections with the trade union movement and had mounted political power over state-funded housing, health, and other services in their community through effective campaigning. By the time of the occupation of Croxteth Comprehensive, the Croxteth community was a force to be reckoned with.

Given the fact that the parents had the last of our three necessary conditions for making community education work (formal power over all aspects of the school and considerable influence over other conditions in their community), it will be of interest to examine the extent to which the other two conditions were affected: the degree of critical awareness residents developed of their cultural interpretative frameworks, and the actual pedagogic and curricular policies that were constructed in the occupied school. This will be the organizing question in the chapters that follow. It will involve a careful analysis of the relationship between forms of power inhering in formal institutional control and those inhering in cultural interpretative frameworks. The frameworks, in turn, will be found to exist because they are related to the ways of life of those who continuously draw upon, adapt, and maintain them, and these ways of life are structured through class positions and social geography. It will finally involve an analysis of the extent to which such cultural frameworks may be changed, as the awareness of those who use them grows through participation in educational and political activity.

Chapters 2 and 3 will set the context for analysis by providing a history of the political campaign for Croxteth Comprehensive. Chapters 4 to 9 will deepen our understanding of urban community–school relationships through an analysis of the complex events which took place during the year in which Croxteth was illegally run under occupation. The reader will find that the highly unusual case of Croxteth can tell us much about more routine forms of urban schooling.

2

Between the jaws of the nutcracker: the closure of Croxteth Comprehensive

There has been a gradually accelerating reduction in rate support grants which is why most local authorities, not only Liverpool, but local authorities generally, have found it more and more difficult. On the one hand the government says, 'we will reduce your rate grant'; on the other hand it says, 'if you levy too high a rate we shall penalise you'. We are caught between the jaws of the nutcracker if you like.

Kenneth Antcliffe, Liverpool Director of Education

Liverpool during the late 1970s found itself squeezed from many directions. The recession, coupled with national government cuts in aid for local governments, steadily reduced the city budget at the same time that unemployment and a host of mounting social problems increased demands for services. Certain areas of the city took the brunt of the pressures. Croxteth was one of them.

This chapter describes the first year of the battle for Croxteth Comprehensive: November 1980 to November 1981. It sets forth the set of conditions and sequence of events that led to the closure of Croxteth Comprehensive. It then describes the first of three distinctive phases in the campaign waged to win the school back. Factors which conditioned the political decision to close Croxteth Comprehensive ranged from structural pressures on the entire British economy through the contingencies of local Liverpool political personalities. Resistance to closure plans during this year was conducted entirely along institutional lines, and was ultimately unsuccessful.

STRUCTURAL PRESSURES AND SCHOOL CLOSURES

Three Rs: recession, rate-capping, and rolls

Educational reorganization was forced upon Liverpool in the late 1970s through three general conditions: economic (the recession), political (rate-capping and national budget cuts), and demographic (roll declines). Although roll declines and of course the recession affected all city governments, both were greatly exacerbated by local conditions in Liverpool. The city had been in general economic decline since the post-World War I era, when over-dependence on its port threw the city into a downward slide as world trade patterns altered (Hyde 1971; Marriner 1982). After World War II Liverpool attempted an economic revival by providing incentives for multinational manufacturing industries to build branch plants along its periphery. Ford, Standard Triumph, Vauxhall, and other firms built plants near newly created peripheral housing estates like Speke, Norris Green, and Croxteth, thus compounding dependence on port activities with dependence on wages from externally controlled corporations. When the recession of the 1970s struck, several of these firms closed down their Liverpool operations and others drastically cut back their employment. This meant that Liverpool had the highest unemployment rate of England by 1978 11.7 per cent throughout the city and much higher percentages in the peripheral estates. With unemployment going up, Liverpool's tax base steadily declined, making spending on services like education an increasing burden.

Neither could Liverpool meet its fiscal crisis by raising rates on more prosperous sections of the city. National government economic policy under Margaret Thatcher's administration restricted local governments through a policy known as 'rate-capping' and at the same time reduced national supportive grants for municipal services. Between 1979 and 1982 Liverpool lost £120 million in government grants. Between 1975 and 1982 the contribution of the rate support grant (a national grant provided to match locally collected taxes, or rates) to Liverpool finances dropped from 40 per cent to 29 per cent of the total income (Liverpool City Local Government Bulletin, Issue 1, January 1984). Yet the British national government, while restricting the total amount it was prepared to give to cities like Liverpool and thus reducing their incomes, simultaneously imposed limits on the amount of money it allowed municipal governments to raise through local rates: it rate-capped city finances. Liverpool was getting pressed both ways.

During this same period, the 1970s and early 1980s, school rolls were dropping throughout Britain in the wake of the baby boom. Once again, a national, and in fact international, trend was exacerbated in Liverpool due to local conditions. Liverpool had had a declining population for some decades because of its faltering economy. During the 1960s a Liverpool slum-clearance policy accelerated migrations out of the city by moving inner-city residents into nearby cities like Kirkby and Skelmersdale. Hence, when the post-baby boom slump in live births reached school age during the 1970s, the result was an exceptionally dramatic fall in Liverpool school rolls. In the primary sector, overall rolls dropped from 76,000 in January 1969 to 39,000 in January 1984 – a drop of 48 per cent. In the secondary sector, rolls dropped 23 per cent from their peak in January 1974 to 40,200 in January 1984 (Liverpool Education Committee, 1965–77, 1978–84; Carspecken 1985). Thus, as the recession and national cuts in grants began to pressure Liverpool to reduce its budget for services, a dramatic drop in school rolls made education the most logical area in which to make such reductions.

Social geographical effects

The decline in Liverpool school rolls had different effects in different parts of the city. To understand what occurred it is necessary to understand something of the different types of schools in Liverpool. There are two dimensions of differentiation: religion and selection. With respect to the first of these, Liverpool has two main categories of secondary schools: Catholic voluntary schools and what the Local Education Authority (LEA) calls 'county secondary' schools (i.e., non-religious state-funded secondaries). Over a third of all secondary schools in Liverpool in the 1970s and 1980s have been Catholic voluntary schools, 60 per cent have been county secondary, and remaining secondary provision has been divided between Church of England and other types of voluntary schools.

In terms of selection, Liverpool initially expanded its secondary educational provision after World War II by creating three types of schools based on 'ability'. Of these, two types of school were dominant: grammar schools for pupils who did well in an examination administered at age 11, and 'secondary modern' schools for those who did not do well in the exam. During the 1960s Liverpool followed England as a whole in abandoning this selective system for its county-secondary sector by creating non-selective comprehensive schools in the buildings of old grammar and secondary modern schools. The Catholic schools remained selective, however, and two selective schools remained as Liverpool county schools as well: the Liverpool Boys' and Girls' Institutes.

When comprehensive schools were created in the 1960s, the prestige associated with the old grammar schools remained. Attending a comprehensive school established in the buildings of what had formerly been a grammar school accorded pupils greater status than attending a comprehensive school in the buildings of a former secondary modern school. This feature of Liverpool secondary education was to have an important effect when rolls began to decline at such steep rates.

The roll decline of the early 1970s was first welcomed as a beneficial trend because many Liverpool schools were very full during the late 1960s and declining rolls meant more space and lower pupil–teacher ratios. A more significant benefit, however, was the increase in parental choice which the lower numbers allowed. In the 1970s all Liverpool schools were surrounded by admission areas which guaranteed places for pupils living within them, but parents were allowed to apply for places in other schools. As rolls dropped, parents were increasingly able to successfully pick schools for their children outside their immediate area. This resulted in a pattern of school attendance favouring comprehensives based in high-status former grammar schools which lay primarily in middle-class suburban neighbourhoods.

This pattern of choice meant that schools lacking the prestige accorded former grammar schools were left to bear the brunt of roll decline. Several of these schools were in the inner city. Others lay at the outer edge of Liverpool in working-class estates built during the 1940s and 1950s. Croxteth, Speke, and Yew Tree Comprehensives all fell into this category. Ellergreen Comprehensive, a school two miles from Croxteth which was to be amalgamated with Croxteth Comprehensive in 1982, suffered similar problems.

By 1975 Liverpool had a suburban belt, the Queen's Drive district, of well-attended, high-status comprehensives sandwiched between seriously depopulated schools in the inner and outer city. Between 1975 and 1982 city-wide secondary rolls dropped by 18 per cent. But during this same period suburban Quarry Bank Comprehensive lost only 7 per cent of its numbers, Childwall Valley, similarly located, lost 8 per cent, and Queen Mary (a voluntary school) actually gained 1 per cent. By contrast, in the outer-city, Croxteth and Ellergreen Comprehensives both lost 41 per cent of their rolls, and Speke Comprehensive lost 48 per cent. In the inner city, Paddington Comprehensive lost 36 per cent of its numbers.

Liverpool director of education, Kenneth Antcliffe, explained in interview what the combination of falling rolls and parental choice did to schools like Croxteth Comprehensive:

> Croxteth was formed out of two secondary modern schools. The comprehensive schools which were founded on secondary modern schools never really took off. Those founded on a grammar school base did.... So it has been those comprehensive schools founded on secondary modern schools which, during a period of falling rolls, have found it very difficult to survive. Because if there was room in the 'preferred schools', in inverted commas, then the parents would opt to send their kids there. And in a system which allowed as free a choice as possible, this meant a constant diminishing for the form entry of schools like Croxteth.

Struggles over reorganization, 1976–80

It was clear by 1975 that reorganization was desirable for both financial and educational reasons. Schools with declining student populations had to narrow their course offerings, for they were staffed by pupil number and lost teachers as they lost pupils. The amount of money spent on heating and staffing only partially filled buildings was a worry to the Education Committee. By 1978 there were 7,500 surplus places in Liverpool schools and the local papers claimed that between £1 and £1.5 million was being lost each year due to inefficient building use (*Liverpool Daily Echo*, 21st July 1978). The pressure to rationalize building use accelerated from 1975 on into the 1980s, corresponding to equally accelerating cuts in national rate support grants.

In 1976 the Local Education Authority formed a subcommittee to make proposals on reorganization. The first proposal offered for the committee's consideration was formulated by director of education, Kenneth Antcliffe. It suggested that limits be set on parental choice in order to halt the excessively rapid depopulation of the inner- and outer-city schools. The proposal was leaked to the press before the subcommittee even met to discuss it, causing immediate controversy. Parents organized to resist anticipated threats to their right to choose schools for their children. Many parents were also worried that certain schools of their liking would be closed down and a city-wide parents' group called the Liverpool Association of Parents (LASPA) formed as a result. As subcommittee discussions proceeded during the following months, at least seven parents' action groups formed around schools whose names came up as possible closures.

It thus became obvious that a reorganization plan of any sort would be met by much resistance and public outcry. Getting a plan through the council would require strong political will. But the Liverpool city council lacked such will. It had been hung between its three major political parties the Liberal, Labour, and Conservative parties – since the early 1970s. Labour had a majority on the council but not an overall majority capable of passing resolutions over combined Liberal and Conservative votes. Labour had decided not to use its simple majority to make it the leading party of the city, the party whose members chair the assembly and all the various committees. They didn't want to appear responsible for their inability to pass legislation. The Liberals, having Liverpool's second largest number of representatives, thus chaired the committees and furnished the city leader, Sir Trevor Jones, though they had to negotiate compromises with the smaller Conservative Party to pass legislation.

Each party had markedly different philosophies of education, making alliances on a city-wide reorganization plan impossible. However, Liberals and Conservatives were able to agree on some piecemeal plans. The different ideologies of educational provision held by each party corresponded to the pattern of school depopulation in the city. Labour advocated a policy for 'community comprehensives' which would require restricting parental choice in order to protect schools like Croxteth, Speke, and others in Labour constituencies. They wished to close and amalgamate schools in a geographically even manner while requiring parents to send their children to the school nearest them (see *Daily Echo* 1st July 1987). The Liberals proposed a contrary policy under the slogan of 'parental choice'. Its basic argument was well expressed in a November 1983 interview with David Alton, Liberal MP for Liverpool and a Liberal councillor on the Liverpool Education Committee during the 1970s:

> The key to our proposals was that parents should vote with their feet, that reorganization should actually be carried out by the parents themselves, that we should look to see which schools they've sent their children to and that on the basis of popular appeal those are the schools that should be built upon. And that if the school is really unsuccessful with the parents, then those are the schools which we should reorganize, amalgamate, close, rationalise.

In practical terms, this approach suggested that the logic of the depopulation trends in the city should guide reorganization. Undersubscribed schools like Paddington in the inner city and Croxteth on the periphery ought to be closed and the popular schools of the Queen's Drive Belt enlarged, if necessary, to take extra numbers.

The Conservatives carried the parental choice argument further than the Liberals by arguing that selective schools like the Liverpool Institutes ought to be retained for those parents who wanted them. Liberals opposed selective education, though some were willing to make it negotiable a possible compromise to win Conservative support for Liberal positions on other issues. Thus Conservatives and Liberals disagreed on specific proposals but their general agreement on the principle of parental choice enabled them eventually to reach some piecemeal compromises. As an overall philosophy for reorganization, moreover, parental choice made it possible to single out specific schools for closure without setting forth an entire city-wide plan, another reason that Conservatives and Liberals could make alliances on specific proposals in council.

THE CLOSURE OF CROXTETH COMPREHENSIVE

Now that the context is set, I will describe the closure of Croxteth Comprehensive. I will first acquaint the reader with the Croxteth housing estate and the nature of the school before its closure, then set forth the series of events that closed Croxteth Comprehensive down.

It's a dump, but I like it

Jackie: The place was supposed to be dead nice ... but when we moved up, like, we had to park down at the bottom and all the shops were closed down and boarded up. They still are. At the bottom we've three shops and a chippy there's supposed to be six shops, one of them was a supermarket. The library used to have books in it [laughs]. It's always been dead grotty, that library.

P.C.: Would you like to leave Croxteth, if you could?

Jackie: No. It's a dump, but I like it. I know everybody here, my mates are all here.

                                                                Jackie Madden

Many residents of Croxteth have their roots in the Scotland Road area along the Mersey River docks of Liverpool. The Croxteth housing estate was developed during the late 1940s in accordance with city policy to develop the periphery. During the 1960s Croxteth became one of the receiving areas for families dislocated by the slum clearance programme. Five miles from Liverpool's centre, Croxteth was planned to be a dormitory suburb with a large percentage of the population travelling to work outside the estate each day. Residents were first attracted to Croxteth from the dockland areas with advertising and later through the forced evacuations of the slum clearance programme. Much initial employment was provided by an industrial estate along the East Lancashire Road containing Napiers, English Electric (subsequently GEC), and Plesseys, along with other firms.

Croxteth is essentially a white, working-class community. In 1981 Croxteth had 12,652 residents living in 4,449 households, 86 per cent of which were council owned (1981 Census). Seventy-eight per cent of those employed worked in the manual unskilled, partly skilled, and armed forces occupational categories. Another 14 per cent worked in non-manual skilled occupations. Typical occupations include lorry-driving, cleaning, unskilled factory work, rubbish pick-up, painting; and in the skilled sector, welding, roofing, and brick-laying. Most residents firmly identify themselves as working class and participate within the cultural traditions of Liverpool workers, long known for their pride and militancy (Marriner 1982).

The only social category that is potentially divisive in the community is religion. The estate is divided about equally between Catholic and Protestant families, some of the Protestant families having Orange Lodge affiliations.

In 1981 Croxteth had four Catholic voluntary secondary schools and only one county secondary school: Croxteth Comprehensive.

Residents who moved into Croxteth during the 1950s report that conditions on the estate looked very promising at first, but as more and more people arrived, conditions on the estate got worse and worse. Promised facilities were never put in, housing conditions deteriorated. The deterioration in housing occurred in specific pockets on the estate, especially the Croxteth Triangle and an area known as 'the Gems'. This had the effect of producing conflicts between those living in nicer areas and those in the areas of deterioration. Residents who were able to maintain their homes in good condition tended to blame the individual residents of the Triangle and Gems for the condition of their homes. But the situation was complex; many single-parent families lived in the deteriorating housing and had few means to keep up their homes. Moreover, the city government was supposed to make repairs but was fairly lax about it.

Housing was particularly bad during the period of the campaign. In 1983 requests for housing repairs averaged 274 a week for 7,108 houses, 30 per cent of which were vacant (Liverpool Planning Department). Houses designed for coal-fire heating have suffered high levels of damp since the introduction of gas fires in the 1960s. Poorly designed rubbish chutes were easily blocked, so that they were eventually bricked off and tenants began putting rubbish out in bags. This practice, combined with delays in refuse collections of up to three weeks (Croxteth Area Working Party 1983: 60) attracted rats and other vermin. Drains were also badly designed, causing the back-up of waste water to increase the damp and create areas ripe for the growth of diseases and infection. Black and green mould abounded.

At the time of my fieldwork, the appearance of the estate struck the outsider with its great contrasts: small sections of the estate had a large number of semi-vacant and decaying buildings peppered amongst many very well-kept homes. The empty buildings and boarded windows were generally sprayed with graffiti, evidence of the restless youth population which managed to win national attention for its high rates of delinquency (*New Statesman*, November 1982). The graffiti often referred to drugs: 'Legalize Heroin Now', 'Crocky Drugs – Speed', 'LSD'. But a large number of slogans also expressed political discontent, stemming from conditions on the estate. On one of the many deteriorated council buildings was written: 'Run by Auschwitch [*sic*] Concentration Camp'. Examples of similar graffiti on the estate include:

'Croxteth the Forgotten Area'

'We supported Labour. They don't support the people, just rats.'

'The council left a 62-year-old woman without water for 6 months. Labour Club never went without beer.'[1]

Local discontent was further inflamed through the lack of general facilities in Croxteth. In 1973 a Liverpool Policy and Finance Committee report stated:

For various reasons, when the Croxteth Estate was constructed emphasis was given to the provision of housing accommodation and the provision of many of the associated environmental and social facilities necessary to provide the basis for a balanced and integrated community had lagged behind.

At the time of the school closure, Croxteth had no swimming baths, no cinema, job centre, bank, restaurant, police station, or adequate shopping centre. Several supermarkets and large shops moved out of the area, leaving small stores with a narrow range of items priced relatively high. Many residents did their shopping by catching the number 14 bus to the Broadway, a shopping area over two miles away.

Unemployment in Croxteth grew enormously with the 1970s recession. The 1981 census indicates an overall rate of 29 per cent in the community, with much higher rates for the 16–29 age group. A report prepared by the Croxteth Working Party in 1983 estimates that real unemployment figures approximated a rate of 40 per cent for the adult population generally and 95 per cent for school-leavers (Croxteth Area Working Party 1983: 49, 25). Decline in Liverpool's industries during the 1970s affected the plants along the East Lancashire Road, many of them merging into national and international conglomerates. In 1961 22,000 worked on the industrial estate along the road; in 1971 14,000 did and by 1981 the figure was 2,000 (Croxteth Area Working Party 1983: 13).

No doubt owing to the combination of high unemployment, poor housing, and few facilities, various social indicators placed Croxteth amongst the most deprived areas in Liverpool. In 1981 44.2 per cent of its school children were receiving free school meals, compared with 27.7 per cent city-wide. The infant mortality rate for the period 1979–82 was 111.9 per cent of that of Liverpool as a whole, and low birth weights were 116.0 per cent of the Liverpool rate during the same period. Eighty-six per cent of the residents of Croxteth were receiving state benefit in 1983 (Croxteth Area Working Party 1983: 25). Local pharmacists report that the highest drug group dispensed between January and October 1982 was that acting on the cardiovascular and respiratory system, because of widespread health problems caused by stress

1 (Pictures of Croxteth housing and graffiti can be found in *Schooling and Culture*, Issue 14, 1984, and *Socialism and Education*, vol. 11, no. 1, 1983).

and damp. The second highest was the hypnotic/central nervous system drug group, indicating high rates of psychological stress and depression (Croxteth Area Working Party 1983: 65).

The Croxteth Area Working Party Report (1983: 49, 51) notes the effects of these conditions on interpersonal relationships and mental health:

> The stress which results in families from such constraints can be linked with an increasing rate of mental and family breakdown and anxiety and depression in both men and women. An indication of the trend already, in the breakdown of family life, is given by the increasing numbers of single homeless young people requesting housing.

> These problems are not mutually exclusive, and the combination of bad housing, unemployment and money problems is often linked with difficulties in domestic situations and to nervous ill-health. This syndrome is by no means unique to this area, but there is a particular concentration of such difficulties, which generalises into a particularly helpless feeling about the whole area, and the situation of all those living within it.

Yet despite the bad conditions in much of Croxteth, most residents interviewed did not want to leave. A common interview was one in which the interviewee first noted many difficulties with living on the estate and then expressed no desire to leave it, as in the quotation at the beginning of this section. Discontent centred on poor housing was often expressed towards neighbours rather than the government. Comments on unemployment, however, often mixed a sort of fatalistic despair with anger directed at Thatcher's national administration. The despairing remarks focused on the plight of men used to work and the plight of youth who had little chance for a job. It was frequently mentioned by those interviewed that the many long-term unemployed people on the estate had high rates of depression, slept long into the mornings, and very often experienced stress in their families. This was discussed with Pat Rigby, Croxteth resident, and secretary of the Croxteth-Gillmoss Federation, who showed considerable acumen as a lay sociologist:

P.C.: What would you say are the key problems in Croxteth?

Pat: If you had full employment here and decent homes, you wouldn't have a lot of the other problems. No doubt about it. There's all the spin-offs in health, depression, physical and mental health both. Unemployment, I think definitely, and then really bad housing. It does, no doubt about it....

I think, especially sort of where the man has used to be working and he's suddenly out of work, and he's at home, know what I mean, with nothing to do. I think that sort of has a worse effect than a family starting off where neither are working and never have worked. It's a completely different lifestyle that the whole family has got to be adjusted to.

In a group conversation with three women residents who volunteered to clean the occupied school every night of the 1982–83 school year, the issue of unemployment came up:

Jean: My lads are out of work, they'd love a job. They haven't had a job for that long, I can not remember. They get fed up, bored to tears but that's as far as it goes.

Sandra: They've got no hope for a job at all. It doesn't worry our Sharon. Our child just thinks she'll get a scheme [a Manpower Services Commission job-training scheme] when she leaves. It's the lads are the worst. I don't think girls worry as much.

Freda: I think they just give up, most people.

P.C.: Is it especially hard with the lack of facilities around here?

Sandra: There's nothing here for them, just nothing at all.

P.C.: A lot of people point out that there's no bank, no sports facilities, no cinema, and so on here.

Jean: God, you couldn't afford to go to the pictures! The price of it! A couple of pounds to get in, isn't it?

Sandra: The main thing we'd want here is a baths [swimming pool]. It's the one thing the kids would love, isn't it?

Croxteth Comprehensive

Croxteth Comprehensive was formed in 1966 with the amalgamation of two secondary modern schools: Croxteth Secondary Girls and Croxteth Secondary Boys. The two buildings are separated by a 32-acre playing field. It was the only county secondary school on the estate, although until 1983 there were four Catholic secondary schools and two of these have remained after a 1983 Catholic school reorganization.

'Crocky Comp' was one of Liverpool's unfortunate comprehensives, suffering a combination of city-wide drops in rolls and a city-wide pattern of parental choice which favoured schools in the wealthier suburban areas. Croxteth Comprehensive was suffering one of the steepest declines in rolls of all schools in the city by the late 1970s. Designed for 750 pupils, it had only 513 or 68 per cent of its places filled in 1982. The numbers of pupils entering the school each year had fallen from approximately 120 at the beginning of the decade to under 90 by 1977. Entry numbers roughly stabilized after 1977, an average of 83 coming each year after to the time of its closure in 1982.

In 1980 one-third of all Croxteth parents with children attending the comprehensive's main feeder-primaries were choosing to send their children outside the estate. In interviews with people sympathetic to Croxteth Comprehensive and opposed to its closure, the main reason usually given for the choice of this large percentage of parents for other schools was the stigma of the Croxteth estate. The former head teacher of Croxteth Comprehensive, George Smith, illustrated the effects of stigma in his account of a meeting he had had with the Liberal leader of the Liverpool city council in 1980:

> I met with Trevor Jones around the time of the education meeting [in December 1980] and he made the comment that if he were hiring and two applicants came to him with equal O levels and A levels [examination results], and one of these came from Croxteth and the other came from some other school, he wouldn't hire the one from Croxteth. I think this is the name Croxteth has had. You know, the area is dark in the eyes of most people in Liverpool.

Those interviewed who did not favour the school tended to emphasize the point that Croxteth examination results were not as good as those of other schools in Liverpool. In 1981, for example, only 22 per cent of all CSE entries (Certificate of Secondary Education examination), and 29 per cent of all O level entries (Ordinary level examinations, more difficult to pass than CSEs) were passed. Only nine pupils made an entry for O level mathematics and only one of these passed with mark C.

Most of the old teaching staff interviewed on the Croxteth Community Action Committee, and the Liverpool director of education, however, expressed high regard for Croxteth Comprehensive. Of course, one would expect positive descriptions from members of the Action Committee. But the comments consistently make the same points of praise: the school maintained high standards of discipline, extended much personal attention to most pupils, and provided services to the community that went beyond examination results. The director of education called Croxteth Comprehensive 'excellent, given its area and circumstances'. Kathy Donovan, full-time volunteer in the school during the occupation and a former pupil of the school herself, had typical memories:

> It was very good. There was no bullies or anything like that. I mean, I'm not just saying that, there really wasn't.... If there was they would be stamped on immediately and they would make sure that it never happened again with that person. Also, each teacher, headmaster, and headmistress

knew every single pupil, personality-wise and all that. They did. The teaching staff in the school were here for 14, 15 years. They weren't just coming in and going, so right through school you knew them – you knew them as a friend.

Nearly all of the residents interviewed described the school as disciplined and considered this very positive. 'Discipline was drummed into us,' said resident and former pupil Ned Kelly, 'They'd look after you. They'd give you a lot of opportunity there – it was great.'

These accounts not only indicate the positive evaluation of the school by those acquainted with it but also the standards by which they judged good schooling generally. The reader should bear these standards in mind when reading future chapters on the nature of the school under occupation. Discipline, school uniforms, and proper regard for school authority all ranked high. Children were caned 'when necessary'. At the same time, close attention was given to pupils, and parents were welcomed into the school for visits. In short, it was very much a school run on traditional lines, and proud of it. As former head teacher George Smith expressed it:

It was a marvellous school. There were no [pause] it wasn't progressive in any way. We did once have many years ago one of those progressive teachers: 'Just call me Joe', something like this. We got rid of him, because the staff was beautifully dressed and the children were beautifully dressed.... The local cowboys may break every window in the district, but not at the school.

In addition, Croxteth Comprehensive served many community functions. The school was used as a youth club and operated services for the elderly at times during the year. Its large playing fields were used for sports activities by all ages and for community fairs and other events. Interviewee after interviewee claimed that Croxteth Comprehensive was the only real facility on the estate. George Smith helped residents with their social security problems, with family counselling, and made sure the school and its grounds were used for local sports, programmes for pensioners, and other community activities.

George Smith was highly regarded as head teacher of the school by parents and staff alike. His ability to keep discipline and his stern but caring relationship with pupils was valued. When Croxteth Comprehensive closed and the former teaching staff had to take jobs in other comprehensive schools, many were dissatisfied. Of the six former teachers interviewed during the research, only one didn't express regrets at having to leave the school.

I will conclude this section with another quotation from the former head:

My best teachers took the slowest learners. On rainy days we'd arrange to pick up the children in cars.... I worked my fingers to the bone for this school, weekends, all night. I never had any social life, my life was the school. Kids loved it. Oh, they knew if they misbehaved they'd get it, there were no bones about it. But they accepted it. If you're capable of getting six O levels and three A levels you're going to get them. If you want help in basic subjects then you'll get help. But you've got to work.... The youngest child in this school is as important as the headmaster, and we've got to treat one another like that, and if anybody steps out of line and doesn't, then heaven help them.

Closing the school

On Monday, 10th November 1982, the early afternoon edition of the *Liverpool Daily Echo* announced a plan, said to have been agreed upon by the Reorganization Working Party of the Education Committee, to close Croxteth Comprehensive and merge it with Ellergreen Comprehensive two miles away. This was the first indication of any such plan that the staff and parents of Croxteth Comprehensive had had. This was also the very day of the Working Party meeting at which the plan was put forth as a proposal. The afternoon edition of the paper must have gone to press sometime that morning but the Working Party's meeting was scheduled for 2:00 p.m. Who leaked the plan to the papers remains unknown, and the reason why the source of the leak was so certain the proposal would be approved before it was actually discussed by the committee made the matter seem suspicious to the parents and staff of Croxteth Comprehensive: 'There must have been something fishy about it because it appeared in a paper which a teacher had read at four o'clock!,' said former headmaster George Smith.

Thanks to carefully kept records of meetings, copies of letters, proposals, and other documents kept by Cyril D'Arcy, the secretary of the parents' action committee, it is possible to trace in detail the events which followed (see Table 2.1). Unfortunately, space constraints force me to be very brief. Readers interested in a detailed history of the school closure must consult other sources (Carspecken 1985, 1987a, b).

George Smith called a meeting for parents concerned about the closure plan on Friday, the 14th of November. Despite bad weather, 650 parents turned up and a parents' committee of roughly 12 members was established to organize resistance to the closure. Its name was the 'Croxteth Parents' Action Group'. Its first secretary was Charles Wallace, a local resident working as a security officer for Dunlops who was also chairman of the school's board of governors. The first chair of the committee was Vic

Rhodes, a local resident and shift worker, who was later replaced during the first phase of the campaign by Tony Blair, a menswear shop manager.

Thus opposition to the plan was to be conducted by two separate groups, parents and staff members. These groups remained autonomous but in good communication. The teachers active in resistance tended to formulate the arguments against closure and determine the tactics to be used by both groups.

On Thursday, the 20th of November, head teacher George Smith received a letter from the Liverpool Education Committee which mentioned the amalgamation plan without providing much explanation. On the same day several parents came to see Mr Smith at the school with letters they had received from the Education Committee explaining the amalgamation proposal and requesting comments. The letters all had return envelopes and requested the parents' opinions. George Smith reacted by sending a circular out to parents urging them to send in their comments. George Smith said that the letters had gone out to parents of 480 or 490 pupils, 'and I got 390 back through me. Every one said that they wanted their children to remain here.' Yet no further consultation with parents was ever arranged, and no attempt was made by the Education Committee to visit the estate to hold a meeting with parents so that the closure could be explained.

Parents and staff were very bitter about what they saw as a circumvention of the consultation process. Absolutely no consultation was made with either parents or staff in formulating the closure plan. Consultation was not part of the plan's rationale, nor part of the research which presumably was carried out before formulating the proposal. The letters came out after the proposal was first voted on, and the use of letters, rather than a meeting at which the proponents of closure could have met face to face with the parents to be affected, was seen as extremely cowardly. The NUT, the National Union of Teachers, eventually forced the Education Committee to hold a consultation meeting with teachers and school governors but the chairman of the Education Committee, Liberal councillor Michael Storey, failed to attend the meeting and little was accomplished at it.

The activities of Education Committee chairman Michael Storey were very much a sore point to staff and parents in Croxteth. Michael Storey was not only the Liberal chairman of the Education Committee, but also a councillor for the ward in which Ellergreen Comprehensive resides. Time after time Mr Storey displayed what appeared to be a cavalier and arrogant attitude towards the community. His use of letters instead of calling a meeting, his absence from the only meeting which was held (and held only because of NUT pressure), his refusal to reply to several letters sent by the teaching staff after the announcement of the closure plan, and various statements he made to the press were found to be infuriating. With respect to the last point, in statements made to the press as late as September 1983, Michael Storey was quoted in the *Liverpool Echo* as saying that the decision to close Croxteth Comprehensive had been 'preceded by massive consultation'. David Alton, when asked about this, called it 'a lie'. George Smith recalled an earlier incident with Michael Storey:

> One of my staff talked to the then secretary of the Education Committee [Michael Storey] and came back with the story that he had visited the school several times and that the closure had been 'well thought-out and planned'. Well, I wrote him and pointed out that I wasn't aware of any visits and the letter I got back from him said something like this: it is not for me to question his visits to the school and he doesn't have to let anyone know when he comes.

A committee of the Croxteth Comprehensive teaching staff wrote a long document several weeks after the closure announcement which was to be the basis of the arguments used by teachers and parents alike for the following year. The arguments in this document fall into four main categories:

1. The Croxteth site and facilities are superior to those of Ellergreen. This argument includes the fact that Croxteth has a 32-acre playing field while Ellergreen has none, that Croxteth has better laboratories and eating areas which were recently modernized at some expense, and that Ellergreen's two buildings are separated by a dual carriageway (a boulevard) which makes travel between them dangerous for pupils.

2. The Croxteth area is unusually deprived and requires the school for reasons of social need. Here the staff pointed out the high unemployment rate in Croxteth, the general lack of facilities on the estate other than the school, and the extra difficulties which transporting children to a school two miles away would entail for parents already under economic and time pressures.

3. Within four to eight years many new pupils could be expected. The staff pointed out that the Croxteth Housing Estate was growing, with the refurbishment of a number of flats and the building of an adjacent new housing estate, Croxteth Park, which was expected to add over 4,000 new homes to the area by 1996.

4. Though not exactly an argument against closure in itself, the document makes much of the lack of consultation given to the community before this proposal was formulated.

These four arguments did not challenge the general approach to school closures taken by the Liberal Party but instead used a horizontally competitive argument and an argument of exception to protect Croxteth Comprehensive from closure. Parents and teachers were willing to compete with Ellergreen and see it closed in order to protect their own school and they also wished to portray their own school as an expectation to general closure criteria for the special services it rendered a community in need. Future chapters will explain how both arguments changed during the second and third phases of the campaign.

On the 28th of January the city council met and voted in favour of closing the school by a majority of four. The proposal was brought up at 11:30 p.m., officially as 'post-business', and no discussion was allowed. Most Liberal and Conservative councillors voted in favour, Labour councillors against. The fact that the proposal was brought up so late, and that conditions of no discussion were imposed, once again gave the strong impression of railroading tactics being used by the Liberals.

Cyril D'Arcy explained the alliance of the Conservative and Liberal parties over the issue of Croxteth Comprehensive in response to a list of questions sent him years later by post. One of the questions in the letter asked what the basis of the Conservative Party's support for the Liberal plan was:

> Deal to be done: The Liverpool Girls' and Boys' Institute [selective schools supported by the Conservatives] were in need of new premises. Both were selective schools, supported by the Conservatives. Close Paddington as a comprehensive because it was undersubscribed – hand the buildings over to the Institute to relocate.

In other words, Cyril believed that Conservatives had agreed to support the closure of Croxteth Comprehensive because the Liberals were also pushing to close down the inner-city school, Paddington Comprehensive, and were willing to relocate Liverpool's two selective schools in its fine buildings. Paddington was also experiencing rapid roll decline.

Cyril D'Arcy also emphasized in this letter the belief, widespread in Croxteth, that the Liberal Party originally intended to sell off the vast Croxteth Comprehensive estate, with its 32 acres of playing fields, to developers: 'We had reliable but unsubstantiated evidence that the Liberals intended to sell off the school property to developers.' Workmen reportedly came into Croxteth to put drainage ditches into the playing fields and make other alterations indicative of an impending sale. Although Cyril's theories on both the intentions of the Liberal Party to sell the Croxteth playing fields and the basis of the Conservative–Liberal alliance over the closure of Croxteth Comprehensive couldn't be verified during the research, both were widely believed in Croxteth itself and both greatly contributed to the anger felt on the estate.

Table 2.1. Summary of events, November 1980–November 1981

10 November 1980	10:00 a.m.: The afternoon edition of the *Liverpool Daily Echo* goes to press with an article announcing the plan to close Croxteth Comprehensive. 2:00 p.m.: The Secondary Reorganization Working Party meets, chaired by Liberal Michael Storey. The committee agrees to present a proposal to close Croxteth Comprehensive at the next full Education Committee meeting.
14 November 1980	A public meeting is held in the school buildings attended by approximately 650 parents. A committee of roughly 12 members is elected to represent the parents and work against the closure.
1 December 1980	The Education Committee votes in favour of closure by one vote. Michael Storey uses his casting vote to break a draw.
8 December 1980	The local NUT (the 'Liverpool Teachers' Association') registers a complaint against the Liverpool Education Committee for making proposals without proper consultation procedures being followed.
17 December 1980	A petition circulated by the Parents' Action Group and bearing 6,000 signatures is submitted to the city council to oppose the closure plans.
7 January 1981	A consultation meeting is held in the buildings of Croxteth Comprehensive. Michael Storey doesn't attend. No resolutions or proposals are generated.
28 January 1981	The City Council votes for the closure of Croxteth Comprehensive at 11:20 p.m. The proposal passes by a majority of 4 votes under conditions of no discussion.
9 February 1981	Cyril D'Arcy writes to Secretary of State for Education Mark Carlisle asking him to visit the school and/or receive a delegation. Warns that parents are 'militant'.
10 February 1981	The Liverpool Deputy City Solicitor, W.I. Murray, signs the official document closing Croxteth Comprehensive.
23 March 1981	SDP MP for Gillmoss, Eric Ogden, requests Mark Carlisle to meet a joint delegation of parents from Liverpool.
26 March 1981	Cyril D'Arcy's request for a visit from the Secretary of State for Education is refused in a letter from Mrs Rudd of the DES. Lack of time is the reason given.
April 1981	MP Eric Ogden's efforts to arrange a meeting between Mark Carlisle and a parents' delegation is successful. Cyril D'Arcy, present at the meeting, felt the Secretary was sympathetic.
Summer 1981	Riots break out in Toxteth.
November 1981	Dr Rhodes Boyson, Parliamentary Under Secretary of State for Education, visits Liverpool to observe the schools affected by the reorganization plan. He doesn't visit Croxteth Comprehensive, causing resentment amongst the parents.
25 November 1981	Secretary of the Parents' Action Committee, Charles Wallace, resigns due to ill health. Cyril D'Arcy replaces him.
30 November 1981	The Parents' Action Group receives a letter from the DES stating that the department had considered all information and objections relevant to the closure of Croxteth Comprehensive School and had approved the plan. Teachers drop out of campaign.

Parents and teachers continued to try to save Croxteth Comprehensive after the council vote through lobbying activities. A city council decision to close a school in England must be approved by the national Department of Education and Science (DES) before it can be implemented. Residents sent a delegation to London to talk to the secretary of education Mark Carlisle, and many letters and petitions were sent as well. At the end of their meeting delegates reported indications of sympathy from Mark Carlisle and were hopeful that he'd decide in their favour.

However, the situation in Liverpool changed during the summer. Riots broke out in Toxteth, the inner-city community from which many pupils attending Paddington Comprehensive come. Paddington had been voted for closure in the same package as Croxteth. After the riots Michael Heseltine, Secretary of State for the Environment at the time, visited Liverpool and was told by the Liverpool Eight Defence Committee (representing Toxteth) that removal of Paddington Comprehensive would fuel conditions for future riots. Heseltine reportedly passed this information over to the Department of Education. The Secretary of State for Education changed, moreover, during this period from Mark Carlisle to Sir Keith Joseph. Keith Joseph decided to keep Paddington open, reportedly because of the threat made by the Liverpool Eight Defence Committee, but approved the proposal to close Croxteth Comprehensive. It was widely believed in Croxteth that rioting in Toxteth had been rewarded while the orderly and well-conducted campaign in Croxteth had been ignored.

On 30th November 1981, a letter was sent from the office of Keith Joseph to the Liverpool LEA stating the secretary's decision to keep Paddington Comprehensive open and to close Croxteth Comprehensive. During this same period the Croxteth teaching staff began to apply for jobs at other school sites for the next autumn, most of them accepting defeat in their efforts to keep Croxteth Comprehensive open. Charles Wallace resigned from the parents' committee and the school's board of governors due to ill health. He was replaced in his secretarial post by Cyril D'Arcy. Croxteth Comprehensive was due to close at the end of the 1981–82 school year, in July 1982.

Why was Croxteth Comprehensive in particular closed?

Given the Liberal Party's ideology of educational provision (parental choice), and the fact that Liberals were nominally in control of Liverpool during 1980, the condition of falling rolls and parents' choices to send their children to schools other than Croxteth Comprehensive made the school a logical target for closure. Yet Ellergreen's fall in school rolls was at exactly the same rate as Croxteth's, so one might wonder why, once the idea of an amalgamation of these two schools came up, Ellergreen rather than Croxteth was the chosen site. One reason given by the Liberals was that Ellergreen's overall numbers were higher than Croxteth's. This meant that the identical rates of depopulation had worse educational effects, by Liberal and Conservative arguments, in Croxteth than in Ellergreen, and that the closure of Croxteth Comprehensive would require the displacement of fewer pupils than would the closure of Ellergreen.

In addition, George Smith, the head teacher, was due for retirement within a year or two and research into primary school closures in Liverpool by Fergusson and Brown (1982) shows that most of the primary schools chosen to close had heads near retirement. A head at the end of her or his career will be less likely to resist a closure than a head in the middle of it, and retirement solves the problem of having to demote someone. The Croxteth Comprehensive teaching staff, moreover, were by and large not members of the NUT but rather of the less militant NASUWT. Ellergreen's staff, by contrast, was well organized by the NUT and it may have been feared that it would have put up a stronger fight.

Undoubtedly, the position of Michael Storey as chairman of the Education Committee at the time and as councillor for the Ellergreen constituency, gave him both an interest in choosing Croxteth over Ellergreen Comprehensive for closure, and the power to pursue it. It would have been politically dangerous for Michael Storey to argue for the closure of a school in his own constituency, and such political pressure couldn't help but influence his decision. Moreover, a merger between the two schools in Ellergreen's buildings would boost Ellergreen's numbers and thus ensure its own future. Michael Story was just one of three Liberal councillors at the time who represented the Clubmore ward in which Ellergreen lies, and one of the other two was the former chairman of the board of governors of Ellergreen (see *Private Eye*, 30th July 1982, for a cynical commentary on these facts).

David Alton, who as member of the Liberal Party and former member of the Liverpool Education Committee could be expected to have had close acquaintance with the manner in which his party reached the decision to close Croxteth Comprehensive, was openly cynical about the motives of his colleagues. He was critical of the Labour Party's stance with respect to the school as well, explaining in interview that Labour had been the first to propose the closure of Croxteth during committee meetings held in the 1970s:

> Yes, it was the Labour Party who first proposed to close Croxteth for all the reasons I've just enunciated. And the whole story's a shabby one. It's one which, for those who care about education, for about the way you arrive at these decisions, [that they should be] on the basis of the arguments about the issues, not about purely political arguments, would go away after having looked at the evidence with a bad taste in their mouths.

And I think it had a lot more to do with what I'd describe as 'porkbarrel politics' than it did with educational factors. Ellergreen School was situated in a Liberal ward, Croxteth school was situated in a Labour ward. The Labour councillors who'd originally advocated closure suddenly got scared because they realized parental support was running the other way. And it was suddenly discovered that the entire estate could be left without a school if Croxteth closed.

I had a stormy argument with Mike Storey at the time about the lack of consultation, the way the decision was announced, the way it was rushed through....

So I personally believe it was a wrong decision. And even if there was justice in some of their arguments about depopulation of the school, which is true, it should have been arrived at in consultation with all the parents involved. And where you have an isolated community, which doesn't have much going for it anyway, you may have to take a decision to keep a very small school open, and maybe that should be part of our reasoning of the future.

David Alton, in other words, believed the primary motivation behind the closure of Croxteth Comprehensive was political, was critical of what he considered an inadequate consultation procedure used by his party, and believed that the school should have been kept open for reasons of social need. He expressed the main arguments put forward by the school staff and parents during the first phase of resistance to closure. Croxteth should have been regarded as an exception because, as a community, it 'didn't have much going for it'.

Thus the choice of Croxteth Comprehensive in particular for closure can be seen as the combination of a number of factors. Some of them were due to general conditions in Liverpool and directly traceable to structural and environmental pressures on the city: to financial pressures, to its social geography, and to its particularly steep decline in live births during the 1960s. But others consisted of highly particular conditions which couldn't be predicted from the structural and demographic pressures alone. The fact that Croxteth Comprehensive, residing in a Labour-controlled ward, was near Ellergreen, residing within a Liberal-controlled ward, was clearly very important, as was the fact that the chairman of the Education Committee, Michael Storey, was a councillor for the Ellergreen constituency. It was also important that head teacher, George Smith, was close to retirement and that the faculty of Croxteth were not on the whole organized by the militant NUT. It was this coincidence of general and particular conditions, of structural and contingent factors, which led to the school's closure.

3
The road to militancy

It really was, you know what I mean; people wanted their school and everybody had to commit themselves to convince the council that the school had to stay, for all different reasons.... Because of all this and everybody saying that the school should remain open because it was clear from the probation, social workers, doctors, health visitors, the police that the closure was a nonsense. And because everybody thought it was a nonsense, it wouldn't happen, the school would remain open.

Until the defeat.... And then there was sort of like an angry reaction, and also there was some feeling that there wasn't much Croxteth could do about it. Angry and discouraged. I thought it was an awful slap-down. People had really thought, because they'd got themselves together, and everybody was supporting them, because of that it seemed obviously sensible to keep it open.

A smaller group it became then, campaigning.
> (Pat Rigby, secretary of the Croxteth-Gillmoss Federation)

The first year of protest against the closure of Croxteth Comprehensive failed. After Sir Keith Joseph's letter of November 1981, many of the original protesters left, accepting defeat. The most significant of the departures from campaign activity were the teachers. For them it was time to prepare pupils for a difficult transition and time to make sure they would have autumn jobs in Ellergreen or some other school of the city. Parents continued to meet but felt demoralized. The year-long campaign had made use of every possible institutional channel – lobbying, letter writing, visits to London, petitioning – all to no avail. There seemed to be no way forward.

Yet a new and spectacular phase of the campaign for Croxteth Comprehensive was about to begin. The first year of protest would soon prove to have been only one of three distinct phases in the battle. Before I continue the chronology let me make the criteria clear by which I've divided the history of the struggle into phases. Each period was unique with respect to four parameters: 1) the arguments used to oppose closure; 2) the participants involved in campaigning; 3) the tactics employed; and 4) the goals that were pursued.

During the first phase arguments against closure were horizontally competitive, urging the closure of another school in a similar situation, Ellergreen Comprehensive, instead of Croxteth. The arguments were also those of exception – supportive of the general definition of schooling and the criteria for school closures used by the Liberal Party, but stressing the exceptional nature of Croxteth Comprehensive because of the other community functions it was serving in an area of unusual need. The participants of phase one consisted of both teachers and parents, with the former generating the campaign ideology and the latter adapting these formulations for their own activities. Tactics were legal and institutional and the goal was straightforward: to keep the school from closing.

The second phase was markedly different. The first variables to change were the participants and the tactics they used. New and more militant residents joined the campaign, portraying it as a *community* movement, as opposed to merely a parents' and teachers' movement, and immediately employed tactics of civil disobedience to get media coverage and make the battle in Croxteth appeal to the sympathies of people throughout Liverpool. As the movement progressed, its arguments lost their horizontally competitive forms. The exceptional needs of Croxteth were still emphasized, but the argument that Ellergreen should close was no longer used. When success seemed at hand and the power of the newly composed action group was at its peak, activists took up other social issues in Croxteth, such as housing and health, and began to campaign for them as well. Thus the very goals of the campaign were to expand.

This chapter is about phase two. Once again I am forced to provide only an outline of the most major events. Many interesting and important details had to be omitted and interested readers will have to consult my larger study for a full account (Carspecken 1987a).

PHASE TWO

The transformation of the Action Committee

The major new figure who arose at the beginning of phase two was Philip Knibb, a local parent in his 30s, and a resident of Croxteth since his youth. Phil was a pipe fitter who had had over ten years' active union experience. His employment history was one of many shifting jobs interspersed with periods of unemployment. He worked in some of the manufacturing firms around Liverpool like Ford and took temporary work in places as far off as Germany and oil rigs in the North Sea. When employed, he very often was elected shop steward, and was well experienced in registering disputes and organizing strike action. Phil once commented during an informal conversation that he used to take a copy of *The Ragged Trousered Philanthropist* with him to new work sites to loan out to other workers. He was several times sacked from jobs for his union activities.

In the autumn of 1981, after a time of living away from the housing estate on a temporary job, Phil returned to his home in Croxteth and heard about the plans to close Croxteth Comprehensive. Although Phil had attended a Catholic secondary school, his wife Carol had gone to Croxteth Comprehensive and the couple had plans to send their own children there when they came of age. Phil began attending meetings about the school closure and immediately felt that the parents' committee was neither imaginative nor militant enough

> mainly because they'd done everything that they were supposed to do, that they knew about, and yet it was still being closed, and they couldn't see any way forward, and yet still had great backing behind them. And I stood up and said, you know, why don't you expand your committee and start taking other action.

A small group of residents, most of whom had also only recently become involved in the campaign, found hope in Phil's suggestions. Cyril D'Arcy was amongst them and the two men quickly formed an effective working relationship. Phil's strengths lay in winning the loyalty and trust of the more militant campaigners as well as in planning tactics. His confidence and past experience, combined with skills at utilizing local norms for winning solidarity, soon put him at the front of the campaign leadership. Cyril was (and still is) an extremely articulate man who could explain the legal and political complexities of the campaign in clear terms to the other activists. He is also an excellent public speaker and letter writer. Cyril became the most visible representative of Croxteth to the media and public at large during the second phase, and did much to improve relations between the campaign organization and other organizations throughout Liverpool.

Cyril's background was similar to Phil's, which is no doubt one reason why they worked well together. About himself Cyril writes:

> I left school at 15 years of age. Twelve months hotel work. Went away to sea I was in the Merchant Navy five years booking. Strike. Went into local mining, 'Bold Colliery', for three years. Joe Gormley was a pit deputy when I was there. Left mines for a job in Bird's Eye Foods. Got caught for two years National Service (Army artillery driver), then 25 years of

age, married, two children. Returned to Bird's Eye, went into dispute later, sacked. Then into selling, demolition, taxi work, driving heavy goods mostly large tapper waggons on civil engineering sites. Motorways, hospital buildings, etc. Housing repairs, etc. ... Unions: Seamans, NUM, T&G.

Like Phil, Cyril had attended a Catholic secondary school but his wife Irene had attended Croxteth Comprehensive. The family, which eventually grew to include seven children, had moved off the estate to nearby Dovecot a number of years before Croxteth Comprehensive was proposed for closure. But the D'Arcys thought highly enough of the school to have two of their children continue to attend it, commuting each day. Cyril was active in the protest from the start, taking on much of the correspondence work and addressing meetings of the Education Committee on the parents' behalf. He officially became secretary of the parents' committee after Charles Wallace resigned.

Phil, Cyril, and Tommy Gannon, another new leading figure who worked for the campaign until summer, organized a demonstration in early December at the *Liverpool Daily Echo*, one of Liverpool's two major newspapers, in order to get more publicity. The *Echo*'s offices were occupied by approximately 50 demonstrators, a large number of them new to the campaign, while a small delegation discussed the school closure with the newspaper staff. The occupation was successful, a promise being made to give more coverage to the plight of residents in Croxteth. The demonstration promptly moved on from the offices of the *Echo* to Radio City and then Radio Merseyside, getting spectacular results when Cyril D'Arcy was allowed to talk live, on the spot, over the radio.

The first demonstration won the backing and increased the morale of many residents in Croxteth. Croxteth resident Mary Kane describes her feelings at the time:

> Well, it picked up when Phil Knibb joined it, and Tommy Gannon. Then it seemed to get more active. You thought, well, we're going to get somewhere now, whereas before you used to think they're just going round in circles, these people. They're saying, 'We'll do this and we'll do that', but they're not taking positive action. And then when the action started it was better anyway. It was being heard anyway, which was one thing about it.... It's changed drastic.

On 10th February 1982, a public meeting was held at the Labour Club in Croxteth about the closure. This was the first time a protest meeting was held outside the school. The location was chosen to emphasize the intentions of the activists to make the struggle a community, rather than merely a parents', struggle. The choice of the Labour Club also reflected the intentions of Phil Knibb and Tommy Gannon to draw the campaign closer to the labour movement. At this meeting a new committee was formed, the Croxteth Community Action Committee (CCAC), again emphasizing the community nature of the struggle. Eventually Phil Knibb became its official chair.

'We won by 31 votes!'

On the 11th, 12th, and 13th of February 1982, the new committee led demonstrations to block traffic on the East Lancashire Road bordering one side of Croxteth. Media coverage was extensive, as hoped. The local papers printed pictures and large headlines accompanied by articles giving the parents' arguments against the closure of their school. The 12th February *Liverpool Post* announced that a 'petticoat blockade', consisting of 'mums and school girls' had stopped traffic on the busy highway for 20 minutes during rush hour. The article draws attention to a consistent feature of the campaign for Croxteth Comprehensive: the majority of participants were at all times women, although the leadership was definitely always male.

In accordance with their strategy of getting maximum community involvement, the Action Committee publicized its meetings and demonstrations widely throughout Croxteth. Leaflets were distributed and put up in shop windows and a car with a loud-hailer drove around the estate. All residents were aware of the demonstrations and many participated, several demonstrations drawing over 200. On the 16th of February between 150 and 200 demonstrators from Croxteth gathered outside the Liverpool City Hall on Dale Street while a meeting of the Education Committee was being held inside. As many of the demonstrators as possible filled the visitors' gallery to watch the proceedings. Michael Storey, chairing the meeting, several times asked the police to clear the gallery because of the noise (*Liverpool Echo*, 17th February 1982). The Education Committee on this occasion voted to give Croxteth a reprieve by 18 to 12, many Conservatives voting along with Labour. But the reprieve was found to be ineffectual soon afterwards, because the council decision of the year before had been ratified by a Secretary of State and was therefore unalterable by the local government.

The turn-around of the Education Committee probably had to do with the publicity generated by the demonstrations. It was probably also significant that the prior decision of the DES in London to retain Paddington Comprehensive removed the basis of a Conservative–Liberal deal over Croxteth: Paddington could no longer be used as a new site for the Liverpool Boys' and Girls' Institutes, the selective schools favoured by the Conservative Party. Public sympathy had been generated through positive press coverage resulting from the acts of civil disobedience. After each demonstration Cyril

D'Arcy, a master of the short and pungent phrase loved by reporters, would be quoted in the papers or over the air. Cyril's statements can be found in many issues of the *Liverpool Daily Echo* and *Post* during 1982. On the occasion of the 16th February demonstration he made a typical statement to the *Post*: 'If you close the school, a sleeping monster will awake. The people of Croxteth have had enough of the political pillage and rape of their community' (*Liverpool Post*, 17th February 1982).

On 2nd March 1982 an important feature article appeared in the *Liverpool Echo* on the Croxteth estate. A brief history of Croxteth was given followed by detailed descriptions of the deprivation and social problems facing residents. The article was accompanied by pictures of some of the worst housing. About the school it stated: 'The school, on a split site joined by a foot path, is seen by the people as one of the threads holding the community together.'

Thus by early March the demonstrations and public statements made by the Croxteth Community Action Committee had succeeded in getting frequent media coverage, culminating in a sympathetic feature article. The feature article presented the school as crucial to local identity and meeting social needs, exactly in accordance with the arguments of exception developed by the Action Committee.

After the vote of the Education Committee to annul the closure of the school proved to be fruitless, the CCAC began to work towards getting a proposal through the council which would create a 'new' school in Croxteth within the buildings of the 'former' comprehensive. This proposal became scheduled for vote by the full council on 3rd March. Phil Knibb took a delegation of councillors from the Liverpool Conservative Party around Croxteth a day before the council vote and these delegates described their impressions to a meeting of their party that night. The Conservatives became convinced that the difficult living conditions in Croxteth justified keeping a school there.

On the next day, the 3rd of March, between 40 and 50 residents of Croxteth again travelled to the city centre and blocked traffic outside the council chambers. Large numbers of the residents made their way into the visitors' chamber as the council considered various proposals on its agenda. When the proposal to reopen a school in Croxteth came up, it was passed with a majority of 31 votes: Conservatives and Labour voting solidly together against the Liberals. It can not be said, moreover, that all Liberals strongly supported the closure at this point. Fifteen Liberal Party members hadn't bothered to come to the meeting and six of those who did come abstained from voting (*Liverpool Echo*, 4th March 1982).

The reaction in Croxteth was euphoric. Pat Rigby described it from her perspective in the Croxteth-Gillmoss Federation office (Pat did not participate in any of the demonstrations and meetings held to oppose the closure because doing so would have put her job in jeopardy; her observations were almost entirely of other residents who were not directly involved):

> Pat: That was great, you know when the council changed its mind. Alright, it [the CCAC] had one smack-down but it actually made the council change its mind.

> P.C.: Did you notice any reaction from residents generally to the news?

> Pat: Oh yeah! Being stopped by people in the street, by youngsters even, actually kids in the street, saying it's actually great. We more or less made them change their minds. And the housing thing was going on. And that was getting momentum up. Well, they've actually done it in the school! Sort of people were saying, 'They've done that against all odds.' We can really go on and we can achieve almost anything now, we've gone that far.

All that was left was for Keith Joseph to agree to the council's new proposal. Cyril D'Arcy wrote to Keith Joseph the day after the council vote in March urging him to uphold the decision. He pointed out in his letter that the people of Croxteth had conducted themselves 'with dignity and responsibility' throughout the 15 months of campaigning. On the 8th of March, the CCAC sent a circular to residents of Croxteth asking them to write to the DES to urge it to uphold the new proposal. The DES later confirmed that 73 objections with 6,481 signatures on them were received (*Liverpool Post*, 21st May 1982).

Expanding the campaign goals

The Croxteth Community Action Committee had little to do during this period other than send letters to the DES and wait for the decision. Many members believed that the struggle was over, the last battle won, and the committee decided to branch out into other areas of activity. The strategy throughout this second phase of the campaign had been to broaden the struggle to the entire Croxteth community and to tie the function of the school to social needs on the estate. This resulted in a growth of awareness of other problems on the estate.

> At first this was purely a fight for the school, but as we began the struggle we became aware of the appalling social deprivation here.... As these facts [unemployment and housing statistics] were emerging we became more aware of the community's needs.
>
> (Cyril D'Arcy)

The Action Committee formed several subcommittees to deal with other social problems in Croxteth. There was a committee for housing, one for youth and recreation, and one called the 'organization committee' which was to tend to general needs in the community like fund raising, arranging dances and other activities. The housing committee soon experienced some success when it managed to get a single parent rehoused who had been living in a dilapidated flat overrun by mice. The committee collected lists of complaints from residents and handed them in to the housing department. It also held meetings on housing which Cyril D'Arcy described as having reasonable turn-outs. Thus the campaign for Croxteth Comprehensive was broadening into a general movement for better living conditions in Croxteth and gaining considerable power in the process.

Taking over the school

And the next thing, bump like, you haven't got the school again.

It's like a see-saw. It's been won, it's lost, it's won, it's lost. I call it bureaucracy like. People in another area like London can say, 'Close that school'. And they don't know the background or the problems. They don't understand the problems of the area.

(June and Ray Harrison, Croxteth residents)

Despite the reversal in the council and the many petitions sent to Sir Keith Joseph, Croxteth was not to win back its school. A letter from Keith Joseph dated April 1982, and sent to Kenneth Antcliffe pointed out that Croxteth Comprehensive had many surplus places, and that it was not attracting many new pupils each year. The letter states that reasons for the change in the authority's view had not been made clear and that the school must close. The letter, in other words, ignored the arguments which had featured most prominently in the March council vote, arguments of social need, and stuck to the figures of forms of entry and surplus places.

Cyril D'Arcy's response to the news was swift; he immediately wrote to the Chief Constable of Liverpool declaring:

All previous unwritten guarantees are withdrawn. Croxteth as one of the most disadvantaged areas of Liverpool has all the ingredients for social unrest. The Minister for Education seems intent on fanning the flames by his decision. The Action Committee realise regretfully that they no longer can be responsible for the future actions of the community.

The Croxteth Community Action Committee ended its new activities over other issues in Croxteth, regrouped, and started another militant campaign. On the 22nd of May members brought between 70 and 100 residents to block traffic on Liverpool's Pier Head, a major bus terminal in the city (*Liverpool Echo*, 23rd May 1982). On the 27th of May two busloads of Croxteth residents drove to London to demonstrate outside the Department of Education and Science. A delegation of parents reportedly managed to get promises from both Keith Joseph and Minister of Environment Michael Heseltine to visit Croxteth. Keith Joseph never honoured his, but Michael Heseltine eventually did, though his office didn't allow him to intervene on behalf of the school.

The CCAC led an occupation of the Education Office buildings in central Liverpool on the 6th of July. Over 200 people participated in this action. Amongst their numbers were many pupils of Croxteth Comprehensive who vandalized offices by destroying notice boards and windows, and by tossing eggs inside the building. These activities greatly embarrassed the Action Committee and were the first in a series of events which soon lost the support of the Conservative Party.

A daily picket of the school buildings was begun soon afterwards. Its main object was to prevent the removal of any equipment from the buildings with the last day of school coming up in just over a week's time. On the 12th of July, before school hours, a number of private cars arrived in front of the Parkstile building and the drivers loaded them with sewing machines from the domestic science rooms. When teachers arrived at opening time they received such strong protests from community pickets that the machines were returned later in the day (*Liverpool Post*, 13th July 1982).

The 13th of July 1982 was a day in which Sir Keith Joseph was scheduled to visit Liverpool for talks about needed educational reorganization and for a visit to several of the schools affected. Despite the invitations to visit Croxteth Comprehensive and his earlier promise to do so, Keith Joseph's tour schedule for the day did not include Croxteth. The CCAC organized a demonstration to take place outside the Liverpool Polytechnic in the afternoon when Joseph was giving a talk there. Residents drove down in a hired bus. Keith Joseph agreed to talk to a delegation of parents, including Phil Knibb and Cyril D'Arcy, for five minutes. 'It was obvious,' said Phil Knibb, 'that he wouldn't change his mind.' The delegation returned and told the waiting demonstrators that Joseph wasn't going to visit the estate or change his mind about the school. Feelings of anger were strongly expressed as the demonstrators got back into the bus. During the drive back to Croxteth, several activists began to urge the immediate occupation of the school buildings. This possibility had been considered in committee meetings and the time seemed to be right as large numbers of the residents were together and the recent appeal to Sir Keith Joseph had failed. A decision was made on the bus and the residents split into two groups, one to enter the Parkstile building and one the Stonebridge:

When we came back from town, when Keith Joseph refused to fund our school, we sent someone in to tell the teachers what we were planning to do, that they could take whatever they wanted and then we would be occupying the school from then.

So we waited. I think it was about a quarter to four and then when the children moved out and the teachers, we just moved in. We were in the foyer. We just occupied the foyer, used the toilets. I think it was to keep the school sort of sealed off, so that not everybody would wander around the building.

(Margaret Gaskell)

On the 14th of July, teachers returning to teach met pickets who turned them back. The vast majority of the teachers were sympathetic to the occupation, including head teacher George Smith and deputy head Leo Bernicoff. The school was in the parents' control with nearly all of its equipment in place.

'Chock-a-block with people'

The occupation of the buildings caused great excitement throughout Croxteth. Many people who hadn't been involved in the campaign before suddenly came over to the school to see what was going on and to see how they could help out. Of these, a good number found the atmosphere exciting and decided to join in the campaign. Twenty-six-year-old Kathy Donovan was one:

We used to sit up all night long, you know, telling stories or playing cards, just getting to know each other. And I got to like them, or most of them, you know, naturally you made friends, you made enemies, but everything and everyone was just great....

It was really great, you know, really electric, so I thought, right, that's it, that's for me [laughing]. And I went in there, stayed, and I've been here ever since.

Kathy actually quit her job to become involved in the school full time.

The people interviewed all remember the first weeks of the occupation as one of the bright points, both of the campaign and of their lives. There were always lots of people in the buildings, many new friendships were made, and something exciting always seemed to be going on, like the expectation of bailiffs, or plans for a new demonstration. The occupation broke for a time the isolation felt by many on the estate, creating new bonds between neighbours.

We brought our kids to the school so it wasn't so difficult. There were loads of kids here. It was more like a social club. We had bingo, we'd take turns nipping to the shop, put our dinner on, get the tea and that, and then come back....

People are isolated in this community. I live near Pat and Sharon but I didn't ever meet them before the occupation. People try to fit in what you miss during the day when you get home. It's a strain on the family life. But in the summer the whole community got to know each other.

(Margaret Gaskell)

The vast numbers of new people taking an interest in the school caused a problem for the CCAC, for it became difficult to control their activities.

I stayed in Parkstile, easier for me to get home from there. First of all, there's too many people there at the beginning. I know the first night we took over, the school was just chock-a-block with people all over the place. And then Phil had to say, like, we didn't need that many, and the day time was still the same, plenty of people there.

(Mary Kane)

Phil Knibb reportedly tried to discourage so many from coming. A rota was established for picket duty which helped to control the numbers somewhat, and some of the new arrivals who showed disorderly or untrustworthy behaviour were forced to leave.

Skirmishes

After the occupation the Action Committee came under attack on many fronts all at once. Several battles immediately took place over the supply of utilities to the school. Manwebb Electricity made an effort to get into the school to shut off the supply soon after the occupation, but pickets blocked the workers and the attempt was unsuccessful. On the 19th of July Manwebb did succeed in shutting off the electricity by sending in one workman dressed in ordinary clothing so as not to be conspicuous. The occupiers used candles at night (reportedly supplied by the local police) until the 4th of August when the power was illegally reconnected by a resident.

Other attempts to cut off resources to the school continued throughout the first term, when the Liberals prevented free meals being served, made parents sending their children to Croxteth Comprehensive ineligible for uniform grants and P.E. kits, and made sure that the Local Education Authority wouldn't pay for the examinations eventually held in the school. Supporters of the school fought back by making every possible effort to have these decisions reversed and by getting as much publicity for their activities as possible. Statements to the media played upon public sentiments by making these council actions seem like attacks on the children when they later enrolled. The opponents of the occupation had every advantage when it came to controlling resources necessary to remain in (and later run) the school. They also had the legal authority to send in bailiffs to cast the activists out at any time. But the media campaign run by the CCAC was highly effective in uniting Liverpool sentiment in their favour. It was the successful use of the media which held the bailiffs at bay for the next nine months.

On the 6th of August 1982 the campaign for Croxteth Comprehensive generated new controversy when it was publicly announced that Vanessa Redgrave, the internationally known actress, was going to perform at the Dockers' Club in Liverpool in support of the occupation. One of Croxteth's three Labour Party councillors, Eddie Roderick, publicly asked Ms Redgrave not to come. The local media made much of Roderick's request, which was based on his worry that receiving help from Vanessa Redgrave would start rumours that the CCAC was being influenced by political extremists. Vanessa Redgrave is well known not only for her career but also for her membership in the Workers' Revolutionary Party (WRP). When asked by the *Liverpool Echo* to comment, Cyril D'Arcy replied:

> We are non-political, non-denominational. We are just a group of parents who have been fighting for more than two years to try and save the school. Miss Redgrave was invited to help us raise money. To be perfectly honest, I don't think any of us are aware of her political affiliations. This is a social evening and I can not see what the controversy is about
>
> (*Liverpool Echo*, 6th August 1982)

In fact, the WRP had been supporting the campaign since the occupation of the school and, as time was to show, did indeed wish to influence the course of the struggle and to recruit members in the process. John Bennett, Merseyside WRP activist, was the main organizer for the party who was involved in the school. Once John arrived, many highly supportive articles appeared in *Newsline*, the colour daily paper of the WRP. Croxteth was featured again and again with large colour photographs of the school and community. Local residents appreciated the support very much, and John made some initial progress in recruiting members. As future chapters describe, however, the presence of the WRP in the school eventually contributed to serious interpersonal conflicts among activists which nearly destroyed the campaign from within.

Compared to the WRP, the Labour Party was doing very little to support the occupation on the grassroots level, though politically their support on the Liverpool city council was unwavering. No councillors or party officials appeared at the school to meet with the local activists and show moral support. Croxteth's three local Labour councillors, Eddie Roderick, Bill Snell and Peter Murphy, stayed away from the school, though they raised various proposals in favour of the campaign on the city council. Residents frequently complained about these three councillors and their absence from the school site. More active supporters of the CCAC kept in communication with the school primarily through the leaders of the campaign, Phil and Cyril. The ordinary parent coming daily to help picket had no contact with them. This no doubt unconscious policy of the Labour Party to establish personal relationships and maintain communication with the campaign only through its leaders, and not its rank and file, was to have important consequences described in future chapters.

Summer school

John Bennett of the WRP, it was claimed by several members of the Action Committee in interviews, was the first to suggest running the school once it had been taken over. He was a lecturer himself, with nine years' experience at a technical college in Birkenhead, and suggested that a pilot summer school scheme be run so that the parents would have some experience before the start of the autumn term. The summer school began on the 9th of August with about 50 residents of all ages taking classes in mathematics, video, poetry, social and economic history, and other subjects. John and ten other volunteers taught classes (*Telegraph*, 10th August 1982). The classes were made up of mixed ages and several parents became inspired to begin work on O levels as a result. The poetry class was especially popular.

During this same period, BBC Open Door television arrived at the school and allowed the Action Committee to plan and film its own 30-minute television programme. John Bennett was also central in organizing this activity. This was the television programme which first informed me of the occupation and drew me to it. The programme included interviews with Vincent Donnelly and Lelia Jennings, both medical doctors on the estate, who described common health problems in the area and their origins in poor housing conditions. The home of the Seniors was visited and filmed, a home which had had no electricity or water for seven months, was extremely damp, and had holes in its windows. Ann McComb, resident of Scone Close in Croxteth, was also interviewed. She had had to wait three years for a new door, was flooded out five times, and her son was on 'nerve medicine'. 'Who's Killing Croxteth?' was shown nationally on the 2nd of September.

PHASE TWO: AN UPWARD AND OUTWARD EXPANSION

A few weeks after the end of summer school, volunteer teachers began arriving to offer their help in running a full school programme for the autumn term. The introduction of a large group of teachers from outside of Croxteth, with the addition of 280 pupils on the first day of classes, greatly altered the nature of the campaign and inaugerated its third phase. Before considering the events of the autumn term, several features of the second phase require emphasis. Phase two was a period in which a parents' and teachers' campaign became supplanted by a purely community movement which had begun to address other issues on the Croxteth estate alongside the removal of the school. During this period the protest ideology ceased to insist that other schools should close instead of Croxteth and focused upon the social needs of Croxteth alone. Tactics involved many illegal public actions, culminating in the take-over of government buildings. At this point, interest throughout the entire Croxteth estate was at a maximum and the school became a symbol of many grievances held by residents.

One of the most significant features of phase two was the great expansion of power which occurred during its course. Power was initially expanded through getting media coverage. The combination of Phil Knibb's tactical planning and Cyril D'Arcy's powers of articulation gained city-wide, and to a certain extent nation-wide, sympathy for the Croxteth campaign. Such sympathy was a powerful tool for influencing politicians and staving off the use of police. Increased visibility also united support throughout the Croxteth estate for the Action Committee.

Towards the end of the summer, the CCAC was able to further expand its power base through making connections with the local and national trade union movement. These connections would prove to be absolutely crucial during the 1982–83 school year when large amounts of money (at times £1,000 per week) were required to heat the school and feed its pupils. Some time during July or August, Phil Knibb began talking with Eddie Roberts, full-time official of the Liverpool Transport and General Workers' Union, and a personality described in some detail by Huw Beynon in *Working for Ford* (Beynon 1973). Eddie and other members of the T&G had already drafted plans to establish union-community linkages and the needs of Croxteth were an excellent reason to bring these plans to fruition. A committee called the 'Merseyside Trade Union-Community Liaison Committee' (MTUCLC) was established in August, drawing representatives from a number of unions around Merseyside. In addition, one of Phil Knibb's brothers, Ron Knibb, was contacted and asked to start drumming up support from different unions, not only on Merseyside but nationally as well. The MTUCLC was an important committee for the remainder of the occupation, managing through the hard work of Eddie Roberts and others on it to collect regular sums of money for the school.

Thus by September 1982 the campaign for Croxteth Comprehensive had expanded outwards towards the community of Croxteth as well as upwards towards the powerful organizations of the labour movement. Unnoticed by the activists at this time was a tension between these two moves, a tension between community and labour movement politics which was to become manifest in a number of powerful conflicts during the months to come. These conflicts were to have important ramifications for the educational features of the campaign. But these conflicts took place only after the campaign was to alter greatly once again, when the addition of teachers and pupils to its ranks inaugurated the third and final phase of the battle for Croxteth Comprehensive.

4
On an express train
going 80 miles an hour

We were on an express train which was careering along at 80 miles an hour. One thing you didn't have was time for a cool appraisal of what you were doing. You didn't have time to get off and look and think. Weekends you were knackered and fell into bed and slept.

(Chris Hawes, first teacher co-ordinator)

Phase three of the campaign for Croxteth Comprehensive began on 23rd September 1982, when the CCAC was suddenly joined by a group of volunteer teachers from outside of Croxteth and over 280 students from the Croxteth estate to start the autumn term. Phase three was thus brought into being through the addition of two new groups of participants. The goals of the campaign also changed at the outset of phase three through the establishment of a sub-objective – the running of a school by the protest group. As time went on, however, the status of this objective came into dispute: should it really be a sub-objective, a mere means to the greater goal of winning back a state-run school? Or should it be an objective in its own right? Tactics were also to shift during this phase, though only after serious disagreements between those involved were resolved. Some wished to expand the community nature of the campaign, using the school as a base for generating more local involvement and for addressing the many other problems affecting residents in Croxteth. Others wished to solidify the linkages which had been made to labour movement organizations and reconstruct the campaign through an identification with their general objectives and party-political tactics.

Phase three thus began with a number of ambiguities which were to lead to a series of intense conflicts among participants. The ambiguities concerned the *political objectives* of the campaign and their problematical relationship to running an educational programme. At the outset these conflicts were submerged and unarticulated. It was assumed by those who had been involved and by those who arrived to volunteer their services as teachers that a consensus existed on campaign objectives. Soon after the first day of school, however, it became increasingly clear that no such consensus existed.

The first realm in which differences in perspectives were manifested had to do with the nature of the school which was to be run. Should it follow traditional or progressive lines? Most residents assumed it would follow the former while many teachers hoped it would follow the latter. Later these different conceptions of the educational objectives of the occupation were found to imply profoundly different political orientations.

In the most general terms, educational practices and campaign policy were shaped by two categories of conditions: 1) constraints acting externally upon the volition of the participants; and 2) intersubjective frameworks which determined the perceptions and interpretations of the participants.

In this chapter I will focus upon the constraints which helped to shape schooling practices in Croxteth during the first half-term. In the next two chapters I will discuss the intersubjective frameworks. Both sets of conditions tell us much about the powers that shape schooling practices generally, not just those which developed within the occupied buildings of Croxteth Comprehensive.

THE FIRST DAYS OF SCHOOL

While the Action Committee fought its skirmishes in the local council and with the media in July and August, it also began to put out a call for volunteer teachers to come to help run the school in the autumn term. Cyril D'Arcy and Phil Knibb travelled about Liverpool and visited other cities to give talks about the campaign and to make it known that graduates were needed to teach in the school. At the same time, word was spread about the Croxteth housing estate that the occupied school would hold classes for secondary pupils beginning in September. Parents were invited to send their children.

I actually missed the first day of school due to an interesting event which throws some light on the paranoia which at times plagued the occupation. To make a long story short, John Bennett of the WRP suspected me of being a CIA agent, sent to undermine or sabotage the occupation. My American accent as well as the way I responded to a question of his about my teaching qualifications were later provided as his grounds for suspicion. He told me during a meeting held the day before classes that the Action Committee held these suspicions and had asked me not to participate. I therefore stayed home the first day, never expecting to see Croxteth again, until I got a message from Cyril D'Arcy that John had made up the story of an Action Committee decision and that I was needed and wanted. I thus began work at Croxteth on the second day, not the first, and will provide some of the flavour of that first day through the accounts of others. As described in chapters ahead, this may not have been the only time that false rumours were circulated about certain activists in order to push them out or curtail their power.

Henry Stewart, a Cambridge graduate in economics and computing who had volunteered in the school after hearing Cyril D'Arcy give a talk at a meeting of the Liverpool TGWU's unemployed branch, was one of the five teachers present on the 23rd of September. He provided a written account of his experiences at my request:

> I went along to the big meeting of local parents [held on the 20th of September], which made me realize the extent of community support, and we assured them of all the teachers we had and all the options we were going to teach (gulp, was that a little dishonest?). And then the big opening day came.

> We had all of five teachers, and these hordes of kids, 280 of them! (We claimed 350 of course, but I counted up the registers; and then there were the ten teachers we told the media about!) And we turned up to find three TV crews, a couple of radio people and probably a dozen other reporters. That always did impress me about the Action Committee: they were very good at involving the media. I think it was Cyril who arranged most of it.

> And I was the teacher who had volunteered to talk to the press on that first day, partially because I wasn't expecting to want a teaching job with the local authority. So this mass of press people packed into my classroom, which already had 48 kids in it (I was lucky, one class had 58 that day) and filmed me and the kids and the other pressmen. *The Times* had a good picture caption: 'Croxteth children get a lesson in media studies' underneath a photo of the assembled ranks of photographers.

> Apart from the media, the most that could be said about that day was that we survived. I doubt anybody learnt anything. Three of my kids left at lunchtime to go to Ellergreen, and then came back Ellergreen was even worse apparently! We didn't have the resources, particularly the teachers, to cope with the mass of students the community had entrusted the school with. Total exhaustion is the main thing I remember feeling after that day.

Henry's account is typical of others taken. The first day was a great surprise to all concerned, with over 62 per cent of the previous year's number of pupils arriving. It was a triumph for the Action Committee, indicating significant parental support and trust. Media coverage was very good with all the major national newspapers, television stations, and BBC Radio Four giving sympathetic reports. The media was still charmed by the novelty of the event and the images of the common person, or 'the community', fighting back against governmental neglect.

But the large numbers caused problems for the small teaching staff of five. The staff were totally unprepared and coped by dividing the day into three very long periods, teaching mainly mathematics, English, and games. Pupils were taught in their year groups, all first years together, all second years together, and so on. The Action Committee helped by staffing the office where the roll registers were kept, getting books from locked rooms for the teachers, teaching games, P.E., sewing, typing, and cooking a free lunch in the kitchen. Some of the food for the lunch was donated from local shops: chips, beans, and sausage being the basic meal from this day on through most of the occupation. The atmosphere was exciting but very confusing, and the pupils, who behaved very well in the presence of TV cameras, were often boisterous and disruptive at other times.

Chris Hawes, an author of children's plays and books and a former teacher with 15 years' experience, was the first teacher co-ordinator. He and his fellow author friend, Graz Monvid, had heard a talk by Cyril during August at a meeting of a national children's theatre group in London, and they eventually decided to lend their support to the campaign by teaching in the school, even though they both lived in Lancaster. Their hope was that enough teachers would eventually volunteer from Liverpool to relieve them of their commitment.

Chris came down from his home in Lancaster and resided with the D'Arcys for the duration of his involvement. Graz commuted by car on the days she worked in the school. Their recollections of the first day correspond to Henry's: too few teachers, poor discipline, and poor preparation were the main problems.

> After the first assembly I think we had about 60 pupils each in a classroom. We didn't know their names, they didn't know us, so they had absolutely no security, no security at all. We had absolutely no security either. There was no structure, there was no equipment, doors were locked and books were we didn't know where. There was no information from past teachers as to what they'd been teaching.
>
> (Graz Monvid)

I arrived to teach on the second day, finding the atmosphere very heightened and exciting. The day began for the teachers in the staffroom where a group of us sat in a semi-circle about Chris who pointed to a crude daily schedule on a blackboard: 'Who can teach English to the third year first period? Henry? O.K.' Chalking Henry's name into a vacant slot, he continued 'Now we've got a problem with the second years. Ernie [a local resident], could you take them onto the field for P.E. and games? Good!' Teachers sat together with local activists as Chris co-ordinated the problem-solving, plenty of suggestions coming from the rest of us. Teaching was difficult because virtually all of us had to invent our lessons as we walked through the corridors towards the rooms of waiting pupils. I remember a three-hour period with the fifth years that day in which I alternated lessons in mathematics with interaction games and values-clarification exercises.

Every few days one or two new teachers arrived, some of them coming from Lancaster through the efforts of Chris Hawes and Graz Monvid. Some came in response to ads placed in the alternative press, publications like *Peace News*, *The Morning Star*, and *Labour Briefing* taking ads willingly. One volunteer, Yola Jacobson, came all the way from Edinburgh to teach history, finding a place to stay in Liverpool and remaining for over seven months after reading such an ad. More and more came from Liverpool itself as ads in restaurants, shops, the Polytechnic, and the University of Liverpool began attracting them. Many members of the teaching staff had to split their time between teaching and making trips into town to try to get more volunteers:

> We were going out during the lunch hours, going literally from table to table at the Everyman Restaurant, the Poly, the University, asking for help, asking for teachers, anyone to come and help. But Liverpudlian militancy was certainly slow in showing itself.
>
> (Graz Monvid)

CONSTRAINTS

The teacher volunteers were a very mixed lot. Most experienced amongst us was Pat Kellet, a retired deputy head who volunteered in the school full time during the first and second terms and then for three days a week in the third. Pat became important to the occupation because he was an excellent teacher and highly respected by the local activists. His classes were popular with the pupils and soon showed results, with well-executed essays and mathematics exercises displayed on his classroom walls. He was very often pointed to with pride by local volunteers describing the occupation to outsiders and definitely served a legitimating role, giving confidence to parents sending their children to the school.

Other teachers included a politically astute immigrant from the Middle East who taught maths and chemistry; a member of the WRP with a master's degree in English (not John Bennett); a member of Big Flame with a degree in economics from one of the Oxbridge universities; two Jesuit priests who advocated liberation theology and had been involved with the radical Catholic publication, *Slant* (actually becoming involved during the second term); a radical Catholic feminist from Lancaster, also closely associated with *Slant*, who taught history for the Open University; a religious studies major from

Lancaster who belonged to the SWP; members of the Merseyside Arts Association; a former member of an animal rights movement; several recent university graduates with no political affiliations; a woman fluent in German and French who worked for 'Left Out'; a number of members of PROUT, an organization promoting a combination of grassroots democracy and local economic control with spiritual ideals from the East; several former teachers (including the former head of an English department) who had been frustrated with traditional teaching practice; several recent education graduates waiting for a school placement with no strong political affiliations; and so on. Nearly all of these volunteers had at least a B.A. or B.Sc. degree; many had masters' degrees and teaching diplomas as well. One-third of the volunteers were experienced teachers, two-thirds were not.

In short, many of the teacher volunteers had affiliations or sympathies with some political organization having a 'far left', libertarian, or new-age ideology, and had come to the school in the service of their ideals. Others lacked any political motivation other than a sympathy for the deprived community in its struggle with the state and came to try teaching or to try alternative forms of teaching after having put in many frustrating years in traditional schools. Almost all had middle-class backgrounds and were coming to Croxteth for the first time. Those who hoped Croxteth would produce alternative forms of education were soon disappointed to find that many constraints acted to give them little time to even think out new forms of schooling practice, much less develop or search for the materials which would have been required.

One of the most fundamental constraints was the serious lack of teachers. The trickle of new volunteers arriving every few days was never enough to staff the school adequately. As new volunteers arrived, others left, finding after only a few days that the situation was too trying for them. Too few teachers was a fundamental constraint which faced the staff, resulting in many secondary constraints and problems.

The first of these secondary constraints was time. With such a small staff, everyone had to focus as much as possible on teaching and teaching alone. None of us had time to do more than take classes, mark books, and plan lessons, usually in several subjects, for the next day. There wasn't enough time to adequately search for more volunteers or to plan innovative and interesting lessons. A traditional curriculum rapidly pervaded the school as a result.

The second major constraint was the timetable. A staff of five teachers means that only five classes can be taught at any one time, and if all five of these classes engages all five volunteers, no teacher is left over to handle the large number of administrative duties required by all schools. Although numbers of volunteers slowly increased, timetables could only be altered occasionally because of the enormous disruption which alterations produced for the pupils. We had a three-period day for several weeks which stressed 'the basics' of mathematics, English, science, and history. We also depended absolutely on local adults from Croxteth to teach classes in P.E., games, sewing, cooking, and crafts. A five-period day was introduced after several weeks, when we had a larger staff to deploy, but the specific subject-period-teacher allocations of this schedule had to be changed several times as teachers left and new teachers arrived. At the beginning of the second term a seven-period day was timetabled which lasted until the end of the school year.

A third initial constraint was the irregular hours of availability of the volunteers. Some could only come one day a week, others two or three. This meant that classes had to be arranged according to the erratic schedules of volunteers two or three periods of a single subject in a day to fit the available time of the volunteer with expertise in it. Students were subjected to very long lessons in some subjects as a result. And when one of these teachers left, the timetable was thrown into chaos. Newly arriving volunteers possess-ing the needed expertise often couldn't match their personal schedules with the empty slots of our current timetable.

To reduce class sizes, measures were taken which introduced a very powerful fourth constraint: streaming. We broke year groups as soon and as efficiently as we could into two classes or 'forms' each. This was done simply by asking students to group themselves into the forms they had been in the previous year. This resulted largely in streamed groups because ability had been the basis of form divisions in previous years. Thus we had form 5A and 5B, 4A and 4B (which were later further broken up into 4A1 and 4A2 largely on gender but partially on ability lines), 3A and 3B, and so on. Streaming was therefore introduced without much thought, a result primarily due to constraints of time, but a result which quickly became a significant constraint in its own right.

Streaming coincided with a decision to teach towards examinations. Those pupils deemed capable of passing examinations were quickly put onto examination syllabuses. The reasons for our decision to teach towards the O level and CSE examinations are discussed in the next chapter. This decision, plus streaming, soon determined the allocation of teachers to forms. The most experienced teacher volunteers took the higher streamed groups because it was decided that they must be taught towards examinations and could not afford to lose time or to be subjected to the most inexperienced teachers. This resulted in many negative effects. The 'B' classes soon became notorious for behaviour problems and their teachers frequently left. Newly arriving tea-chers were often surprised, when they offered to teach drama or English or some other subject they were acquainted with, to discover that these subjects were already covered or couldn't be scheduled without a revision of the entire timetable. In consequence, many were very often asked to take classes on the basis of vacancies, frequently in subjects other than their own areas of expertise, and very often for 'B' classes. This often happened within minutes of their arrival and it caused many of them to leave after only a brief period. The pupils in the 'B' classes became even more rebellious and resentful as a result.

The experience of being put immediately into a classroom with one of the 'B' groups always presented the new volunteer with problems of establishing authority. Barry Kushner, a recent sociology graduate at the time, describes his arrival at the school with his friend Paul:

> I went to see Chris Hawes and was sent back to the car to get my qualifications. We showed our qualifications and were found to be O.K. Then Chris asked me if I wanted to take this 5th year class. Straight off!

> I remember Mick and Joe [two community volunteers] were there. I felt it was very difficult. I'd been there a quarter of an hour only and found it hard to impose any organization [on the pupils]. Hour and a half lessons and I'd never taught before properly in a school. It was terrible. And I was given 3B [later in the day], and they were absolutely abysmal, a really mean class, about 20 to 24 boys....

> Sometimes we managed and sometimes we didn't. Because I was young I used to wear jeans then. I think I was pretty idealistic in those days. I was really pleasant. There's a period when they sus you out. I think they could sus you out. I wasn't obviously very autocratic and they were calling me Barry. We just managed to get them working.

Although Barry stayed, many did not, and the holes left in the timetable caused daily aggravation for the entire school.

A fifth constraint was inexperience. Two-thirds of the volunteers were university graduates with no training or experience in teaching. The combination of inexperience plus tight constraints on time meant that these teachers usually depended upon what they remembered of their own experiences in secondary school for their pedagogy. Curriculum had to be rapidly constructed and standard examination syllabuses and traditional textbooks found in the school were heavily relied upon. Peter Clarke, an inexperienced volunteer with a master's degree in English who remained on the staff for the entire year, explained his own method of surviving the first weeks during an April 1983 interview:

> Well, I was taken to Chris Hawes, the co-ordinator at the time, and he shook my hand and took me into a classroom [laughs]. Instantly! The 5B

girls as well, as it so happened. The 5B girls at that time were quite a large class. And I was very easy-going about it, which I think helped. If I had had the sort of attitude, 'I must do my best', you know expecting a 100 per cent response [pause], I think you'd be very quickly discouraged. You couldn't plan ahead back then like you can at this time. You had to remember what you were doing at a comparable age at school and hope they would like it, which wasn't very satisfactory.

Thus constraints in numbers of teachers, time, inexperience, the limitations imposed by the timetable, and the high volunteer turnover rate resulted in streamed classes, a traditional curriculum, an emphasis on examinations, and a fairly traditional, though more informal, pedagogic practice. None of these results, aside from the informal pedagogy, were planned or consciously sought in any way. All were the product of people trying to survive in a difficult situation.

INNOVATIONS

While the educational content of most classes was generally very traditional, innovations rose spontaneously at once in many classrooms. The volunteer teachers, despite the constraints, certainly differed from Croxteth's former teaching staff. They immediately abolished the practice of caning pupils, to the horror of many local activists from Croxteth. They dressed informally and did not require pupils to wear uniforms. They introduced themselves to pupils with their first names. During the first days, many teachers made efforts to discuss the significance of the occupation with pupils, or have them talk about, or even act out, their views on life in Croxteth. Early English classes invariably assigned essays on the occupation of Croxteth Comprehensive. Such discussions and activities were at first popular with the pupils, many of whom were particularly keen to talk or write about drugs and the police. Henry Stewart recalls an English class he had with the 4Bs early in the term. His account reflects some of his own political and educational orientations as well:

The 4Bs, I certainly remember them. A great bunch of kids but no interest in school. And we spent those first few weeks stuffing them full of maths and English. I remember one good English lesson where got talking about the police, and also about their attitudes to blacks, but I'd rather forget about that. Although there was a grudging respect for the way they'd hammered the police in Liverpool 8 [Toxteth, during the 1981 riots], they came out with all the standard phrases about flooding our country and so on. And they seemed to think that Liverpool 8 was paved with 5-a-side football pitches and every resource young people could want. I asked them to do an essay on the police and every one of them did it. You have to know 4B to understand what a rare event that was. I remember the impeccable logic of Neville [pseudonym]: 'If the police can kill people on the street, like Jimmy Kelly, then the people on the street should be able to kill the police.' There was a deep sense of injustice about the way they were treated, and the times they'd been picked up for doing nothing, although most of them readily admitted, boasted of, the things they'd got away with, like setting fire to local unoccupied flats, which a parent helping out confirmed.

Henry, and some other teachers, also found they didn't have to depend entirely upon what they remembered from their own schooling to develop their pedagogic practice.

And there was the 3C, before they were renamed the 3B. They were very lively, and intelligent, although they directed most of their intelligence at outwitting the teacher. There was the time I was trying to teach some basic algebra; I don't remember it exactly but things like $7x = 42$, what is x? And they were getting them all correct. I soon noticed the smirks around the classroom and discovered that they had those times-table books under their desks. However, what they didn't realize was that it wasn't the calculation I was trying to teach them, it was understanding how x represented a number. Inspired by the thought that they were cheating, they had quite happily coped with that. Could I lead them unwittingly into other concepts by somehow allowing them to 'cheat' in other ways, I wondered.

And there was the time I promised 3C they could sing songs at the end of the lesson if they did the maths I set them. They did all their maths and so I told them, yes now they could sing. Without hesitation they broke into:

We don't need no education
We don't need no thought control....

by Pink Floyd, 'The Wall'. A parent came running up the stairs, preparing to tell off a class she thought had gone wild.

By mid-October I had come to occupy a fairly central position on the staff by putting in long hours on the timetable and using my own past experiences as a teacher in making contributions to staff discussions. I had become one of the stable core of teachers and had managed to establish control and consistency in my own mathematics classes. Eventually (in mid-October) I would become the second teacher co-ordinator after Chris Hawes left. I shared timetable work with Henry Stewart, who had quickly become a good friend. We worked in liaison with Chris Hawes, who specialized in other aspects of co-ordination such as giving the daily assemblies and serving as the communication link between staff and Action Committee. The confusion and poor organization in the school during these days sometimes resulted in help from the pupils as well as disruption. An account of one of my own days, recorded in the field note books, gives a not atypical picture of the first half-term. On this day fifth-years acted very supportively. Following are selected portions of my notes for 18th October 1982, the first day in which the five-period-day timetable was introduced:

> Henry [Stewart] and I arrived early to plan the day's schedule, which we did. The entire Lancaster contingent didn't arrive, however, which completely ruined the schedule. Only Chris [Hawes] arrived by train to say the others couldn't make it, the car had broken down. So we made last-minute changes as best we could. Eight teachers showed up during the course of the day, two of them very late.

> I had to take 5A and 5B simultaneously, a task made easier by the fact that they were in adjacent rooms. I had a double period of maths with both. I first set a lesson with the 5B class, left them with their text books, and started giving a lecture to 5A. Paula [a pupil from 5B] watched over her class, a role she has taken for some time. Paula had originally been a member of 5A but had been very disruptive and uncomfortable in the class because of difficulties she was having with the work. Since her change to 5B she's become a strong leader, negotiating between them and teachers frequently, much as Gerard Irving does for the 4Bs. She regularly came into the 5A room today to ask me how to work certain problems in the assignment and then went back to explain it to the others and help them with their work. Once she came in to ask me where she could get materials.

> I had to stay with 5A longer than I felt comfortable with because the lesson was rather difficult in trigonometry and I had to go from desk to desk showing individuals how to work the problems. At one point Paula came and warned me that I'd been with 5A too long: 'They're getting restless, Phil!', so I left 5A a few minutes later to see about the situation with 5B. When I came in the room, Paula was going over answers at the board with a relatively quiet and attentive class.

Although some classes were conducted well in the difficult conditions which existed during this period, with teachers and pupils taking innovative and effective action, discipline problems eventually curbed many of the innovations, forcing teachers to fall back continuously on more traditional approaches. The 4B and 3B classes were especially difficult, and it was not uncommon to hear teachers shouting loudly for order when walking past these classes along the school's corridors. As the novelty of the occupation wore off, the use of discussions about day-to-day life and unconventional rewards for good work lost appeal to the pupils. Pupils were regularly sent out of classrooms to report to the office for offences in the classroom, but parents in the corridors frequently resented this practice, not really knowing what to do with pupils sent out in this way and often expressing their belief that teachers were showing incompetence in having to put pupils out. Those pupils sent out would also sometimes find an empty room in the building in which to hide from adults, waiting for the bell to ring to go to their next class. Detention classes were set up after school to keep disruptive pupils in as a punishment.

THE LOCAL ACTIVISTS

During this period the local activists were also very busy under conditions of stress. They were divided into a number of groups based on where they worked and what they did. A number remained at the Parkstile building where few classes were actually held. They kept a picket up in that building, kept the premises clean, and were present and helpful when a few specialist classes like domestic science and, for a time, typing were held there to take advantage of the extra facilities of that building. The rest worked in Stone-bridge. A kitchen crew consisting of Molly, Marty McArdle, Irene D'Arcy, and Carol Knibb was established which cooked lunch for all pupils, staff, and local volunteers every day. Tommy Maher became the school's main-tenance man and general trouble-shooter if anything mechanical started to fail. Three women from the estate, Freda, Sandra, and Jean, who all worked day-time jobs, came to the school every single evening for the entire year to clean every classroom and corridor.

Several activists, particularly Ann Abercromby and Ev Loftus, worked in the office, keeping the registers and handling the large amount of correspond-ence necessary for the campaign. A large part of the correspondence consisted of requests for funds from trade union branches and thank-you letters when such funds came in. The Action Committee also sent speakers to various meetings around the country, usually describing the struggle and requesting help but sometimes actually advising others in similar situations on possible strategy. Still other volunteers from Croxteth worked in the corridors to keep order during class changes and at the day's beginning, break time, lunch time and after school. These volunteers not infrequently were called upon by teachers for help during class hours, to quiet down a noisy class, remove a troublesome pupil, or get needed materials. Sometimes they sat in difficult classes, like the 4Bs or 3Bs, for an entire period to aid the teacher in keeping order, and many times they actually took classes for exercises set by a teacher who was occupied elsewhere. I several times had

Ernie Jones, Margaret Gaskell, and Pat Brennen take mathematics classes based on textbook exercises I first explained to them. These activists had little trouble keeping control, though over-dependence on the textbooks limited the educational value of the lessons.

The office became a room not only of business but of leisure and conversation during the day. When not required for any job or duty, volunteers often sat together in the office to drink tea and chat. The room always had people in it, staff and community volunteers, and one could hear the latest facts and rumours there or express one's frustrations to sympathetic ears. Pupils also continuously showed up at the office during the day, explaining that their teacher needed this or that material or that they'd been kicked out of a room for causing trouble. Some pupils became regular visitors to the office, exchanging gossip and jokes with adults in the room. While the conversations went on, with people coming in and going out, Ann or Ev or both would usually be sitting at a typewriter, joining in the conversations while typing away and answering the telephone. Ann and Ev were good friends; both had children in the school, were popular with most teachers and local activists, and together maintained what became the social centre of the school during the first months.

After school and on weekends local residents supervised children on the trampolines or at football matches. Many students remained after school to participate in these activities. Spirits were high at such times and rapport between pupils and adults was excellent.

There was a small number of local volunteers who actually became permanent teachers. Mick Checkland and Joey Jacobs took games and P.E. from the start of the year to the very end. Ernie Jones, in addition to collecting food each morning from local shops to bring to the kitchen, frequently took P.E. and lessons in maths, English, and history, set by teachers. Kathy Donovan took sewing with girls, Rose took needlework. Some of the locals took classes for short periods of time, Tommy Maher taking woodwork for a period; even Phil Knibb, who was always busy both inside and outside the school with campaign work, took a few classes of welding. By the end of the first term this group was joined by Keith and Frank Leatherbarrow and Paul Gerard who daily taught science or assisted other science teachers as lab technicians. These three volunteers came from Liverpool communities outside Croxteth which were similar in socio-economic make-up and culture. The Leatherbarrows had grown up in Croxteth but had moved out in later years.

Phil Knibb's role during this part of the occupation was to do what was needed in the school and to spend much time going to meetings of various types in town. He maintained contacts with the Merseyside Trade Union Community Liaison Committee and kept in communication with the local

Labour Party, getting to know key members. In the school he could be seen on a typical day discussing strategy with the office workers, handing out registers to arriving teachers, leaving and returning in his car to attend some meeting in town, and helping with the washing-up in the kitchen after lunch. He also spent a couple of nights a week sleeping at the school for picket duty and more than once had to get up in the middle of the night to visit the school after receiving a phone call from a picket that vandals or thieves had been around. His wife Carol worked in the kitchen every day as did Cyril's wife, Irene. Cyril himself was seldom in the school during the day. He continued in his role of correspondent for the committee and travelled alone or with Phil to give talks about the occupation. Cyril also took several overnight picket duties a week, along with Irene D'Arcy and their daughter, Collette.

LOSING THE BATTLE FOR PUPIL CONSENT

From the first day pupil disruptions were a major problem in Croxteth. Discipline problems were concentrated in the B classes, with 4B and 3B (13–14 year olds and 12–13 year olds respectively) especially difficult. While other classes went well and some, especially 4A, displayed exceptionally high levels of motivation on the students' part, disruptions in the corridors and in the B classes began to dominate the entire school atmosphere.

Reasons for these disruptions were complex. Initially, however, it seemed clear to many teachers that the problem was at least partially rooted in the traditional curriculum offered and the use of streaming, which caused resentment in the lower streams. The lower streams were also the streams that suffered most from teacher inexperience and turnover and the streams most in need of an alternative curriculum of some kind.

While teachers disagreed on the relationship of pedagogy and curriculum to disruption, some believing that an alternative curriculum was necessary while some were sceptical, all believed that if the sense of common purpose and excitement they felt amongst themselves could be extended to the pupils, disruptions and discipline problems would diminish. This was the reason for the policy of a daily assembly. The hope was that assemblies would break the fragmented nature of the pupil's experience in the school by bringing everyone together and reminding them of the common purpose everyone supposedly shared. Chris Hawes began giving the assemblies every morning. On Fridays he was joined by Paul Shackley, another volunteer commuting from Lancaster who had majored in philosophy and religious studies at university, to give a religious reading. The practice of giving religious readings at assemblies was another move in the direction of very traditional

British schooling practice, though Paul read not only from the Bible but from the Bhagavad Gita and the Koran as well.

Chris gave reports on political developments at assembly and frequently strove to produce a feeling of unity in the hall by calling for group cheers and clapping for the successes of the campaign. He also repeatedly stressed the difficulties of the situation and complimented the pupils on how well they were doing. But invariably, assemblies also contained strong condemnations of disruptive pupils, the 'minority who are trying to ruin it for all of us', and called on the well behaved to help control the trouble-makers. Chris's hope, and the staff's generally, was that pupils would come to share the adults' feeling of commitment to an important cause.

But discipline continued to be the major problem in the school just the same. Class disruptions were one problem; outside the classroom there were incidents of vandalism, petty theft, and fighting that caused great concern. When the first-years were taken to a public baths to swim on 20th October, they were kicked out for unruly behaviour and told not to come back. A major theft brought a police officer to visit the school in mid-October. Chemicals stolen from the chemistry storerooms threw everyone into a panic and the police were again called, though in the end the items were recovered through the efforts of local adults. Chris often expressed anger and outrage on the mornings after such incidents. He kept calling on the pupils to understand the political importance of running the school successfully and to identify with the work of the occupation in opposition to the government trying to shut the school down.

However, the efforts of Chris and other teachers to get pupils to share in the sense of commitment to the occupation was really an effort to get pupils to obey teachers and do school work. Although many adult volunteers in the school interpreted pupil disruptions in terms of their age, as 'immature behaviour' which indicated their 'lack of understanding' of the situation (see next chapter), it was in fact the discrepancy experienced by pupils between the authority relations and school work of the classroom, and the occupation of the buildings and the confrontation with the local government, which seemed to be the problem. Pupils did support the latter aspects of the occupation. They expressed in exhaustive interviews taken during the course of the year with nearly all of them a great deal of loyalty and enthusiasm for the campaign to keep Croxteth Comprehensive. Many of the older ones helped in demonstrations by making banners and actually coming along. They certainly shared in the atmosphere of the school; however, this atmosphere didn't extend very far into the classroom. In the classroom pupils faced a single teacher asking them to do work which had no obvious connection to the occupation itself.

Thus the appeals by teachers during the first weeks of the occupation for commitment and responsible behaviour on the part of pupils most often took the form of a stern demand for pupils to realize that they had a duty to behave in the school. The pedagogy and curriculum in the school did not draw upon the political context of the occupation; in many ways it contradicted it. Over time, appeals to pupils to take schooling seriously began more frequently to take the form of trying to convince pupils that school work was for their benefit, rather than the futile attempt to get them to link school work with support for the campaign. A substitution of 'exchange' incentives for 'moral' incentives was taking place. The explanation usually given to pupils from teachers and parents alike soon took the form of a promise that school work would one day translate into a good job.

Efforts to control pupils thus shifted not only in their method (sanctions), but eventually in their rationale, towards the traditional promise of the 'good job'. Pupils, however, were well aware of two facts which made the employability argument unconvincing. First, for most of them jobs didn't seem a likely outcome for school work as their parents and older sisters and brothers couldn't get them, with or without examinations. Second, most believed, despite the protestations of teachers, that few would get good examination results. The British CSE and O level examinations are difficult for working-class children to pass, not having the cultural capital of their middle-class competitors. There was thus a tension built into the situation, which manifested itself primarily in the classroom.

SLIDING TO–1OWARDS CRISIS

As the weeks continued during the first half-term, discipline problems became a matter of increasingly great concern to the Action Committee. There is no record of how many local activists volunteered in the school during the first weeks, though it is clear that the number had fallen greatly from the large numbers who had come just after the occupation in July. Whatever the number was at the beginning of term, it steadily fell as the half-term approached. Like many of the volunteer teachers, local activists got tired of the constant problems with pupils and with the disorganization caused by poor teacher discipline (late arrivals) and the impossibility of establishing a working timetable. As the numbers decreased, the situation got more difficult. Those who remained had extra burdens, and everyone was worried about the quality of education which was being provided.

By the first half-term the campaign was generally acknowledged to be in another crisis. Chris Hawes was in a key position to perceive the development of this crisis as he was the chief liaison between the staff and the parents during this period. His account of its development is worth quoting in full.

In it he gives his perceptions of the roots of the discipline problems in the type of education that was being provided. He also mentions problems the Action Committee was having with 'the far left', which was primarily a problem with the WRP:

I was lodging with Cyril D'Arcy and going back to Lancaster at weekends which was a good idea. It gave me a lot more to go on because in the evenings I was drinking with Cyril mostly in the Lobster [local pub near the school]. Those amazing sing-songs, mixing with the people socially, that was a great pleasure because you know what those people are like, they can show you a good time....

I was there, I was living in Crocky. That became the line of communication between the Action Committee and the teachers. We were trying to hammer out those questions of discipline and how to control the situation. We, the teachers, needed more help. The number of parents began to dwindle away. We actually needed that presence in the school and it wasn't there and people were drifting away. It was quite understandable, people were picketing the school 24 hours a day. The same small few people were holding the line, living in the building, staying over night. They were absolutely knackered.

Tempers were getting frayed and ragged. Discipline was a problem and got people onto the edge. People were shouting when they felt very threatened within and without. And that was why discipline problems became worse. A lot of things that happened in the school in those early days was entirely a result of that. It was actually about a bunch of people feeling extremely threatened. Things were happening within the school that were causing people to worry. Vandalism from the kids, items being stolen, a feeling of suspicion that things being stolen from the school with the connivance of certain parents.

There was also a certain amount of political paranoia – people looking with suspicion in the direction of the far left. I always felt the involvement of the far left in the occupation had been positive, but at times they were unhelpful, insensitive, and clumsy. It was pointed out to them and they ceased to be so.

I strongly felt that there were contradictions set up in the situation which were causing problems within ourselves. For me personally there was a major contradiction in terms of the actual quality of the teaching we were able to provide.... With hindsight one of the problems was that the teaching style we adopted was not appropriate to the situation. Not a less disciplined but a more informal approach should have been used. We should have used the situation, we should have done more work centred around the occupation....

In general, there was a sense in which the parents – this came up at Action Committee meetings – expected too much of the teaching staff. Expecting the staff to re-establish the kind of regime which had existed in the school, and this was a very cruel expectation to have of these teachers who were struggling away. I was very used to having to constantly defend the teachers, actually to make appeals to parents to come in and help, and to not have those parents come forward. That was very demoralizing at times....

The pressure was unbelievable and there were times when you thought you were just over the hump, times when you'd congratulate yourself. You'd get through the day, you'd achieved a school day without a riot breaking out and you'd go down to the pub to celebrate. Two or three days of that in the school and you'd think, we've achieved it, it's actually working as a school now, it's operating as a school. And then some disaster would happen. Things like (pause), some kids broke into the science labs and stole chemicals, the implications of that, all the time too you were conscious of what the press could make out of that. They could cut the teaching off any time, anyone could be arrested for trespass.

Chris attended an Action Committee meeting on the evening of Monday, 18th October and, next day, reported to the staff that quite a few of the Action Committee members had expressed grave concern about the quality of education in the school. He himself had told the committee that the teaching was going very poorly and the education of the pupils was in danger. Action Committee members later called this Chris's 'message of doom'. The suggestion came up at this meeting to close the school down at the half-term break, one week away. Chris reported that the consensus by the end of the meeting had been to keep the educational provision in the school going if at all possible, but he had been asked to tell the teachers that the Action Committee had to depend on them to make this possible, to get control of the situation. Chris's suggestion was that both the Action Committee and the teaching staff hold long post-mortem meetings during the holiday break, to use the week off as a time to regroup and 'start a new phase, a completely different phase in this occupation'.

The week before the holiday break was one of the most difficult. Wednesday was the day the first year were thrown out of the public baths, making it impossible for any Croxteth Comprehensive classes to use the swimming facility for the remainder of the year. On Thursday, at a general lunch-time staff meeting, disputes between Croxteth volunteers and teaching staff over discipline broke out. The two P.E. teachers, Mick and Joey who both came from Croxteth, were being criticized for slapping children and making entire classes take detention when only some of the pupils had misbehaved. Mick and Joe retaliated by demanding that the cane be used to keep order. Both teachers and community volunteers at this meeting expressed feeling totally fed up with the erratic timetable which they believed was one of the main causes of the poor discipline. Volunteer teacher Liila said she wouldn't teach another class until she was given a personal schedule; she had been used as a substitute teacher for several weeks. Ernie said the local volunteers were tired of having classes suddenly shoved on them for games and complained that some classes were getting many more games than others. Henry Stewart reported that his 4B maths class 'went on strike' in the morning because they believed they weren't getting their fair share of games per week.

On Friday the 4As threatened me with going to Ellergreen unless they could be given something other than art with the 4Bs, and the 4B girls refused to go to needlework and demanded a games lesson instead. While I was teaching a class in the physics lab, local volunteer Margaret Gaskell twice interrupted to tell me she'd discovered small pockets of pupils hiding in the library, the hall, and other areas of the school, and what should she do with them? She later told me she found out what subjects they were supposed to be in and shoved them into the appropriate classrooms, probably to the dismay of the respective teachers who no doubt had been glad to be rid of 'trouble-makers'.

The last paragraph in my diary for Friday, 22nd October 1982, reads:

> In general today there was a breakdown in class attendance and everything else. Attempts by staff to get a sense of emergency across to the pupils, and thus appeal for their co-operation, failed. Control over pupils is breaking down, they often simply don't obey a teacher or a helper [community volunteer], no matter how nicely or menacingly it's put.

As teachers gathered in the staff room at the end of the last day of the first half-term, Cyril D'Arcy expressed the growing worries of the Action Committee to us:

> I'm concerned about using kids as pawns in a political game. We told the parents that if we couldn't provide a standard education we would close. I don't want to close but I don't want to see the situation crumble about our feet.

SUMMARY: CONSTRAINTS AND PRACTICE

This chapter began with a description of the enormous confusion and stress felt by all participants in the occupation of Croxteth Comprehensive during its first half-term. It ended with the campaign entering a full-blown crisis, the Action Committee seriously considering whether or not to close the educational operation down.

Although the word 'chaos' was frequently used by participants during this period and in later recollections of it, there was actually a good deal of structure underlying the activities of the participants. The conditions structuring the situation included a number of constraints which limited the resources available to the activists in forming their daily routines. The chief constraint which existed all along was the lack of sufficient teachers. This constraint resulted in a serious time shortage, for those teachers who were available didn't have enough time for proper planning or for recruiting other teachers. Combined with limited educational materials available to teachers, time constraints led to the implementation of a traditional curriculum and a school structure geared to get those few pupils capable of examination passes ready for the spring examinations, with negative consequences for other pupils deemed incapable of academic work. Hence newly arriving volunteers with little experience of teaching were either given permanent classes with the 3Bs and 4Bs or used as substitutes to fill in the vacant slots of an outdated timetable. Either way such teachers were given little of the support they needed and many soon left in consequence. The small number of teachers also meant that the timetable was very inadequate for an extended time, producing long periods and dull classes. Pupils, in turn, left the school or participated in escalating incidents of disruption. They failed to give their consent to the objectives of the occupation as defined by the adults in the school.

On the other hand, *attitudes* of teachers to education with respect to teacher–pupil relations were more determinant than constraints for the initial development of pedagogic relations in the school. Pupil defiance, however, forced these informal practices to change in the direction of increasingly stronger sanctions against disruptive behaviour.

Thus routines formed in the school largely despite the discussions which took place about what forms they *ought* to take. The intersubjective conditions which influenced routines in the school will be given detailed analysis in the next chapter. I have shown in this chapter that the slide towards traditional forms of education during the first weeks of the occupation was primarily due to constraints of time, numbers of teachers, and existing materials.

5
The field of interaction

While the most fundamental features of the educational programme in occupied Croxteth Comprehensive were determined by constraints, another set of conditions structured relationships between teachers and local activists. These conditions grew in importance as the first term moved on, for they shaped the diverse ways in which each group perceived and conceptualized the constraints described in the last chapter. In this chapter I will freeze the chronology, leaving the events which took place just after the crisis at the end of the half-term break for future chapters, in order to describe and analyse what I shall call 'the field of interaction' in the school: the intersubjective terrain through which actors made their way as the months moved on. The reader will find that it was a terrain rife with potential conflict between teachers and local Croxteth activists due to the profoundly different ways in which each group perceived the educational and political features of the occupation. The different ways each group viewed their situation owed much to the cultures from which each group came.

I will be concerned with interpretative schemes relevant to three areas of potential conflict:

- The form of schooling to be provided to the pupils a – constant question even as constraints shaped schooling practices;

- The direction the political campaign for the school would take – an important question since running the school had added a new dimension to the movement and since the previous political strategies had not worked;

- The question of who should determine solutions to these problems. When disagreements arose, it was not clear what decision-making rights teachers and local activists had over political and educational issues.

INTERSUBJECTIVE STRUCTURE

'Interpretative framework', or 'interpretative scheme', are terms used by various social theorists but represent very general concepts which must be delineated to be useful. In the analysis ahead I will focus primarily upon components of interpretative schemes and show how they are connected to form broader structures. The primary unit I will focus upon is termed 'ideological theme' here. In my usage, ideological themes will refer to clusters of norms, values, and assumptions which condition activity and thought in certain areas of social life. They are ideological because they shape perceptions along limited lines, silencing possible alternative views. I call them themes because they are capable of being articulated into diverse theories: a single theme may be used by different activists to produce different articulated theories of events and desired activity. Yet, personal theorizing aside, activists sharing a particular theme will agree on general courses of action and will find themselves in common disagreement with others who draw upon different themes.

Much of the following analysis will consist of isolating and clarifying ideological themes used by the participants in the occupation. As the discussion proceeds, however, two other features of interpretative frameworks will come to light. The first is the extent to which actors were aware of the themes through which they interpreted events. In some cases themes were deeply embedded features of the common sense of the activists. These themes shaped perceptions and gave rise to forms of discourse but were not themselves discursively formulated and thus tended to be hidden from the activists' consciousness. They influenced perceptions and framed certain objects of the actors' consciousness without themselves becoming objects of their consciousness. At the other extreme were themes of which activists were very aware. They had words for these themes and they were conscious of alternatives though they aligned themselves with themes of their choice. There were many themes which fell between these extreme cases, which I shall call partially articulated, or 'under-articulated', themes.

Second, I will be concerned to show the way in which themes were related to each other. A particular theme conditioning the perception of authority relations in school, for example, may be related to a theme determining an actor's concept of school knowledge. Actors possessed sets of themes, some of them linked together through rational implication and some of them in implicit tension. These relationships were important for they structured the ability of actors to translate interpretations into practice and helped to determine the way in which conflicts were resolved. I will have much more to say about the nature of connections between various themes in the pages to follow.

Thus the analysis in this chapter will focus upon: ideological themes held by the activists; the awareness actors had of these themes; and the connections which existed between themes.

ORIGINS AND ORGANIZATION

Teachers and local Croxteth activists differed in their perceptions of the occupation largely because of their different backgrounds. They had been socialized into diverse patterns of routine activity and routine perceptions which corresponded to both their economic positions in society and the cultural traditions passed on by others who had historically lived within those, or similar, social environments. Most of the teachers came from middle-class backgrounds and had high levels of education. All the local residents from Croxteth were steeped in working-class culture and had had less formal education. Differences in the cultures of the two groups quickly led to different organizational structures. This section is concerned solely with the origins and organizational forms of the teachers and Croxteth residents.

The local activists

Charismatic authority

By the first half-term the numbers of community activists in the school had stabilized at about 40. These residents were divided formally into those who belonged to the CCAC and those who did not. The latter were called 'helpers', had no voting rights on the committee, and had to pay higher fees for the meals served by the school. There were roughly 25 helpers working in the school on a daily basis. A similar number of residents belonged to the CCAC, but a portion of these did not work in the school on a daily basis.

The Croxteth Community Action Committee was formally democratic. It met regularly (fortnightly, on average, in the first term) to review and plan its course of action, all decisions being presented as proposals through a strict formal procedure and voted on. However, it was apparent to all who attended Action Committee meetings that only a few members actually made the key campaign decisions, with Phil Knibb enjoying the greatest degree of influence. Most residents on the committee did not understand many of the issues proposed and chose to support the ideas of Phil as he presented them. Discussion of campaign issues at meetings usually consisted of presentations by Phil Knibb, often followed by further explanations of the key issues by Cyril D'Arcy, and a following vote in favour of the suggestion. If an issue was discussed, the form of discussion generally consisted of questions put from members present to Phil or Cyril, followed by an answer. Rarely were residents found to be debating points between themselves; Phil was almost always at the centre, answering one person at a time.

Phil Knibb had, in fact, a great deal of charismatic authority. He was very skilful at using cultural norms for winning loyalty, norms which included a return of loyalty and solidarity from his side. And Phil was unwavering in his support of fellow comrades when, as at times occurred during the course of the campaign, some of us were attacked by the media or encountered other difficulties. Phil's skill in leading the campaign was frequently proven; his judgments on which courses of action to take appeared to be sound. He was thus respected, trusted, and seldom challenged by other activists. Phil could, and not infrequently did, make snap decisions on major issues without consulting the CCAC. The entire informal organization of the local residents was partially structured around this authority, and status was distributed according to how socially close people were with the Knibbs or D'Arcys.

This informal organization of the Croxteth activists about the charismatic authority of Phil Knibb was also partially related to gender roles in Croxteth, for most helpers and CCAC members were women and gender roles on the estate tended to ascribe authority to males. As resident Pat Brennen (female) expressed it: 'Most on the committee are women and they want to be told what to do.' Thus through a combination of factors, Phil Knibb was the unquestioned leader for most of the local residents who gave their full consent to his role.

Class backgrounds and education

Most of the activists from Croxteth had been unemployed at the time of the occupation and the majority of these were unemployed for over five years. Of those unemployed who were women, all were either single parents or had husbands who had been out of work for over five years. A few had part-time and/or temporary work during the occupation. The employment backgrounds of these participants and their parents were all in the unskilled, semi-skilled, or skilled manual labour categories.

With respect to education, virtually all of the local Croxteth activists had taken no examinations in secondary school. Six had attended Croxteth Comprehensive itself, one had gone to a grammar school, and the rest had attended other secondary modern schools and comprehensives.

Volunteer teachers

Consensus decision-making

During the year of occupation over 100 teacher volunteers came to help at Croxteth for some period of time, but most of these left after a short period. Just under 30 teachers worked in the school for significantly long periods of time, and it was this group of long-serving teachers which participated most in the decision-making procedures of the school and which found themselves taking sides in some of the conflicts to be described ahead. Twenty-seven of these teachers were intensively interviewed for this study and it is about them that the following regularities are noted.

The teachers rather spontaneously established a democratic decision-making structure using rotating facilitators and seeking, whenever possible, consensus on all issues. There were no formal rules for decision-making of the sort used by the Action Committee. There were two teacher co-ordinators during the course of the year, the first being Chris Hawes and the second myself. The role of the teacher co-ordinator was precisely that of co-ordination and not one of authority.

Although an informal status structure was always in existence amongst the teachers, the groups at the top of it shifted not infrequently and access to it was open. In terms of gender, several female teachers reported sexist attitudes on the part of male volunteers which acted to reduce their influence in decision-making. Gender roles on the teaching staff, however, were not as obviously demarcated as they were in the case of the Croxteth activists and several female teacher volunteers played highly influential roles at various times during the occupation.

Teachers' meetings differed markedly from Action Committee meetings through their much longer discussions and debates. Meetings were never dominated by a single personality. For many teachers such meetings were a key part of their involvement in the school, stages upon which they could express themselves and debate with others. They were exciting and involved most present in the discussions.

Class backgrounds and education

While nearly all of the local activists were long-term residents of Croxteth, with periods of residence varying from 10 to 30 years, most of the teacher volunteers had grown up in areas outside of Liverpool altogether. Their socioeconomic backgrounds were primarily middle class; 15 of them had parents in professional or semi-professional occupations. A few had been born into working-class families but had been upwardly mobile and had training and work experience in education. Four, however, had grown up in Croxteth itself and worked in the school as teachers of science, games, and P.E. They came to identify themselves primarily as teachers and usually took the teacher's side in those disputes which polarized roughly along teacher/resident lines.

Of the 27 teachers interviewed, 22 had completed a B.A. degree or equivalent. Seven either had, or were working on, post-graduate degrees, and seven had taken teacher training courses. Of 18 asked about their experience of secondary education, 12 had attended either grammar or private boarding schools. Three of the four teachers from Croxteth had taken no examinations in secondary school, but their involvement during the occupation led all three to enrol for O levels, and in one case eventually A levels and then university, during the years immediately following the occupation. Roughly one-third of the core teaching staff had previous training and/or work experience in education.

Thus, to summarize, teacher volunteers and local residents differed in their class backgrounds and formal education. The first organized decision-making through values of consensus and participation and used few formal rules to structure their meetings. The second used a formal democratic decision-making structure but produced decisions largely through an informal organization about the charismatic authority of Phil Knibb.

IDEOLOGICAL THEMES

Different backgrounds were associated with different interpretative frameworks. In this section I will describe how activists perceived the political and educational features of the campaign. I will note the degree of awareness activists had of their themes and as the discussion proceeds it will become clear that linkages existed between the themes I describe. The structure of connections between themes will be also be described and further elaborated in the section following this one.

Political themes

'Community power'

The bulk of the teacher volunteers explained their involvement in the occupation through an ideological theme I shall term 'community power'. To repeat a point made within a more abstract context earlier, this orientation is termed an 'ideological theme' because it was a cluster of values and assumptions which were discursively drawn upon by most of the teachers when offering explanations and justifications for their active support of the occupation (hence 'ideological'), and yet were used to support differing theories by different teachers (hence 'theme'). Thus while nearly all the teachers interviewed accounted for their involvement in the school as resulting from their belief that the assertion of grassroots or 'community' power was to be valued in itself, some theorized this through the imagery of 'class struggle' and others simply as the stance of 'common people' (rather than specifically working-class people) against government.

Regardless of the way in which the community power theme was used to support personal theories, its values and many of its most immediate implications were shared by those who held to it. These activists agreed that the occupation of the school was at least potentially a positive step in itself, not just a defensive step, nor a mere means for party-political goals; that it was a 'proactive', rather than a 'reactive' movement (Tilly *et al.* 1975). They agreed that the injustice which had been committed in Croxteth wasn't just the fact that a school had been shut down, but was rooted in the lack of control the community had had over its school in the first place, even while it was officially there. Later in the first term, those who adhered to the community power theme were to argue politically for more community involvement in the school, and some even for an alteration of educational practices to make them consistent with the political nature of the occupation. They were opposed in these arguments by members of the community who wished only to get their state-run school back and who wished to emphasize a tight liaison with the Labour Party in order to do so.

'The social wage'

The Action Committee members also made use of the term 'community', especially in their statements to the media aimed to justify their illegal action. Their use of this term certainly drew upon many of the same associated values as those tied to the teachers' use of the term. But local activists rarely emphasized community power as the teachers did. Community 'rights' rather than power was their central concern. To most of them, the occupation was not an end in itself but rather a 'holding operation', as it was often to be called, to be continued until the state was forced into taking back its obligations to the community and providing it with a school. The view was markedly different, one which I shall term 'the social wage'.

The social wage theme was a way of justifying and interpreting the occupation which emphasized the duties and obligations of the state. It is a justification which has been aptly described by Manuel Castells as 'trade union consumerism' (Castells 1977, 1978). Implicit in this view is the client–administrator relationship inherent in most welfare services, which parallels in many respects the employer–employee relationship on the shopfloor. The purposes for which the activities of the shopfloor are organized are primarily the purposes of the employers, not the employees. The latter organize in unions to negotiate the conditions in which they work and the amount of pay they receive; they do not control the basic logic by which production quotas, type of product produced, and so on are determined. With respect to social movements over welfare services, those movements which fall into the category of trade union consumerism similarly don't challenge the actual nature and form of services, but rather the amounts and 'quality' of services being supplied. State definitions of quality remain unchallenged; in this case they consisted of the condition of the school buildings, the number of teachers, and the amount of money allocated. The key relationships involved are not opposed by this ideological theme.

Both the community power and the social wage themes were frequently theoretical objects of the participants themselves. This meant that, unlike features of 'common sense' which are so taken for granted that serious alternatives are invisible to those drawing upon them, the proponents of the community power and social wage themes were able to articulate and argue for their points of view with full awareness of alternative positions. The articulation of these themes took a particular direction and became elaborated during the second half-term (Chapter 7). Their high level of discursivity was in stark contrast to many of the conditions which will be discussed below, conditions which fell more within the deeper realms of 'common sense' and which thus exerted their influences in less visible or controllable ways.

Educational themes

The community volunteers

On the whole, the community volunteers began their occupation of the school with an unquestioning attitude towards schooling. They desired their school to be restored to them, and their children to attend it, and they did not really question what went on inside it. They had their own 'black box' theory of educational equality (Karabel and Halsey 1977), a theory which emphasizes the equal provision of schools and does not examine the inequalities which may be perpetrated within them. This was, of course, consistent with their social-wage orientation to politics. Moreover, the residents felt themselves unqualified to criticize or comment on schooling. Virtually all of them, as shown above, had been school-leavers, had gained no formal qualifications, and this led most of them to regard themselves as incompetent to criticize schooling or to have any say in the curricular and pedagogic policy of Croxteth Comprehensive. When the teacher volunteers first arrived, the community volunteers insisted on deferring to them on all questions of actual educational practice, to the embarrassment of some of the teachers.

While noting this perhaps unsurprising attitude of the community volunteers, it is important to consider what memories they had of their own schooling years. Most of them were prepared to tell a number of personal stories which illustrated a generally unpleasant experience during their school years. Since memories and stories are not only related to actual events in the past but also to presently held frameworks which place patterns of selection and emphasis upon past events, it is important to consider these stories of the past for what they can tell us of the present. In this case the interest is in how an unquestioning attitude towards schooling could coexist with negative personal memories of being in school. By examining the situation it is possible to assemble various elements of the subjective attitudes held by the Croxteth activists towards education into a model of the interpretative framework these activists possessed.

Employability and resistance

Croxteth volunteers conjoined negative memories of school with present attitudes towards education in several ways. One was to identify inadequacies in their youthful understanding of the purpose of schooling, their personal 'failure' to see how schooling could help them. This almost always revolved around the theme of employability. The reason schooling should be taken seriously is that it is something which can help one get jobs. The following quotation given by Margaret Gaskell, a local activist with two children in the school, illustrates her negative memories of school given alongside regrets that she hadn't understood the importance of a qualification for getting a job.

> I didn't really take it seriously. I'm sorry now I didn't, really. I didn't do any examinations. I did hate the school. I thought when you left school you'd just go and get a job and if you didn't like that job you could just change it, go from one job to another.

Margaret's comments were not atypical. Many community volunteers noted that schooling was important for getting jobs, especially in the 1980s when qualifications were being demanded for more types of jobs than was the case when they were themselves pupils. In so far as this explanation of the usefulness of an education almost never included things like personal growth or critical social awareness or other educational goals formulated and widely propagated by the progressive movement in education, it is another ideological theme, one labelled with the shorthand of 'employability' here.

A major purpose of schooling was seen to be to make youth employable. Not to realize the importance of this feature of schooling was interpreted as unfortunate, a product of immaturity.

Another way in which local activists recalled their previous dislike of school and yet affirmed its importance uncritically was provided by many of the males. A large number of them affirmed their previous dislike of schooling and their corresponding involvement in resistance activities with some pride. They retained positive memories of their own resistance activities in school, but did not interpret these previous activities in a way which found any fault with the schooling process. For example, kitchen helper Marty McArdle had been expelled from three schools for hitting teachers. P.E. teacher and former Croxteth resident Mick Checkland had played truant and 'got drunk as much as I possibly could'. George Knibb, a brother of Action Committee chair Philip Knibb and a worker in the school corridors, noted:

> We used to do the same as this lot, Phil. I mean, we would take our books and work and tear it up and hide it in a hole in the floor. The teacher would go the whole year without knowing. So I can understand them [the disruptive pupils of the occupation].

But Margaret, George, Marty, and others who reported either unpleasant experiences in school or their involvement in resistance activities (or both) did not initially question the validity of traditional teaching, in terms of content, assessment, or teacher–pupil authority relationships. Their own negative experiences in school were not the basis, at first, of any critique of school practice. On the contrary, the very experience of 'failing' at school, of not taking the examinations and leaving at the earliest possible age, helped to solidify an unquestioning belief in the competence of those who had not failed. There were several reasons for this, such as the lack of an articulated critique of schooling within their own culture, or, indeed, within the labour movement itself. Progressivism had been confined as a movement to largely middle-class populations and had not been taken up and rearticulated along working-class lines.

The most fundamental reason, however, why local residents hadn't developed critical attitudes to traditional schooling from their personal experiences of it was that these experiences had been absorbed and interpreted in conjunction with two features of their local culture: a particular view of *school knowledge*, and the customary pattern of *adult–youth authority relationships* on the estate. I will look more closely at each of these.

Reified knowledge: being 'ordinary'

While a principal purpose of schooling was seen to be employability, school knowledge was seen as the instrument to get jobs. In fact, it wasn't anything specific to school knowledge itself which appeared to serve the purpose of getting a job, but simply its possession, as indicated by examination passes. School knowledge was not viewed as something related to the considerable knowledge required and used in daily life, even in this situation of social disruption in which a group of people were carrying out a campaign that required significant amounts of new knowledge and processes of learning. School knowledge didn't have value as something which could enrich an individual, alter identities, or serve to promote social change. Rather, it was best acquired as a possession to increase employability.

Corresponding to this view of school knowledge was an acceptance of certain authority relations which went with it. Some people had school knowledge and some people did not have it. Those who had it were believed to be entitled to a certain amount of authority, in some realms of life, over those who didn't have it. For example, the local activists, having no qualifications, didn't feel they had the competence or the authority to question schooling practice:

> Actual standards of teaching are not up to me to criticize, 'cause I don't think I can. I can not say that the kids are doing the right work or the wrong work 'cause I've got no, I don't know, CSEs or O levels meself, I'm just ordinary....
>
> So actually as criticizing educational standards, I couldn't do it. And I don't think there's anyone else in the school that can, on the Action Committee. The only thing we can criticize is the handling of the kids. I don't think we can criticize anyone on work standards, I don't think we have the authority to.

(George Knibb)

This passage is pregnant with meanings which were expressed by nearly all the community volunteers talking about schools. George uses the term 'standards', not suggested to him by the interviewer. 'Standards' is a term which we often come across in policy statements, media presentations, and professional articles about education. It is itself a product of the education system: a view of schooling which suggests that very clear objective criteria exist by which schooling practice can be judged and assessed (just as the transmission of school knowledge can be assessed with examinations). It implies that only those qualified can make judgments about standards or even know what they are (like teachers and examination boards). George calls himself 'ordinary' in this passage. Those who have school knowledge are not ordinary, those who don't have it are. A distinction is created, based on possession of qualifications, which has authority implications. George himself uses the term 'authority'. The experience of being a school-leaver is an experience which disqualifies one, subjectively, from criticizing educational practice. School-leavers are 'ordinary', 'thick', or 'slow', terms which many volunteers used to describe themselves and which point back to a particular view of school knowledge, tightly related to the way in which school knowledge is organized and presented.

This view of school knowledge is one more of our ideological themes, called 'reified knowledge' here. It is a view of knowledge as something external, not in an obvious relationship to the sorts of knowledge all people master in conducting their daily lives, but possessed through the completion of schooling. Several things work together to produce the reified view of knowledge. One pertains to the cultural form of school knowledge, which many sociologists of education have noted to be fairly class-specific (e.g. Bernstein 1977; Bourdieu 1977). Thus when a disjunction exists between home cultures and school cultures, the latter will appear more foreign and 'thinglike' – more separate from the forms of knowledge used outside of school in conducting everyday affairs of life.

However, other and possibly more determinant factors help to generate a reified view of knowledge which have nothing to do with the cultural form of the knowledge *per se*. It must be stressed that what is meant by reified knowledge here is an orientation, rather than anything intrinsic to the knowledge itself, even though cultural disjunctions between home and school help to produce this orientation. As argued below, middle-class volunteers in Croxteth also had a reified view of knowledge even though they were fairly fluent with it. The first of these is the process of certification mentioned above, of getting qualifications which immediately translate into opportunities on the occupational structure of society. Because an examination pass is a 'thing' which serves as currency on the job market, the knowledge which it represents is easily viewed instrumentally: a possession which can be cashed in for jobs, 'commodity knowledge' (Whitty 1976; Apple 1982). The second of these determining factors concerns the advantages gained by those who take an instrumental orientation to knowledge. For the working class, the view that knowledge is a possession useful mainly for getting jobs may be a form of resistance to a schooling situation which is difficult because of the cultural disjunctions of community and school mentioned above. It may be a way of retaining cultural identity by distancing oneself from the values and general culture of the school, since identifying too closely with these may undermine local cultural modes of attaining dignity (Hargreaves 1982). For complex reasons, entering too intimately into the middle-class culture of the school was viewed by many in Croxteth as an effort to be 'posh', a breach of solidarity which incurred various informal sanctions in the community.

As a brief summary, let me list the ideological themes shaping the residents' perceptions of schooling I've discussed so far. They include employability and reified knowledge, and are linked to the social wage political theme through the association of authority with possession of school knowledge. I call the authority features of this string of themes 'school authority'. School authority operated as an autonomous theme to structure relations between residents and teacher volunteers and to determine residents' perceptions of pupil–teacher relations in the school. School authority, determined by possession of school knowledge, was connected to another complex of themes, described just below.

Schooling for discipline and control

In the quotation above, George Knibb also mentions the one area in which he does feel competent to make judgments about what was occurring in the school: 'the handling of the kids', the state of discipline in the school. He is correct in speaking for all the community volunteers on this. They did, as a group, feel competent to make judgments on how teachers were handling pupils and were in fact very critical of how it was being done. The feeling of competence with respect to judging teacher–pupil relationships is related to the second cultural factor which mediated the negative experience of secondary schooling reported by most of the activists: adult–youth authority relationships.

Adult–youth authority relationships in Croxteth involve a style of interaction in which rough language, and sometimes rough physical actions, are often skilfully combined with humour and affection as well as disapproval. Adults in Croxteth have to negotiate and maintain their authority over youth, who frequently challenge it. Thus it was not seen as unusual but was rather to a certain extent expected that pupils would be disruptive, and would challenge authority whether in school or outside of it.

When George Knibb, Mick Checkland, Marty McArdle, and others from Croxteth were themselves pupils, they were very much 'lads'. They challenged school authority frequently. But they didn't interpret this in a way which could have led to a critique of school authority. They didn't like school, just as they didn't like other situations in which authority was exercised over them. But this dislike, displayed in disruptive and defiant activity, was .expected cultural behaviour, expected especially of youth. The existence of authority was accepted as given and the way in which they had resisted it as pupils was a way in which youth were expected to act. Hence when these individuals crossed the cultural line between youth and adult, they looked upon their past behaviour as behaviour typical of many youths. As adults they could understand pupils carrying out the same sorts of disruptive activities but they opposed it just the same in their role as adults. Most significantly, they didn't see the behaviour as justifiable in terms that would have criticized schooling but in terms that related the behaviour to expected cultural roles.

Teacher–pupil relationships in Croxteth Comprehensive before the occupation (see Chapter 2) were reported to have been 'strict', 'firm', and yet caring by community volunteers, former pupils and staff. As George Smith, the former head teacher put it, 'If they [pupils] step out of line, God help them.' And the cane was used regularly in Croxteth before the occupation. Although some former pupils like Mick Checkland and Marty McArdle explicitly stated their dislike of this type of authority, it was a style of teacher–pupil relationship which worked in Croxteth because it was in harmony with the adult–youth relationships on the estate. The two reinforced each other. They reinforced each other not only in the sense of a continuity, a similarity of form, between adult–youth and teacher–pupil styles of interaction (a subjective and normative reinforcement), but in the sense of the school actually bolstering efforts of parents to extend authority over youth (a reinforcement of practice).

The challenge of youth in Croxteth to adult authority is not always contained within the cultural style of interaction. There is in Croxteth a high rate of vandalism and, now, drug usage. Fears for the welfare of their children translate quickly into demands from Croxteth parents for discipline.

Thus school authority, a norm which consents to the authority of those possessing school knowledge, was expected to be imposed over Croxteth youth in a form corresponding to adult–youth authority relations on the Croxteth estate. For the Croxteth activists the imposition of such authority in such a form was felt to be an important purpose of schooling itself, not as a means for getting pupils to learn but as a way of introducing self-discipline into the subjectivity of pupils. The result is yet another ideological theme, one having its own autonomy, and termed here 'schooling for discipline and control'. There is much evidence to suggest that this view of the purpose of schooling was held by many adults in Croxteth, both amongst the community volunteers and the parents sending their children to the school. In a number of incidents, for example, parents actually took pupils out of Croxteth Comprehensive and sent them to other schools, not because of concern about how much they were learning in the school, but explicitly because of their fear that their sons or daughters were not being disciplined enough. Discipline was seen not as a mere means to learning, but as a goal in itself.

Examinations

In the beginning examinations, like other features of schooling, were not questioned by the community volunteers. Examinations were a part of schooling practice which teachers, not parents, ought to make decisions about. Examination results were a way of getting jobs and were therefore valuable for those who could pass them. This uncritical attitude towards examinations changed for some of the volunteers as the year went on and the plight of the non-examination pupils became more visible to them. Initially, however, the educational value of examinations was not in question.

Added to this was the strategic value of introducing examinations into the school for the campaign. Teaching towards examinations did two things: it legitimized the occupation to parents sending their children to the school, and it served as a weapon in the media battles taking place. Occupied Croxteth Comprehensive was virtually forced into competition with other schools over examination results. Hence there were reasons for offering examinations in the school which made the option of not doing so completely impractical. But what should be noted here is that community volunteers didn't reluctantly concede to necessity in this case; rather, they did not question examinations initially at all. This is in contrast, as discussed below, to some of the teachers.

A reinforcing chain

In summary, I have listed and analysed a number of significant features of the attitude of the community volunteers to education. They took examinations for granted, had a view of school knowledge which I have called 'reified' and which formed the basis for teacher and school authority in the perceptions of the community activists. They also believed that education served two principal purposes: to increase employability and to discipline and control pupils. Moreover, I have suggested some explanations of why the community activists held the views they did. Their own experience of schooling had made them feel unqualified to criticize school practice and thus unqualified to challenge the authority of those who had succeeded in school. There were good reasons to worry about the discipline of youth on the Croxteth estate and the school discipline of which they approved was a form that corresponded in style to adult–youth relationships in the culture of Croxteth. In addition, there were no clearly expressed or widely available alternatives in the residents' culture, or in the culture of the labour movement generally, which could have helped them articulate an alternative to the examination system or to the form and content of schooling. Finally, it is obvious that this unquestioning attitude towards schooling practice was consistent with the political orientation of the social wage.

The subjective structure of this cluster of orientations can be represented as a series of *reinforcing links* in a chain. Indeed, I have discussed and explained each theme in relation to other themes already. Reified knowledge, examinations, and employability were very tightly linked; each could be used as an argument to support the other two. School authority was supported by reified knowledge, and the form in which Croxteth residents thought school authority should be exercised over pupils was shaped by adult–youth authority relations on the Croxteth estate – both were purely normative, enforced by coercive styles of sanction. All of these links worked under an umbrella of the social wage orientation and all served to mark out and pattern activities around class relationships. The state took a specific class relation to the Croxteth residents as a power which must be met with trade union-like demands and yet which retained the power to define the purposes of service institutions like the school. Teachers, as embodiments of school authority, were outsiders, 'not ordinary', were class others. The themes were linked together in a supportive system which structured the social relationships within the school and which had for a long time structured relationships between the homes, the school, and the occupations of residents as they moved through the life-cycle.

The teacher volunteers

The teaching staff displayed more diversity of opinion on educational issues than did the community volunteers. The schooling practice they established during the first weeks of school was homogeneous primarily because of the constraints which they faced in common (Chapter 4). Most teachers relied upon their own memories of what had happened when they were in secondary school and on available textbooks and standard syllabuses to plan their lessons and organize their classroom practice. The experienced teachers on staff were constrained to use similar methods. If these teachers had had time to develop educational policies of their choice, more differences would have emerged, especially with respect to the curriculum and the decision to teach towards examinations. The one area on most teachers did agree was pedagogy. I will consider the perspectives of teachers in each of these areas below.

Examinations and knowledge

Examinations played a major role in the attitudes of teachers towards the curriculum. It was agreed by the staff that examinations were important and must be offered, for much the same reasons as those voiced by the community volunteers. Examinations were necessary in order to legitimize the occupation in the eyes of the public and to retain the trust given the occupation by parents in Croxteth. It would also have seemed unjust to deny pupils the opportunity to take examinations when successful scores could in principle do so much to alter their future lives.

However, a number of teachers wished the situation could have been otherwise, and although these were in a minority they were all in highly influential positions on the staff during the first term of school. An interesting contrast exists between the data collected in the field notebooks on ongoing events in the school and the responses given by teachers in interviews on the question of examinations. In the field notebooks there is virtually no significant record of any debates over the question of examinations, though stormy debates took place frequently on many other issues. It seemed to be taken as a matter of course by the teachers that examinations were a major educational goal of the school. In the taped interviews, however, a number of teachers claimed that they were very much opposed to examinations in principle. Their failure to emphasize this at staff meetings no doubt came from their perceptions of the enormous constraints which existed for developing a non-examination-based curriculum. (Most of those who expressed objections to the examinations in interview were not at all restrained from engaging in staff discussions and debates.) Drama teacher Graz Monvid expressed their view as follows:

Then the decision was made that in order to prove the school's worth we had to totally orientate it towards examination results – our first step towards lunacy. Trying to carry that led to the point where kids were being expelled. Smaller and smaller numbers of kids were there because you have to exclude the ones who won't conform to what you've decided is the aim of the occupation: examination results. More and more of the teachers, as far as I could see, spent their time mainly with kids who wanted them [examinations]. The others, as in traditional parts of the education system, were being forced out.

Graz's observations were to a large extent correct. Once examinations were accepted as a goal of the school, the use of a traditional academic curriculum was strongly reinforced. Although traditional curricular practice became adopted in the school primarily for reasons of time constraints, examinations firmly entrenched its usage. As long as the major currency for the job market remains examination results, no single school can ignore them, even if it is known that only a small minority of the school's population have any chance of passing them. And in Croxteth, examinations meant a curriculum based on standard syllabuses, streaming, and the skewed allocation of experienced teachers to favour higher streams.

Most teachers, however, expressed either moderate or enthusiastic support of examinations. Some in the strongly approving category tended to equate successful education with passing examinations. Others argued, and the argument is not an invalid one, that examinations allow pupils from deprived areas to rise above the stigmas of their local schools by proving themselves on nationally competitive tests. But the counter argument made by teachers like Graz was that very few pupils in a school like Croxteth can actually pass examinations, largely due to differences between home and school culture. Most don't even try them, and most who do try them do poorly on them. Meanwhile, making examinations a goal of the school reinforced all the problems mentioned by Graz, the creation of sink classes and increasing disruption.

In the moderate category were teachers who were less quick to automatically associate 'good schooling' with work towards examinations, but most of these felt they were an important part of what schools do. They recognized the problems which streaming introduced into the school and were aware of the fact that Croxteth pupils tended not to pass examinations. The most frequent explanation they offered for these problems was put in terms of a believed discrepancy between the pupils' 'actual ability' and their self-confidence and/or work habits. Many teachers saw the examination question in terms of 'potential' versus 'self-image', rather than in terms of cultural disjunctions between deprived communities and school culture. 'There is a certain false mystique about these exams, most of these kids could pass them', was a comment made at one staff meeting, expressing a not uncommon view. Angela Cunningham, a history teacher in the school, gave a more elaborated version of this belief:

> They've got the ability [to pass examinations], but they haven't got any of the kinds of attitudes to work with to get through.... It's a long process getting your child to believe he can do it or that it matters.

Here the ideological theme of 'reified knowledge' arises once again but in a new context. Teachers tended on the whole to think that cultural differences between home and school were not great enough to rethink assessment procedures. They tended to think that the same knowledge in the same form and taught largely in the same way could be transmitted to children of any cultural group as long as the barriers of self-image and attitude were mastered. They had a sort of 'cultural deprivation' model for explaining the difficulties faced by Croxteth youth.

Lest this point be viewed as an implicit argument for a totally separate curriculum for the working class, let me make it clear that it need be nothing of the kind. Within Croxteth a number of students excelled in traditional academic work (see chapters ahead), and it was surely a good thing that the school provided them with the opportunity to pursue such work. But the examination system made it very difficult to respond to the needs, interests, cultural styles, and capabilities of other students in the school. Reification takes a limited form of knowledge, ties the definition of its possession or non-possession to examination skills, and regards that knowledge as fixed, as all that is meant by 'knowledge'. Attempts at flexibility suffer from the ranking of knowledge which results. A non-reified orientation to knowledge is flexible, regards knowledge as a social product which changes continuously, and reflects the socially influenced orientations of those who produce it. For a non-reified orientation to knowledge to characterize a curriculum, a flexible assessment procedure is needed as well, so that the ranking of knowledge may be lessened.

Purposes of schooling

With respect to purposes of education, teachers tended to stress employability but would often mention other purposes of education as well, such as the development of 'personality' and 'character'. Character, for them, was not the product of imposing discipline upon pupils but rather the result of exposing pupils to opportunities to increase their personal and social awareness. Employability became an argument to use against persistent objections made by pupils about the point of doing school work. Amongst themselves, however, many teachers also stated their belief that pupils in occupied Croxteth Comprehensive were learning 'special' things just from the atmosphere and the unique political situation of the school. These additional social and political 'lessons' were never specified very clearly, and they weren't believed to be a part of any deliberate teaching practice, but they were believed to be present all the same. Indeed, teachers often said that these lessons were possibly more important than academic knowledge. Ian Tulip, a former head of a secondary English department, commented:

> [The pupils] are getting a minimal education of a formal sort, an academic sort obviously because of all the sorts of constraints.... And what they are getting [in addition] is again something which isn't normally tangible, which is just the stimulus of the people involved and ... well, there are, I wouldn't say *political* [pause]; the fact of working in a sort of heightened atmosphere, with the parents involved in an intense way which they normally wouldn't be.

Such statements played the role of justifying the continuation of the occupation under its difficult conditions – conditions which possibly lowered the quality of classroom practice in the occupied school according to traditional criteria and also to justify teachers' own classroom practices when many did, in fact, doubt the usefulness of what they taught.

Teacher–pupil relations: 'progressivism'

The realm in which teachers did attempt to introduce innovations in the school was that of authority relationships. When the teachers first arrived they introduced themselves to pupils by their first names, attempting to establish warm and friendly relationships with them. They also dressed informally and insisted, over the objections of many local residents, on banning the cane as a form of punishment. Pupils were allowed to sit where they liked in most classrooms and were not required to wear ties or uniforms. Teachers attempted to give pupils power in school decision-making processes by having a school student council with representation on the staff and Action Committee (to which the Action Committee agreed). These practices illustrate the teachers' commitment to another ideological theme: 'progressivism'.

The progressivism of the teachers was employed in a truncated manner, limited largely to the form of authority relationships and not encompassing other features of schooling. Teachers soon found, however, that Croxteth pupils were extremely difficult to contain with such informal authority relationships, as shown in the last chapter. Pupils liked their new teachers and supported the political campaign to save Croxteth Comprehensive, but resisted classroom activities strongly and all the more successfully for the lack of coercive sanctions which they were used to, both in school and at home. Teachers soon found it impossible not to employ various coercive methods but then discovered that they weren't very skilful in their use. Meanwhile, the student council, and student representation on the Action Committee, failed to win lasting enthusiasm from pupils and were both dropped within a matter of months. However, although they moved towards the use of various coercive methods, teachers managed to maintain a basically informal approach with pupils throughout the year. First names continued to be used and pupils were allowed to have a greater say in classroom affairs than they were used to.

Themes in tension

To summarize this section, teachers differed from the community activists in their advocacy of informal pupil–teacher relationships and some of them were more critical of traditional methods of assessment. But on the whole they subscribed to traditional educational practice and had their own versions of a reified view of school knowledge. They saw an important purpose of

Table 5.1 Conditions of action and their degree of articulation

Conditions of Action	Degree of Articulation
Age relations in Croxteth	Not articulated for community volunteers and teachers; uncontested and not in discursive formulation.
Traditional curriculum reified knowledge, and examinations	Not articulated for most community activists and teachers; uncontested and not in discursive formulation. Where articulated and contested by minority, no articulated alternative.
Schooling for employability	Not articulated and uncontested for both groups. No clear alternatives.
Schooling for discipline/control	Under-articulated for community volunteers; contested by teachers. Alternative partially formulated.
Progressivism (informal teacher–pupil relationships)	Discursive and contested. Held by many teachers; opposed by many community activists.
Community power	Discursive and contested. Held by teachers; opposed by many community activists.
Social wage	Discursive and contested. Held by many community activists.

Source: Compiled by author.

education to be making pupils employable but mentioned other, less tangible, purposes of education as well.

In looking at relationships between the ideological themes of the teachers we find more relations of tension than of reinforcement. A traditional curriculum has been shown to be in tension with informal teacher–pupil relationships by other sociologists of education. Bernstein (1979), for example, predicts that strong classification (knowledge presented in a sharply defined and categorized form) accompanied by weak framing (classroom activities not subject to a highly visible teacher authority) will produce a tendency to move towards strong framing. This did occur to a certain extent in the school with teachers increasingly making use of coercive sanctions to curb disruption, sanctions such as writing lines, detention after school, suspensions, expulsions, and the creation of a discipline room where disruptive pupils were sent during the day. But this tension was resolved in more complex ways involving the intervention of local adults, as discussed in Chapter 6. Though the implementation of examinations and a traditional curriculum was largely due to constraints of time, materials, and the lack of an alternative, it was reinforced by the view of school knowledge held by teachers. This chain of reinforcing relationships between practices and ideological themes was in tension with the themes of community power and progressivism held by the teachers.

Thus teachers drew upon subjective orientations which clustered into two mutually antagonistic groups. While a reified view of knowledge reinforced and was reinforced by the adaptation of a traditional curriculum along examination syllabus lines, it existed in implicit conflict with the values of progressivism and community power held by the teachers. The progressivist theme was used by teachers initially to establish informal relationships with their pupils, but as shown above, this produced problems as soon as a traditional curriculum was introduced. The community power theme, moreover, was used by teachers to emphasize, among other things, the value of the school occupation in itself: the fact that parents now 'controlled' their own school was deemed a positive end in its own right. However, the use of examinations and the stress on academic forms of knowledge helped to keep parents away from the schooling practices of most impact on their children.

Unlike the conditions discussed which were drawn upon by community activists, these orientations of the teachers were not tightly connected to systems of practice between the school and other social sites in which these

Table 5.2 Orientations of community activists and teacher volunteers concerning politics and education

	Community Volunteers	*Teachers*
Justification of Involvement	Community deprivation implies demand for state provision (social wage)	Community deprivation implies demand for community control (community power)
	Knowledge reified and basis for authority of educationalists	Knowledge reified but transmittable to any group (cultural deprivation)
Attitudes on Education	Examinations important	Examinations important and/or inevitable
	Schooling for discipline and control of pupils	Informal teacher–pupil relationships desirable (progressivism)
	Schooling for employability	Schooling for employability and intangible goals

Source: compiled by author.

teachers were involved, at least not in the same way or to the same degree that attitudes of the local residents corresponded to systems of practice between home and school, and the cultural past (being a pupil) and cultural present (being an adult). They were related, of course, to these volunteer teachers' own previous success in schooling and examinations, and thus to an investment they had made earlier in traditional forms of education which had yielded certain pay-offs. These orientations on the part of the teacher volunteers, in other words, were related to their middle-class backgrounds and tied to very broad systems of practice which did not involve the Croxteth community in an immediate way.

THE INTERSUBJECTIVE TERRAIN

Table 5.2 lists key ideological themes held by activists in the school and contrasts them according to whether they were drawn upon mostly by teachers or local residents.

In reviewing these themes it is important to bear in mind differences in the extent to which actors were themselves aware of them. I have already indicated that the social wage and community power themes were fairly highly articulated and that activists were aware of their contested nature and of the existence of alternatives. I haven't yet said much about the degree of awareness actors had over the ideological themes pertaining to education. These themes, in the case of both teachers and Croxteth residents, were not initially at high levels of articulation but existed rather on either *tacit* or what I will call *under-articulated* levels. Tacit conditions included reified knowledge for nearly all participants, age relations in Croxteth, and schooling for employability. These orientations informed discourse and practice without themselves becoming objects of discourse. They were largely uncontested conditions as well, shared by most of those involved. Progressivism and schooling for discipline and control, on the other hand, were in tension with each other, generated conflicts as a consequence, and led correspondingly to some articulation of each orientation (conflict requires verbal justifications). Yet neither of these orientations was ever given a very clear articulation and thus no clear theoretical positions were formulated about which sides could form in the disputes. These orientations were therefore under-articulated. Table 5.1 indicates the degree of awareness actors had of each theme.

In addition to the specific themes and the level of awareness actors had of them, I have promised to indicate the relations which existed between themes. I have already done this to a certain extent, showing how certain themes were linked together in reinforcing ways, one supporting another, and how other themes were in at least implicit tension. Let me say a bit more about these types of relationship.

Relationships of reinforcement may be of at least two subjectively different kinds. One theme may *logically imply* another, or one theme may be *similar in form* to another. Examples will illustrate this difference. There is a logical relationship between schooling for employability, examinations, and a reified view of knowledge. If one's support for examinations is questioned, one could draw up arguments of employability and at least implicitly refer to a reified conception of knowledge to defend one's position. On the other hand, the reinforcement between norms governing adult–youth authority relationships in Croxteth and expectations of teacher–pupil relations within the school is not one of logical implication but is rather based on a similarity in form between the two. The reinforcement between the two affected the perceptions of teacher–pupil relations in Croxteth in a direct and normative manner but did not lend itself to an articulated defence of one theme through the use of the other. I have elsewhere elaborated upon these two different types of reinforcement, calling the first a paradigmatic reinforcement and the second a homologous one (Carspecken 1987). I will say no more about the differences between the two here for concerns of space. The distinction becomes useful when analysing the relationship of intersubjective structures to systems of practice, and in predicting how the related themes will enter into discourse if the associated practices become contested.

Tensions between themes refer to expected conflicts in practices associated with one theme and those practices associated with another. In the occupied buildings of Croxteth Comprehensive there were community activists who interpreted schooling in a way which made the discipline and control of pupils one of the purposes of education, alongside a large number of teachers who valued informal teacher–pupil relationships. 'Progressivism' was in tension with 'discipline and control', and one could expect, simply by carrying out the sorts of interviews made in this study and the inferences to ideological themes I have conducted, that the practices of these two groups in the school would lead to disagreements and interpersonal disputes. In this particular example the tension was one between distinct groups of people holding to ideological themes in an acknowledged tension because the ideological themes existed at relatively high levels of discursiveness.

Tensions may also involve low levels of discursiveness and may exist between themes held simultaneously by the same group of people. Many teachers in Croxteth Comprehensive, for example, held to a form of progressivism at the same time that they held to a reified view of knowledge. Because reified knowledge was never itself an object of discourse, these teachers could hold to both themes without much subjective conflict. But the activities generated through the simultaneous possession of both themes created problems, especially because of the chain of conditions within which reified knowledge was located for pupils and parents. Reified knowledge supported

Table 5.3 Sets of tension and reinforcement

Sets of tension		
social wage	——	community power
charismatic authority	——	community power
traditional curriculum	——	progressivism
discipline and control	——	progressivism
reified school knowledge	——	community power, progressivism

Sets of reinforcement
social wage/reified school knowledge
discipline & control/reified knowledge/examinations/employability
community power/consensus decision-making
reified school knowledge/discipline and control/age relations

schoolroom practices which entailed a relationship of authority between teacher and pupil contradicted by the ideological theme of progressivism. Teachers thus acted out one set of practices pertaining to the presentation and evaluation of knowledge which stemmed from their reified view of school knowledge, at the same time that they invited pupils to call them by their first names, have a say in classroom desk arrangements, and so on. The two sorts of practice did not work well together, given the general intersubjective structure within the school.

There were several sets of tensions between ideological themes held by activists as well as the sets of reinforcing themes I have discussed. Table 5.3 displays some of these tensions and it should not be necessary to elaborate on them beyond presenting them in this table. I will include some themes discussed at the beginning of this chapter in relation to the formal and informal organization of the activists.

ROUTES FOR CONFLICT RESOLUTION

Tensions between themes are potential areas of interpersonal conflicts, and both the extent to which themes are articulated and the position of contested themes within sets of reinforcing themes will influence the form of the conflicts and the routes through which they may be resolved. In a situation of interpersonal conflict in which the participants attempt to resolve the disputes *rationally* rather than through the use of coercion or manipulation, the background conditions of the practices in dispute will become thematized: they will be drawn into discourse, made problematic, and discussed (see also Habermas 1981b). Thus interpersonal conflicts, where attempts are made to resolve them purely through discourse, could be expected to draw up structures of conditions for rational examination. And these intersubjective structures are usually linked to systems of practice which may extend beyond the particular practices in a dispute (recall the relationship of reified knowledge and school authority to the life-cycle of Croxteth residents from home to school to work).

I will take another example to make these points clear. I will here consider only what is rationally implicit and possible in the situation rather than what actually happened – what happened is the subject of the next few chapters and it will be understood most clearly by considering what *could* have happened. Disputes between teachers and community activists over what form teacher–pupil relationships in the occupied school ought to take may be expected to begin initially over specific practices like whether or not teachers ought to use the cane, whether or not they should be called by their first names, and so on. But if those in dispute are in a situation facilitative of full rational discourse over the issue, other themes involved in the formation of authority relationships between teachers and pupils could be expected to be drawn into the arguments. Community activists, for example, perceived the basis of teachers' authority to lie in their possession of school knowledge. This is what distinguishes a teacher from an ordinary adult and it is what constitutes the essence of the teacher–pupil relation within this view. Norms and identities first come into conflict: teachers are not 'ordinary' and should control pupils. To explain why, it could be pointed out that for pupils to learn and for pupils to stay out of trouble they must be disciplined. This would be an empirically referenced claim and a specific elaboration of the theme. To explain why pupils need to learn, it could be argued that pupils need to possess knowledge to pass examinations to get jobs. All of these arguments draw from the same interpretative scheme, and link specific formulations into a logical chain.

To counter these arguments, teachers could argue that in general teachers are not so distinguishable from other adults, that possession of school knowledge is not worthy of such differences of status. They could also argue that teachers should not be coercively authoritative with pupils. This is a conflict of norms and identities, consistent with the interpretative scheme of the teachers. The overt and most discursive features of both schemes begin the conflict. But then teachers would have to claim either that non-authoritative styles of teaching produce at least as much learning in pupils as authoritative methods, or that learning itself needs to be conceived differently; that its goals include more than passing examinations in order to get jobs. Here the teachers would have to take steps away from other themes they held at the same time as their progressivism, for as has been shown, the volunteer teachers in the campaign for Croxteth Comprehensive held many of the same ideological themes pertaining to education as did the community activists: reified knowledge, examinations, and schooling for employability among them. The empirically referenced claim that informal teaching styles could work was clearly invalidated by events in the school (Chapter 4) and teachers would thus be forced either to reject their progressivist ideals or start to rethink the nature of knowledge and the purposes of schooling.

It is not necessary to work out any other possibilities, for the main point is that interpersonal conflicts originating over overt practices and their associated discursive justifications will of necessity draw tacit and unacknowledged conditions into discourse if these conflicts are to be resolved through discussion and debate. But rational discussion is only one way of resolving conflicts; other possible routes to conflict resolution exist as well. Conflicts can be resolved through the use of coercion and manipulation, or through a consensus which gives some individuals or groups more decision-making power than others. Conflicts can also be resolved through toleration, itself drawing upon certain values and norms. Actual resolution is likely to involve a combination of rational discussion and these other means.

A number of conditions can be expected to determine routes taken to resolve conflicts: the organization of the group of people involved in the conflicts is one, as for example, an organization based on charismatic authority is not as likely to lead to debate as is an organization based on consensus decision-making. The extent of articulation of the themes in conflict is another such condition: under-articulated themes in conflict can allow for resolution to take place in practice, through 'compromise routines', at the same time that verbal disputes take place (see below).

In general, conflicts which existed between participants in the occupation of Croxteth Comprehensive had three main courses through which they could be resolved:

1. If some of the conditions were in discursive conflict, they could be openly and rationally discussed with the aim of resolving them at the level of discourse. This would require equal access to decision-making power on the part of all participants in conflict and would lead to a progressive drawing out, into discourse, of the previously unarticulated conditions related to the conditions in overt conflict.

2. If some of the conditions were in discursive conflict, one group could make use of other conditions (articulated or not) to exclude the group with which it was in conflict from legitimate decision-making power. In this case unarticulated conditions in relationship to those in overt

conflict might not be drawn into discourse at all, but be tacitly drawn nevertheless into some of the action.

3. If the conditions in conflict never reached clear enough discursive formulation to allow competing groups to take positions with respect to them, the conflict could be resolved through the establishment of routines which draw from both sets of conditions. These routines might not appear satisfying to any of the actors involved in the conflict but would resolve the situation nevertheless through the establishment of stable routines and co-ordinated action. Conflicts would be expected to continue in discourse, but since discourse would not be clearly formulated enough for antagonistic positions to be taken, the question of formal access to decision-making power wouldn't be an issue. The conditions which were unarticulated but in relationship to those in conflict would be expected to contribute to the outcome of the conflicts in practice without being drawn into discourse. The resolution in practice could in principle also correspond to a rational but unarticulated resolution of the conditions of action, *if tacit schemes shifted to match the new routines*. This would result in a decrease in the verbal conflicts conducted over the development of stable 'compromise' routines.

The actual conflicts which arose in the school and the ways in which they were resolved are the subject of the next two chapters. It will be shown that educational conflicts were resolved largely through the third route, described above, while political conflicts were resolved primarily through the second route. The last two chapters of the book describe how themes which tacitly underlay many of the conflicts occurring during the first school term eventually became articulated and critically examined by the participants.

6
A dual system of authority

There was a complete clash, really, with mainly middle-class teachers coming in with certain views of how, if it were an independent school, different methods of education could be carried out. For instance, right at the beginning it was decided there wouldn't be caning. But we had no tradition to draw upon. We were trying to devise completely different social norms which the kids weren't used to.

(Graz Monvid)

The chronology of the campaign for Croxteth Comprehensive was left at the end of Chapter 4 with the beginning of the first half-term break. The reader will recall that the most fundamental features of the educational practices in the school were determined through the presence of constraints during the first weeks of term, but that there were problems associated with the resulting regime. Teachers and Croxteth activists failed to win the consensus of pupils to their goals and objectives in running the campaign, and many pupils, especially in the 'B' streams, were highly disruptive. By the end of the first half-term most participants felt the occupation had entered a full-blown crisis and some were questioning the sense of continuing to try to run an educational programme.

Both teachers and local residents believed the problem of disorder was related to technical problems, especially to the limited number of teachers, the lack of a permanent timetable, and the high turnover rate of volunteers. However, Croxteth activists also believed disruptions were the result of the inability or unwillingness of the teacher volunteers to assume a strict enough role with their pupils, though they simultaneously appreciated the warmth of the relationships which had developed. Most teachers felt strongly that stricter methods, such as use of the cane, were not appropriate and ought not to be employed. Yet they were at a loss to explain disruptions in the school and devise a strategy to curb them. They felt vulnerable to criticisms from the parents while remaining firm in their belief that less formal and warmer relationships were good, in principle, for pupils.

The two groups interpreted the situation through different ideological themes: progressivism from the side of the teachers, and schooling for discipline and control from the side of the local activists. As the last chapter argued, these themes were not highly articulated. Both groups interpreted events through their respective sets of values but both saw some sense in the views of the others. Members of each group frequently complained about the attitudes and practices of the other, but neither group came forth with an articulated policy which could be debated through the decision-making structures of the school. Hence bickering persisted throughout the year. But the problems of discipline demanded solutions in practice on a minute-by-minute basis, each group responding as their views and abilities allowed. Gradually a stable system of practices developed which curbed the disruptions, but it was a system which did not fully satisfy anyone. It was a set of compromise routines, attained in practice while the verbal disputes ran on.

THE 'PROPER TEACHER'

On the 23rd of October, during the first half-term break, teachers and parents met separately to decide whether or not the school could and should continue to run. The teaching staff met first and passed a number of resolutions based on the technical aspects of the discipline problem. By this time a stable core of teachers had volunteered their services and the week-long break allowed some breathing time in which to restructure the timetable around their personal schedules. Subject departments were also created with a department head for each who would take responsibility to ensure consistent teaching for all classes in that subject area. CSE and O level syllabuses were used to plan curricular programmes for the older years and set textbooks were used to standardize instruction for the younger. Some of the more experienced teachers (John Bennett amongst them) agreed to give workshops on classroom management to the less experienced.

The morale of the teachers was high after their meeting. The feeling was that improved organization and renewed commitment would solve the bulk of the discipline problems. Representatives were chosen to report the teachers' commitment to continue the educational programme to the Action Committee later that day. During their evening meeting, the Action Committee became swayed by the optimism of the teacher representatives and voted in favour of at least finishing the first term.

When classes began again after the week-long break the improved staff organization had immediately visible effects, with fewer disruptions and the beginnings of more consistent educational programmes for the 'B' streams.

But disruptions were only curbed, not eliminated, and as the days rolled on local activists began to complain again about the pedagogic styles adopted by most teachers. Many continued to believe that it was a mistake not to use physical punishment like the cane and blamed the prevalent discipline problems in the school on this. Cyril D'Arcy, for example, once commented: 'I don't see why the cane isn't used. I found a kid vandalizing a door and I cuffed him around the ears. It worked, and the kids don't think anything of it. Something has to be done!' In other incidents criticism of teachers for not using physical punishments was more direct. Yola Jacobson, a history graduate who had come all the way from Edinburgh to volunteer her time in the school, was having trouble with the daughter of one of the Croxteth helpers, Tommy, who worked in the school every day:

She was just giving me hell in a class, just not doing any work, so I asked her to leave the room. Later I said to Tommy, 'Look I'm worried about Annette, she's not doing work, she's being a nuisance.' He said, 'Well, you've got two hands, clip her.' I said, 'No, I don't hit kids.' He said, 'I give you permission, you keep control! If you've got two hands why can not you just whack them? You call yourself a teacher?!'

There were a number of similar incidents involving other teachers, pupils, and local residents which caused not a few teachers to stop appealing to the parents of disruptive pupils for help. Local residents saw most of the teacher volunteers as 'soft' and thus as not 'proper teachers', though their school knowledge still didn't relegate them to the status of 'ordinary' and still caused local residents to defer to them on issues of curriculum and standards. Local resident Kathy Donovan explained her own position on the matter:

I think the worse thing that happened was when they came back on the 22nd of September and it was announced that there would be no cane. The kids sort of thought that 'no cane, well then they can not hit us' ... And they thought, 'You know this is going to be great and we can get away with murder.'

Many local activists also stressed the need for teachers to maintain traditional indicators of superior status with proper dress and with the insistence that pupils address teachers with 'Sir' or 'Miss.' The practice of allowing pupils to call teachers by their first names was seen as a grave mistake:

I don't think it's strict enough, me. But that's because you all started off with this, without the 'Sirs' and the 'Misters' and that was it. So the kids just think we're just pals, aren't we?

(Mary Kane)

These criticisms from the helpers and Action Committee caused resentment in many teachers. Some expressed disgust at what they took to be old-fashioned and barbaric methods of discipline advocated by the local activists. Many noted something like a dilemma in the situation:

> We had parents in the classrooms or helpers who'd be screaming at the kids and dragging them out by the hair, thinking they were helping! But in fact they were helping. In fact I can remember fleeing from a class when my helper didn't turn up. They thought I could control the class and didn't need a helper. I thought it was deliberate sabotage at the time. There were real problems.

(Graz Monvid)

Yet the community volunteers also frequently praised the warmth of the relationships between teachers and pupils, and the pupils themselves often stated they liked these teachers better than the ones they'd had before. As 4th year Steven put it: 'Some of them care about you, a lot of them do!' Like the local adults in the school, however, most pupils felt the cane should be used, both those who were disruptive and those who were not. None of those interviewed, neither pupils nor local activists, seemed to see any contradiction between their appreciation of the warm relations and their criticism of the poor discipline. Teachers were blamed for not being able to provide discipline and warmth, both at the same time. They weren't 'proper'.

THE DUAL SYSTEM

As teachers and local activists responded to disruptions in the school an informal, dual authority system slowly attained stability. Parents constantly disciplined pupils by giving them a severe scolding, often mixed with threats of physical punishment. But usually this sort of discipline was carried out with the assumed authority of the teachers in the background. The most common way the community volunteers disciplined pupils was to give them a 'good rollicking' and then take them over to a teacher for the 'real' punishment.

The irony in this situation was that it was the methods used by the local activists, not the teachers, which were most effective in keeping control. The pupils clearly recognized this fact: 'Without the parents this school would be torn apart,' one of them said. But the community volunteers, despite awareness of their superior abilities, would consistently refer back to the authority of the teachers when carrying out their own castigations of pupils. Local activists used adult–youth forms of authority from their culture, not just to discipline pupils, but to try to force pupils to defer to school authority. 'That's no way to talk to your teacher!' could often be heard during a scolding session, 'I'm going to take you to see your teacher!' and so on.

On the pupils' side

This usage of adult–youth authority relations to bolster traditional relations of school authority (and this usage of school authority to justify local methods of control in the occupied school) didn't always work so directly. There are several incidents recorded in my field notebooks in which community volunteers administered their own punishments on pupils, which were effective because they agreed not to tell any of the teachers about it. A good example was referred to earlier. During the first half-term some pupils broke into the chemistry room and stole a number of laboratory materials. Two community volunteers discovered who the thieves were and steps were taken by these two to get the items back and admonish the offenders. Yet at a joint teacher–parent meeting held after the incident, these two helpers refused to reveal the names of those who had been involved. 'We can not break confidence,' one explained. This was crucial to the form of discipline these community volunteers could hold over the pupils within the school. They would have been seen as 'grassing' if they'd given the names. 'Grassing' is a term which has meaning only in a 'them–us' situation. The pupils saw the teachers as 'them' and the community volunteers, or at least some of them, as part of 'us', even though they were still seen as adults in opposition to their own status as youth. Many other incidents of this nature occurred during the course of the year.

What is noteworthy about these incidents is that, first, pupils were more successfully disciplined by community volunteers when it came to face-to-face confrontations. Yet, second, the form in which many of these successful confrontations took place referred back to what was really a symbolic and greater authority which was not that of the individual teachers but rather what the teachers represented: school authority. Pupils responded well to promises not to break confidence, because their misbehaviour was often a resistance to the symbolic authority of the school. Not breaking confidence meant that the resistance had still in some ways succeeded, and the pupils could feel, even when punished by a community volunteer, that they and the community volunteer were in some ways on the same side. Order was maintained in this way, disruptions were controlled, and thus school authority prevailed under the prop of adult–youth authority relations drawn from the culture of Croxteth.

As time went on during the occupation, certain figures from the Croxteth community took on more visible roles as disciplinarians in the school. George Knibb in particular began to handle many of the discipline problems which came up. He stood in the corridors every day to make sure pupils went to their classes between periods, and he was approached by many of the pupils themselves over disciplinary matters. George began to think of himself, only partially in jest, as 'headmaster'. He was very confident that he could handle the kids better than any other adult in the school, including the various figures on the staff who temporarily occupied highly visible positions, such as myself and his brother Phil, the Action Committee chair. Yet he still held himself below the status of a teacher, a 'proper teacher', even if he believed that no teacher in the school was really competent to fill that status either. The following lengthy quotation illustrates both his self-confidence in matters of discipline and his simultaneous insistence that he was not a teacher but was rather 'just ordinary'. The passage also illustrates the style of adult–youth authority relations in Croxteth, its physically aggressive tones which served more to win the consensus of pupils than to frighten them:

> I try to talk to kids as they talk to themselves. I mean, in words that they use like, if they want someone to go away, they'll say 'Do one!', you know, or 'Turn it in!'. I mean if they think somebody's snitched on them, they'll say, 'He's a grass', you know. So if you talk to kids in their language, you get more response out of them. I'm not saying that's the right language to talk to them in, but I mean just for the time being if a certain situation explodes and it needs quieting down there and then. If you walk into a class and say, 'Now look, kids!', like a lot of teachers do in this school, and it's not the teacher's fault, the teachers don't come from this area so they don't know the kids' language....
>
> And you've got to bring them down in the class and let the class see that you can stop any of them, no matter if it's a 16-year-old who is 6'6", which we've got in this school, who's twice as big as me. But I'll walk up to him and I'll tell him, you know, that if he wants to walk outside, I'll go outside and I'll knock his head off. But I would never hit a kid, but they think I would. And then when you get hold of them and you sort the situation out and start talking to them, then you find out you've got their respect. 'Cause I think I know why I've got the respect of the kids ... I mean, I won't allow them to call me 'sir', I mean I won't allow them to because I'm just an ordinary, well, local person myself. So if I go walking around the streets of Croxteth ... and I hear kids call, 'Hello, sir', you know though the people I'm with know I'm doing a decent job in the school, but you know I make sure they call me George.

This quotation refers to a complexity of things, three of which particularly stand out. It begins with George's emphasis on the importance of knowing the kids' language, winning authority over them through their own cultural terms. But as George himself says a little later, these terms are not simply of the youth culture, they are of the culture of Croxteth generally, and the confrontational style which George employs is not a style limited to the youth culture but one characteristic of Croxteth adult–youth relations (and partially of Croxteth adult-adult relations) generally. George next describes the confrontational style: his skill at communicating a readiness to come to physical blows if necessary. George, it must be kept in mind, was better than most community volunteers at disciplining pupils and part of the reason for this was his ability to combine features of the youth culture with features of Croxteth adult–youth authority relations in a skilful way.

Finally, George says he refuses to allow pupils to call him 'sir' and stresses that this is one of the main ways in which he has won the respect of the pupils. George was drawing upon the identity which was most acceptable, according to his interpretative scheme, for him. He avoided putting himself into a position of directly representing school authority, and thus he was perceived as united with the pupils in some ways against that authority, against it in the sense of being on the same side with respect to it, though as an adult he used his authority to support and defer to it. George also sees himself in this way, as just 'ordinary', and he feels he earns respect by openly acknowledging that he is just ordinary. He insists that pupils call him 'George' rather than Mr Knibb, again allowing pupils to see him as one of them with respect to school authority. The roles and standards of behaviour prescribed by the culture of Croxteth to differentiate between adult and youth were less of a division than those indicated by the expected behaviour of teachers and pupils.

George's practice of not allowing children to call him 'sir' or to consider him a real representative of school authority was widespread in the school. Many other volunteers from Croxteth took on activities within the school which overlapped with activities expected of teachers, and they also insisted that pupils refrain from using the linguistic forms which would have ascribed school authority to them. Although the community volunteers were for the most part critical of the teachers in the school in questions of discipline, they held the position of teacher in esteem, didn't feel it was a position they themselves could even in limited senses occupy, and used their authority over the pupils to try to get pupils to hold it in esteem too.

Thus teachers were expected to be authoritative with pupils, or at the very least to have control over them one way or another. But successfully controlling pupils was not seen as the essence of being a teacher; it was rather the teachers' possession of school knowledge, indicated by their prior success in examinations, which was seen as the ultimate basis of teachers' authority, the ultimate criteria by which the teachers and the 'ordinary' were distinguished. And, to point it out once more, those who had this knowledge were outsiders, territorial and class others. A coincidence of terms existed, aligning broad class relations with more micro-social relations of authority.

A dual system in a dual sense

A dual system thus emerged, unplanned and not clearly recognized by anyone. It was a dual system in a dual sense. It juxtaposed traditional school authority with local cultural forms of establishing authority in a way which bolstered the former through the use of the latter (sense one). It resulted in a harmonious pattern in which the way community volunteers took on relations with pupils and the way teacher volunteers took on relations with pupils supported each other in the creation of routines (sense two). A feature of the stability which resulted was continuous argument and conflicts between adults and pupils in the school throughout the year, and worries about discipline which never ceased. But the routines were stable even though few people were satisfied with them. Pupil–teacher relations were often warm and liked by both teachers and pupils, but failed to get as much 'work' out of the pupils as the teachers desired. Community volunteers found themselves intervening in the activities of the school more often than they thought proper, and everyone seemed to think that daily classroom disruption was at an unacceptable level, pupils as well as adults. Yet the social relationships had taken on stable forms, just the same, compromise routines which resolved in practice certain conflicts inherent in the situation, and which did curb disruptions in the school.

The establishment of a dual system of authority within the occupied buildings of Croxteth Comprehensive is of interest for two reasons. First, it was the under-articulated nature of the themes in conflict, progressivism and schooling for discipline and control, which allowed this conflict to be resolved in practice while verbal disputes continued. If the themes had been fully articulated into educational positions, these disputes would have to have been resolved in another way either through debates leading to a clear policy position or through the exercise of authority by one group upon the other. Second, the residents of Croxteth basically reconstituted old themes and relationships through a new and more complex set of practices. They bolstered school authority and through it the client–administator relationship implied in their social wage political orientation by using local adult–youth authority norms to get pupils to defer to school authority and by refusing to allow themselves to represent that authority. The dual system, unique in form, fell between a mere reproduction of traditional school relations and an alternative, unplanned but more 'community', form of schooling. But it fell far closer to the former, to a reproduction of normal schooling practice in Croxteth, because it enabled a traditional curriculum and a traditional definition of schooling purpose to survive the challenges presented by pupils, some of which were clearly rooted in the inappropriateness of the classroom practices. The reader will nevertheless find by Chapter 9 that certain spaces opened by this dual authority system were slowly to become important conditions for change.

7
The community or
the Labour Party?

Thus far I have described the effects of external constraints upon the development of schooling practices in Croxteth Comprehensive (Chapter 4) and the manner in which conflicting, but under-articulated perspectives on pedagogy were resolved (Chapter 6). In this chapter I examine another set of conflicts which arose between teachers and local residents over the political goals and strategy of the campaign. These conflicts were conditioned by the same structure of ideological themes which gave rise to the disputes over educational practice discussed in previous chapters. But the intersubjective field in this case shaped the conflicts along different lines. While conflicts over the form of social relationships within the school were a retrospective affair – involving commentary on routines which were already being established – conflicts over political strategy involved a prior, rather than a retrospective, relationship of thought and discourse to action. This meant that competing positions reached a higher degree of articulation, that two distinctive positions could form, and that conflict resolution was consequently related to the formal and informal decision-making structures within the school. In the course of my analysis, I resume the chronology of the battle for Croxteth Comprehensive, left at the end of Chapter 4. As the reader will recall, conditions within the school had become so stressful by the end of the first half-term that many residents were considering an end to the educational programme. The matter was to be discussed during the half-term break, which is where I shall resume the story.

CONFLICTS OVER CAMPAIGN STRATEGY AND GOALS

The beginnings of polarization

The social wage and the community power themes worked implicitly to structure conflicts and disagreements between activists from the first day of school on, but it was only during the first half-term break that these orientations began to rise into clearly articulated positions. Even then the process of articulation was slow, beginning with disagreements over the appropriate ways to handle very specific problems. The problem of central concern to all participants during the half-term break was that of pupil discipline, and some solutions proposed by the teachers implied their political orientation to the occupation.

In particular, most teachers felt that discipline problems would definitely improve through increasing the involvement of the Croxteth community in the school. Increased participation was seen as a way of solving some of the technical problems resulting from the limited number of teacher volunteers. More local residents were needed both to help control pupils and to perform many necessary tasks, like visiting the homes of the disruptive pupils and of the pupils threatening to leave, taking classes in crafts and other subjects, taking pupils on field trips, and assisting teachers in getting supplies, setting up displays, and so forth.

Though not immediately obvious to the pro-community camp, these proposals for greater community participation had fundamental implications for the general campaign strategy of the occupation. They were being put forth at a time in which the Action Committee was under pressure to recognize the failure of its earlier effort to exploit the hung Liverpool council and take a clear new position. Its earlier strategy, the effort to obtain a Liverpool council vote in its favour, had proved fruitless. The enemy now was the DES in London. If the main goal of the campaign was to remain that of getting back a state-funded school, the Action Committee would have to try to build its power base from that of a community pressure group towards a political party capable of altering national policy. That party would be the Labour Party, the only party which had provided consistent support from the beginning and which already enjoyed the allegiance of all local activists on most issues.

Many teachers, however, viewed the main campaign objectives differently and actually feared too close a link with the Labour Party. Their desire to appeal to the community as a resource for mastering the discipline problems in the school was consistent with their political instincts. They realized that the power base must be expanded but felt expansion should go towards the neighbourhood, not the Labour Party. This desire on their part went much deeper than their concern with the technical problems of running the school. It was connected to the way in which most teachers justified their own involvement in the occupation, an involvement to support the principle of community power, not to support the Labour Party.

Moreover, by the first half-term many teachers were beginning to question the relationship between the Croxteth community as a whole and the Action Committee which claimed to represent it. During the teachers' meeting of the half-term break Kate, the staff's German teacher, asked rhetorically, 'Where is the community?!' A helper joined in, 'We're on an island here!' To many teachers, the 40-odd residents active in supporting the campaign seemed to have no clear mandate from the Croxteth estate.

Teachers accordingly began passing proposals urging the Action Committee to take steps to get more local residents into the school on a daily basis. Mass leafleting was suggested, as were home visits to parents to see if they could come into the school to help. Parents could be invited to join in classroom activities, it was suggested, and a PTA established. John Bennett began to pressure for the establishment of street committees in Croxteth. Henry Stewart offered to start a community newspaper, called *Crocky News*, partially in order to increase community involvement. There were also proposals to provide educational opportunities for adults in Croxteth: adults could learn alongside pupils, as was already occurring in some classrooms with helpers and CCAC members taking an interest in science, computing, and engaging in preparation work to teach basic mathematics and English skills. Most of these suggestions were appealing to the teachers and to the community helpers attending the meeting.

These October proposals were an early sign of an articulation of the community power ideology into a specific position, a position which was to become more clearly formulated in time. Its most extreme articulation at this meeting was put forth by Henry Stewart, who suggested that Croxteth Comprehensive register as a 'community school', along the lines of other alternative schools in Britain, such as 'free schools'. If the goal of the campaign was to be the establishment of an alternative community school with legal recognition (but of course without legal funding), the entire emphasis of the occupation would necessarily turn towards issues of greater local involvement and alterations of schooling practice to better meet local needs. A number of teachers immediately indicated that this sounded like a good idea to them as well.

However, any extreme articulation of the community power position was destined to run into a dilemma. As Cyril D'Arcy, supported by John Bennett, pointed out at the 23rd October meeting, the government would have liked nothing better than to recognize a community school in Croxteth, though eventually not within government buildings. Their concern was to end the financial burden which Croxteth Comprehensive had become. It would thus be a tactical error to register. Better officially to regard the occupation as a holding operation designed to pressure the government into once again funding and staffing a school for the community.

Teachers immediately recognized the sense of Cyril's objection and agreed to it. But Cyril's argument involved more than just an argument of good tactics. The Action Committee didn't want to run its own school.

Members wanted a return of 'proper teachers', paid for by the state. They saw any effort to develop an alternative community-run school as far too akin to the government's policy of privatisation, which was removing government funds from many essential services and disadvantaging the working class.

Hence not only strategy but the basic meaning of the campaign had begun to emerge as an issue, but only in very murky forms at this point. On the level of tactics alone, the two positions could coexist: many social-wage activists could see sense in getting more local adults in to help with the work, and the pro-community activists could see the sense of keeping up the pressure on the state, including a liaison with the Labour Party. But those who saw the campaign through the lens of the social wage didn't have much commitment to getting more local people into the school and could find many reasons why efforts to do so would be a waste of time, while those who thought along the contours of community power *had* to insist on more involvement to maintain their perception of the occupation as legitimate.

At their own, separate, 23rd October meeting, (held after the teachers' meeting), the Action Committee agreed to try to get more residents involved in the occupation at the teachers' request. But it became evident during the succeeding days and weeks that the CCAC had little resolve to pursue the idea. The reason for this was simply that most of the community volunteers felt efforts to involve residents of Croxteth further ranked as a very low priority. Few expected much of a response from the community and time was needed for the many other activities which had to be done daily to maintain the school. Community helper Eddie Pines expressed the general belief: 'Everyone supports this school except the community.' Another helper said about the community: 'They don't care, they can not be bothered.' When John Bennett kept stressing his idea of street committees he was given a very lukewarm response by local activists, sometimes drawing cynical laughter and negative comments: '[Laughing] You just try to get the people on my street into a committee!' Phil and Cyril frequently said that they'd 'tried everything, leaflets, posters, public meetings, they just don't want to know.' And Phil explained further that frequently calling public meetings was dangerous because low turnouts to these meetings, which is what he expected, could be latched upon by the press. Liberals were already saying in council that Croxteth Comprehensive wasn't being occupied by the community but by a very small minority of people from Croxteth. A crucial tactic, Phil implied, was to stress constantly in the media that the community was running the school and not to provide any incidents which could contradict it.

There were more deep-seated reasons, however, for the reluctance of some of the social-wage activists to appeal to the community. Since teachers, 'proper teachers' that is, were seen as the only adults really capable of running a school effectively, it was feared that more residents in the school might contribute to the problems rather than solve them. There was an organizational problem as well. 'If we get more people in here it would be difficult to control the situation,' Phil Knibb commented.

This state of affairs clearly constituted a legitimacy problem. How can a group of residents take over a school for the sake of their community, run it in an effort to win it state support for the sake of the community, and then state their belief that the community wasn't really interested? It would seem that a fundamental justification for being involved was undermined in such a view. However, many helpers who held this pessimistic view did think that 'the community' (the term became used so frequently in the discourse of the activists that a reified entity was created) would rally to defend the school during an emergency, like a raid of bailiffs, but that it wasn't normally motivated enough to work in the school on a day-to-day basis. Their pessimism didn't involve doubts about community support, but about the willingness of the community to move from passive to active forms of support. Others said that although most people in the community were opposed to the closure, they didn't believe that the occupation could possibly win and thus would not support it. Still others reported firmly negative attitudes on the part of people in the community towards the occupation. One helper mentioned an incident during an interview in which people had told her they thought the school was being run by 'a bunch of scallywags', that the pupils were allowed to smoke in classrooms, and that all in all it was 'a free school' having a very bad influence. Similar incidents experienced by other volunteers were reported during the research.

Thus there was an ambiguity in the relationship between the Croxteth Community Action Committee and the other residents in Croxteth. Activists, especially teachers, worried about the nature of the relationship. Those who did not worry disagreed with each other about what the community actually thought. Community opinion was gauged through anecdotes and rumours; no one really knew what the community thought.

Where is the community?

It is not possible, from the data collected, to determine precisely what general attitudes towards the occupation prevailed in Croxteth. It would have been necessary to conduct a survey on a sample of the housing estate to get the information required, and I wasn't able to conduct a survey during the occupation as my time was filled with qualitative studies of events within the school while serving as staff co-ordinator and teacher.

However, there were a number of indicators that community feeling towards the occupation was itself ambiguous. The original closure of the school reportedly sparked indignation throughout Croxteth, even in old age pensioners and families who sent their children to the local Catholic secondary schools. Pat Rigby, the secretary for the Croxteth-Gillmoss Federation which co-ordinates activities of many diverse organizations on the estate, and Effie Sherlock, a health visitor who regularly entered the homes of many residences on the estate, were both convinced that feelings were explosively high over the closure. However, both Pat and Effie observed residents expressing feelings of suspicion with respect to the occupation. Many people thought it had little chance of succeeding and declined to support it actively for that reason. Others felt that the Knibbs had taken complete control of the campaign and had made participation a matter of invitation for their selected few friends and relatives. At a Croxteth housing meeting I attended, for example, I heard the school cynically referred to as 'the Knibb kingdom'. When visiting the homes of a few parents with children in the school, I discovered formerly active campaigners who felt squeezed out of the campaign and unwelcome at the school. Pat, Effie, and I talked to others who supported the occupation wholeheartedly but who were unwilling to devote time and energy to it unless a crisis, like an invasion of bailiffs, required it.

The ambiguity of community feeling is well summarized with remarks made by Pat Rigby in an interview:

P.C.: So what did people think about the occupation?

Pat: I think they were admired for it but a lot of people thought that at the end of the day they couldn't really win with it. That was a task that was really too impossible. They might be able to hold out there for a few weeks, but gradually everyone would fall off, one by one. And there was really nothing at the end of the day that could save the school. I honestly thought, they're doing their best down there but they're on a hide into nothing.

P.C.: Were there rumours about what was going on inside the school?

Pat: All sorts of rumours. And that would get interest going again. You know, the bailiffs are coming down and you're all going to be shoved out. You would get support back then and people were more prepared to go and help out on pickets. But I think that was really, some people just done it as an act of defiance. But it was eventually going to happen by one means or another, that they would be eventually out of the school. Like they would get them at a weak time. There was a big rumour going around during Christmas that they would either come, maybe on Christmas Eve or even Christmas Day itself. The bailiffs would go in then. And I think people thought it was the end of the story. Like it was a very gallant effort but the odds were just too much stacked against them and they would not win.

P.C.: I've heard that there were rumours that a sort of a 'free school' was being run, and that some residents thought the people in the school were sort of soft. Did you hear anything like that?

Pat: You'd hear like a little story that might have some basis in fact and be exaggerated. They'd say things like there were teachers down there who'd been on probation. You could retaliate against that sort of thing like with someone like Pat Kellet [the retired deputy head] and then you've got your Jesuits [two Jesuit fathers who volunteered two days a week] down there and all this, know what I mean. Then, like, the rumour would swing to it's all ex-priests teaching down there. The community sort of in the main, I would say, have been behind them.

What is most clear from Pat's observations is that during the occupation communication between the activists and the other residents in the community was very poor. Newspaper articles attacking the school by claiming that it was damaging the pupils' education caused genuine worry in Croxteth and knowledge of the character of the teacher volunteers was based only on rumour. Pat held the same belief that many of the local activists in the school expressed frequently: that if bailiffs were sent in many residents would have rallied to the school's support. She believed that sentiment in the community was still supportive of the school, but that the competence of the volunteer staff to teach pupils was often in question.

My impression was that more community support could have been stimulated and maintained if the Action Committee had pursued it, especially during the weeks just after the July take-over when many people displayed interest and enthusiasm by coming to the school. How much more support could have been generated is unknown and must remain so. However, the Action Committee seemed to fear extensive interest more than welcome it. Some of the residents who came over just after the occupation acted in disreputable ways, making sexual advances on other pickets, drinking, and possibly even thieving equipment. The Action Committee was anxious not to lose control of the situation and discouraged massive involvement. This disappointed some, as an interview with Ray and June Harrison during the occupation illustrates:

June: I was there then, I was one of the first people that were occupying it.

Ray: At the time there was help coming from everywhere. I don't know if the help's still coming in or not. The talk of Croxteth School was on everyone's lips, you know, the talk of the day – Crocky School. And then of course you got the media coming in, the press and the television.

June: But now, this is what I mean about the school, they've let it slip, they've let it all slip. Not many people talk about the school. I mean I'd be on the van [a vegetable and fruit van run by the Harrisons on the estate]. I mean, I work on the van. I've lived here, I know nearly everyone. There used to be something from somebody everyday but there's nothing now.

They should have kept it up, they should have kept it going, these meetings and that. You know, inform people – public meetings, keep it going, keep the spirit up.

At any rate, after the autumn term started, boundaries between the school and the community thickened once again and the Action Committee was probably correct, during the disputes with the pro-community group, to claim that extensive home visits or leafleting would be futile. A public meeting called for 29th October 1982, for example, to explain what had been occurring in the school and what the Action Committee's hopes and aims were had a very small turnout. Other incidents like this seemed to confirm the feelings of pessimism.

Polarization

The pro-community group, however, believed that the community could be further involved, was badly needed, and even *should* be involved for the campaign to be in line with their personal political objectives. The vast majority of teachers, as noted already, had little interest in party politics and had no wish to make the struggle for the school a merely party-political affair. They supported grassroot struggles, community power, and were dismayed at the evidently poor relations between the Action Committee and the community. Many mentioned the belief on the part of helpers that the community was ready to rally for the sake of the school in a crisis as evidence that there was a vast potential waiting to be tapped if only the right effort was made. As it became increasingly clear that the hung council in Liverpool was no longer an exploitable resource for the campaign and that therefore an electoral victory of the Labour Party was the only political hope left, a fear grew amongst many teachers that the campaign would come to depend too much on the Labour Party for its support and lose its base in the community as a result. Rose Goodwin, English and music teacher, gave her views during the final days of the occupation:

Rose: I think that the kind of struggle there was over which way the campaign should go was basically fought and in my view lost before I came. You know which was, should it be strongly community-based or should it rely on the Labour Party? And ... it was resolved in favour of relying on the Labour Party. You know my view is that their record is such that they don't deserve any different treatment from the working class than the Liberals or the Tories. I think that they supported the school simply because it was necessary for them.

P.C.: Well, people on the Action Committee claim that the community hasn't shown much interest in the school.

Rose: All community struggles have a hard-core minority that does all the work and then, at special moments, everyone joins in for a time. The point is, the hard-core minority must represent the community: struggles must proceed in relationship to the community, and that relationship has to be maintained.

P.C.: And you think that this hard-core minority has lost touch with the community?

Rose: That's what I feel.

As the second half-term progressed, this conflict over campaign objectives and strategy became heightened and took very specific forms. An early incident involved the request for help from a parents' committee which had formed to prevent the closure of a school on the other side of the Mersey, Bromborough School. John Bennett first got in touch with the school and suggested that talks between Action Committee representatives and Bromborough parents begin. Phil Knibb stated on 2nd November that their request should be answered by the Merseyside Trade Union Community Liaison Committee, instead of by the Croxteth Community Action Committee, because the MTUCLC wished to expand itself from the case of Croxteth Comprehensive to many other community struggles. He pointed out that the MTUCLC was planning to establish branches in Birmingham and other cities. His statement was met with much grumbling on the part of many teachers, who discussed it informally over lunch and during staff meetings. There was even more grumbling on the part of the volunteers running the school office: Ev Loftus, Ann Abercromby, as well as Ann Pines, a friend of Ev's and Ann's who spent much time in the school office. It was opposed by John Bennett as well.

'We have run this occupation and have the experience, we should be the ones who talk with these people,' said Ann Pines one afternoon in the office. Those opposed to Phil's suggestion said they felt that referring such matters to the MTUCLC would rob Croxteth of its leading role in community struggles and cut the volunteers in the school off from other political developments. In fact, this incident does represent importantly different conceptions of the campaign and its relationship to other struggles. Shifting the matter to the MTUCLC in which only Phil and a few others from Croxteth were involved represented a loss of power and the loss of an opportunity for developing direct connections between the majority of the activists and the world outside the school. It would create a dependency of the local volunteers on the MTUCLC, and even though the local activists had representation on the committee, it would mean a shift of power and initiative away from the grassroots to formal union organizations.

In addition to the Bromborough dispute, teachers found themselves at odds with Philip Knibb and other local volunteers when they began to make lists of proposals on campaign strategy for presentation at Action Committee meetings. This first occurred after a staff meeting held on the 9th of November, when the teachers agreed to ask the Action Committee to have pupils more involved in demonstrations and other political activities, to co-opt teachers onto the CCAC with voting rights, and once again to begin door-to-door efforts to get more helpers. This list of proposals also included a statement urging the Action Committee to begin discussing campaign goals more itself, to clarify the goals of the campaign instead of taking them for granted. The proposal to have pupils involved in campaign activities was a step further in clarifying the link that many teachers believed ought to exist between educational and political activities.

This list provoked a very angry response from Philip Knibb, Cyril D'Arcy, and others on the Action Committee, although the request to have three staff members co-opted onto the CCAC was honoured. Pressure from the teaching staff to adopt certain strategies or even to introduce explicit discussions on campaign goals was seen as overstepping the teachers' legitimate realm within the school and conflicts began to take the form of arguments over *who* had rights in decision-making over *which* aspects of the occupation. However, before this turn in the conflicts between pro-community and pro-Labour Party activists can be described, the rise of certain rumours and scandals which became enmeshed with rational argumentation on strategy must be mentioned, for these had a decisive influence on the final resolution of the conflict.

Entanglements

On the day that Philip Knibb gave his views about Bromborough School, 2nd November 1982, I recorded for the first time evidence of rumours pertaining to Phil which had been exchanged for several days previously. One rumour was that he actually wished the campaign to fail so that he could get an £8,000 per year job with the Manpower Service Commission (MSC) which would start projects in the Parkstile building. A few days later this rumour was changed slightly: he would be put in charge of a grant of some £60,000 to co-ordinate the MSC project, which of course would include a salaried position for himself. The rumour was elaborated by the contention that Phil had been approaching the parents of a number of pupils in the school and advising them to put their children in Ellergreen, thus deliberately weakening the campaign by lowering pupil numbers in the school. Finally, there were vague statements about a conflict between Phil and Ev Loftus in which Phil was claimed to have behaved in an unacceptable way: what it was had not yet been communicated to me. Phil was said to be centralizing his power as the campaign leader and acting increasingly for his own interests, not for those of the community.

It is not clear what the origins of these rumours were. Phil, Cyril, and others were eventually to express their belief that they had been deliberately started as part of a WRP strategy to gain more control over the campaign. In the end the rumours proved to be false: Philip Knibb had many opportunities after the success of the campaign to get himself a job in the school but he never took them. He did his best instead to get other activists from Croxteth jobs and became employed in the community of Netherley himself. Moreover, before the start of the rumours in November, no expressions of dissatisfaction with Philip Knibb had ever approached anything like the attack on his character which these rumours represented. It seems very improbable that they arose through a simple misunderstanding. If they were started deliberately, then they were the result of strategic conduct on the part of one or a few people intending to move Phil Knibb out of his powerful position on the Action Committee.

Ev Loftus, though clearly not the originator of the rumours about Phil, was believed to hold 'far left' views by a number of other community activists and to be in sympathy with the ideology of the WRP. I never learned what Ev's relationship to the WRP was but it was obvious that she supported her own version of a community power strategy at odds with Phil's political views. Ev had a warm and winning personality, was well liked by most activists from both Croxteth and the teaching staff, and had done much important work for the campaign, including raising funds and running the school office daily. Ev and Phil had become rivals in a struggle to determine the course of the campaign, creating personality problems between them which lent themselves to rumours and hints of scandal.

Whatever their origins, this nest of rumours wove genuine disagreements between participants about the campaign strategy with scandal and mistrust. As the two camps formed over what direction the campaign ought to take, competing positions on the validity of the rumours tended to associate themselves with the competing strategies, so that arguments against Phil

Knibb's political ideas became confusingly mixed with arguments against his character. The rumours were taken very seriously by a small number of helpers and Action Committee members, most obviously by those socially close to Ev Loftus but possibly by others giving less visible support. On the teachers' side, a small number of the more radical volunteers were starting to talk about them as confirmation of their belief that Phil Knibb didn't really want to involve the community in the school in order to secure his own position of power. Most of these teachers didn't seem to take the specific details of the rumours literally, but contributed to the climate of doubt beginning to form concerning Phil Knibb by voicing their own complaints about Phil's powerful position on the Action Committee and the failure of the Action Committee, as a result, to get the community of Croxteth involved in the school. Tensions were growing and groups of both teachers and local activists were beginning to talk in hostile terms about each other as sides formed.

Shortly after these notes of rumours in my field notebooks are records of comments made by Phil Knibb about the school office. He began expressing criticisms of the inefficiency of the office, the usual presence of many teachers and local activists talking and drinking tea which obstructed its functions. His criticisms were related to the growth of negative rumours about himself, for the office was usually occupied by the very volunteers who were discussing the rumours. The office also happened to be the place at which incoming mail and telephone calls were received. Phil stated that it would have to be 'reorganized'.

One evening in November Phil and Cyril had a private talk with me to express their belief that certain local residents had been recruited by the WRP and that they were intercepting mail and telephone calls in the office in an effort to shift control of the campaign. 'I haven't had a letter for weeks,' said Cyril, 'but I know there must have been plenty of letters.' The articles about Croxteth for *Newsline*, the WRP daily newspaper, were being written in that office, they also claimed. They commented as well on the rumours about Phil Knibb, stating their own belief that the WRP, through the activities of John Bennett, had deliberately started them in an effort to take power away from Phil: 'They're saying that I want the campaign to fail so that I can get a job out of it and the people are believing it!' said Phil. 'They want to start a revolution, I just want to get the school back, that's all,' added Cyril. Phil and Cyril said that many members of the Action Committee were disturbed by the 'far left' views of Ev Loftus and Ann Abercromby and a number had ended their involvement as a result. Cyril had taken the extreme step of offering his resignation to the Action Committee to get a vote of confidence, which he got, a week before. They said that they intended to ban the selling of *Newsline* in the school and that they were close to putting a proposal onto the committee to ban WRP activists from further involvement.

Thus added to the conflict over campaign strategy and the climate of rumours about Phil Knibb were doubts about the role which the WRP was trying to take in the school. The sentiments created linked all these things together in a way which polarized the participants. The disputes between activists over two possible courses for the campaign to pursue began to combine many other factors, and the form of this polarization was to have an influence on the way the disputes were to be resolved in the end.

Legitimate decision-making power

The 9th November staff meeting was a peak in expressions of teacher discontent with the way the campaign was being run. The Bromborough decision was highly criticized and Phil Knibb was accused by many present of not sharing decision-making enough with other activists. People present at this meeting were not all members of the teaching staff; several helpers, particularly those who worked regularly in the school office, were present and joined in the criticism. A proposal was made to bring pupils along on a demonstration planned for the following day and most present voted in favour of it. Reza, a science teacher, agreed to arrange transportation for pupils by hiring a couple of coaches. Teachers believed that involving pupils in the political aspects of the occupation would be an educational experience for them, and would help to win their support for the daily educational activities of the school.

The morning after this meeting Phil Knibb approached me to say that under no conditions would pupils be allowed to go to the demonstration scheduled for that afternoon. After some discussion I agreed with his views, which were mainly put with respect to legitimate decision-making processes in the school. The teaching staff didn't have the right, he claimed, to make a decision on as sensitive an issue as involving pupils in demonstrations. Phil was sure the parents of the community would be outraged to learn that their children had been sent on a demonstration, and he was convinced that the Action Committee, which was the only body that should have made such a decision, would not have approved of it. 'I know what they think,' he said, 'the kids are not going!'

Slowly this information circulated amongst the staff. Several teachers became very angry about it. On my way to lunch I was approached by Yola and Reza who told me they intended to act against Phil's wishes. 'Just one man!' Reza said, very incensed, 'Action Committee members were at that meeting and they agreed with the idea.' Yola told me that the previous day she had had lunch with some of the community volunteers, which I inferred had included Ev Loftus and Ann Abercromby. 'You wouldn't believe what I've learned!' she said, 'Phil and Cyril have been doing things which will really hurt this campaign.' Cyril was apparently included in versions of the rumours now. She went on into some of the same rumours I'd already heard and implied that there was 'even more', but failed to elaborate. I discovered later what this 'even more' was. Phil was said to have started acting in extremely petty and spiteful ways towards Ev Loftus in an effort to drive her off the Action Committee.

While eating lunch, George Knibb approached me to say that he and Margaret, present at the staff meeting the evening before, had changed their minds about having pupils on the demonstration after talking to Phil about it and now believed that it would be a poor move. George said that Reza was going ahead, telling his pupils to go to the demonstration, and he urged me to call a quick lunchtime meeting to put a stop to it. I agreed with his arguments and called the meeting, facing some bitter complaints from those present. No coach was hired in consequence (whether there actually would have been time to arrange a coach was questionable anyway).

The demonstration, in the end, did have a large number of pupils present. They had found their way downtown after school on public buses. Large numbers of local activists and pupils stood outside the town hall with placards. The vote was not in favour of Croxteth, but the Action Committee and its sympathizers in the Labour Party intended to bring another proposal up at an Education Committee meeting on the 30th of November. These proposals called for the Liverpool City Council to send a new demand to the DES to re-establish a school in Croxteth.

After the demonstration I returned to the school and found a large number of people complaining about Phil in the office. An article on Croxteth had just come out in the *Liverpool Daily Post* (10th November) which no one had had previous knowledge of and which seemed to feature Phil Knibb entirely. It had a large picture of Phil, sitting alone in the school with a despondent look on his face. It described how difficult the occupation was becoming and could be read as implying that things couldn't go on much longer. The people in the office felt it confirmed their suspicions that Phil was trying to do it all on his own and was beginning to paint a very pessimistic picture of the campaign – 'defeatist' was the word which was used several times. The people in the office also freely discussed the rumours about Phil's desire to get a job and let the occupation fail. Cyril was reportedly 'in on it' too.

Over the weekend Phil took further steps to halt what he saw as a growing and conscious plan to challenge his power. Somehow he persuaded or forced Ev Loftus and Ann Abercromby to agree not to work in the office any longer. He reported to the staff on Monday, 15th November that they had left 'on their own accord', taking their things with them. Ann Pines left (temporarily, it turned out) as well. Phil now took possession of the office himself and a volunteer from outside of Liverpool, a new acquaintance of mine whom I'd asked to help with the school, was to act as the school administrator. His name was Kevin Stannard. As the days followed it was evident that most of the teaching staff accepted Phil's decision though a few complained. The resolutions passed by the staff on the 9th November meeting, to go door-to-door visiting parents and to try to establish street committees in Croxteth, were never really acted upon. Calls for increased community support continued in the staff meetings, but for a time were less hopefully discussed. There was simply not enough time for teachers to take the necessary steps themselves and the Action Committee wasn't showing much support. The teachers' main concern continued to be the problems of maintaining discipline and teaching adequately.

As the first term progressed there were a large number of activities which occupied the staff other than their concerns with the campaign strategy. The first issues of *Crocky News* came out and enjoyed some success. They included articles by students and were distributed throughout the shops of the estate, some of which advertised in it, as well as to various places in town. Requests for more teacher volunteers were printed in the paper in large letters surrounded by lines to draw the attention of readers, but though such ads specifically appealed to people in Croxteth, no significant response resulted. The hopes of involving residents in the production of the newspaper as writers, illustrators, editors, and so on never drew in more community involvement. But the *Crocky News* continued throughout the rest of the occupation and was supported by the Action Committee.

New disputes broke out between teachers and the CCAC over a request by 20/20 Television to film a future programme on the occupation. Most teachers felt strongly that the camera crew should not have free access to everything in the school but should discuss all their filming intentions with the staff first. The reasons for this included the reluctance of many teacher volunteers to appear on television. More significantly, the teachers felt they knew more about the actual educational activities in the school than did the Action Committee and they didn't want particularly disruptive classes or classes taught by especially incompetent substitute teachers filmed.

Phil responded to this demand of the teachers again with anger. 'The teachers have no right to make such demands,' he said, 'this is our campaign, not theirs.' The issue, again, was over which group of people had decision-making rights over which sections of the campaign. Phil's views prevailed, simply because he told 20/20 Television to go ahead with free access to the school. No effort was made to win the staff over to his views, and no power existed on the staff to oppose him. The programme was shown during the second week of December and in fact gave a very sympathetic view of the occupation.

Another event captured the interest of the teachers and Action Committee as well. Through the efforts of Henry Stewart and Julie Meakin, Selwyn and King's Colleges of Cambridge University invited 40 Croxteth pupils to visit their campus for one day and one night. Julie was a student at Cambridge at the time and a friend of Henry Stewart's. There was much discussion about what criteria to use in choosing the 40 pupils and most Action Committee and staff members were anxious to be on the list of chaperones. Chaperones were chosen by drawing names out of a hat but a rather humorous and revealing discussion preceded the decision for a drawing during an Action Committee meeting. When Phil Knibb put the question to the committee of who should go with the kids on the trip, someone called out, 'Michael Storey'. This produced some laughter and other people called out names like 'Trevor Jones', 'Margaret Thatcher', and so on. Then someone called out 'John Bennett' and the whole Action Committee burst into loud laughter. The incident is significant because the humour which the committee found in the suggestion to send John Bennett along to Cambridge was a first public indication that the bulk of the local activists were not happy with suggestions of street committees and rumours about Phil Knibb, which appeared to have origins with John. Another humorous comment was made during this discussion of the Action Committee. When the four local volunteers were chosen from the hat someone said, 'I hope they come back, they might find jobs over there!', again resulting in general laughter.

The Cambridge trip was yet another instance of conflict between teachers and Phil Knibb. After long discussions, the teachers worked out a method of selecting pupils for the trip. Their method was based on getting equal representation among the girls and boys and also of rewarding pupils for non-academic (as well as academic) contributions to the school. After the method was finally agreed upon, Phil Knibb approached me to say that he didn't agree with it and that he had drawn up his own list of pupils he felt should go. This time, however, his opinion was blocked successfully by the staff, Phil agreeing in the end that it was a domain of decision-making in which teachers should have priority over his own views.

The conflicts between Phil and teachers were thus beginning to take the form of negotiations over decision-making rights. Phil, Cyril, and other less vocal local activists felt that teachers had no right to make decisions which affected the course of the campaign. At each confrontation over campaign issues Phil had taken actions, often without any prior discussion with other Action Committee members and certainly without a preceding discussion between himself and the teachers. He was acting strategically, rather than through efforts to gain a consensus on his views. He justified these actions by pointing out that teachers did not belong to the community and, aside from three co-opted representatives (myself, Reza, and Yola), did not even belong to the Action Committee. He thus drew upon the very ideological theme which teachers used in formulating their suggestions for campaign strategy: *community power*. This invariably worked as the teachers could hardly oppose the argument, though they often grumbled that Phil Knibb was not the community either. Phil frequently stated that he knew what the Action Committee wanted, but this didn't sound convincing to most of the teaching staff.

These disputes over legitimate decision-making pulled several of the formerly tacit conditions underlying the disputes into the discourses of those originally least influenced by them. Community power, which had existed largely on the level of tacit norms for most of the local activists at the onset of their involvement, became articulated in ways which legitimated Phil's claims to decision-making rights. School authority, a cluster of tacit norms adhered to more by the local activists at the start than the teachers, now became more clearly articulated to delineate certain realms in which teachers' opinions were granted priority. Examples of the latter include an incident in which a teacher volunteer was 'sacked' by Phil in December for showing inappropriate videos in the school after hours. Many teachers felt that this volunteer should have been reprimanded for running the videos, but believed that banning him from the school was too severe. They believed Phil had acted outside his legitimate areas of authority in this case and Phil was eventually persuaded to change his decision. Phil once suspended a pupil who had come late to school, which again was seen as outside his authority, and the decision was changed. He took school keys from two teacher volunteers, Mick Checkland and Joey Jacobs, which produced a similar uproar and the return of the keys in the end.

Hence the negotiations over legitimate realms of decision-making power began to clarify informally the realm of schooling issues as the legitimate domain of the teacher volunteers, and the realm of campaign strategy as the domain of the Action Committee, or Phil Knibb. Community power and school authority (based on possession of knowledge) were used by the groups least adhering to them to win the consent of the other to claims of decision-making rights.

Towards the Labour Party

On 20th November a meeting was held in the school for the purpose of promoting objectives of the MTUCLC, the Merseyside Trade Union–Community Liaison Committee. The November meeting alarmed many teachers because it made it apparent that the activities of Phil Knibb weren't simply obstructive to their own efforts to influence the campaign but were actually taking the campaign in a different direction altogether, without any input from themselves or, it seemed, from the Action Committee. No teacher was involved in the planning of this meeting and none seemed to understand its emphasis until they attended it. In addition, the community of Croxteth also seemed to have little role in the meeting. It was another sign that Phil Knibb, in the opinion of many, was becoming too powerful, with no account-ability.

The 20th November meeting was divided into a morning and an afternoon session. The morning featured a panel of speakers. Two were local Labour Party leaders (Tony Mulhearn, the president of the district Labour Party, and Bob Wareing, the Labour county councillor), one was from the MTUCLC (ironically Bill Hunter, not only a very active member of the MTUCLC but a long-time member of the WRP as well), and one was a 4B pupil, selected to talk by George Knibb, from Croxteth. The talks given, other than Gerard Irving's (the pupil from 4B) all stressed the need for supporting the labour movement in its campaign against cuts. The speakers stressed Labour Party policy and tended to refer to the closure of Croxteth Comprehensive as an example of what they could put to right with a Labour government: 'The community movement must work hand in hand with the broader labour movement,' said Bob Wareing. 'Education is linked to jobs and social service. We've got to get Labour back in the May elections,' said Tony Mulhearn (May 1983 was the month for local elections in Liverpool).

These speakers spoke of 'the community's fight for this school' in approving and glowing terms but for many teachers present it seemed that 'the community' they referred to was more a mythical entity than anything else, especially since no effort had been made to get local residents to attend this particular meeting. The audience consisted of local Labour Party activ-ists, a few former teachers from the original Croxteth Comprehensive faculty, a number of WRP supporters (some of whom had come up all the way from London), representatives from the Cockpit group within the London Local Education Authority, and many teachers and local activists who had been working in the school. But it included very few residents of Croxteth or even parents of children in the school.

After the speeches Dominic Brady, local Labour spokesperson on educa-tion, rose and stated:

The Labour Group has plans for 11–18 comprehensives throughout Liverpool. The only way this campaign is going to do any good at all is if a Labour majority on the council is secured. The Labour Group has plans for housing and unemployment and related issues.

Thus the strategy being pursued by Phil Knibb became very clear: to work with the local Labour Party and trade union movement to get a full majority on the city council in the May 1983 elections. In this way a proposal to reinstate Croxteth Comprehensive could be just one part of an overall city reorganization of education, something the DES was extremely anxious to get as it would reduce the city budget considerably.

During the lunch break a group of teachers including Reza, Yola, Graz Monvid, John Bennett, and myself animatedly discussed the fact that the community hadn't even been invited and that no teacher volunteer had been asked to speak. We all felt concerned for the campaign, seeing that it could become co-opted by the Labour Party, taking the initiative away from the community. We decided to approach Phil Knibb and insist that a teacher be allowed to speak in the afternoon session. Phil was approached and he agreed. I was chosen to speak.

After lunch several more representatives from the Labour Party gave speeches, as well as Felicity Dawling, a teacher, member of the NUT, and Militant supporter. Bob Parry pointed out the links between this struggle and unemployment. Eddie Loyden, Labour MP, gave an interesting talk:

> Industrial struggles have failed in Britain because of the lack of links to community struggles like this one. This is therefore a unique situation. It is the first time in my experience that trade unions have taken an interest in community action.

Eddie Loyden's talk pointed out something very significant which was indeed taking place: the link between the labour movement with its traditional concerns over purely industrial struggles, and an urban protest movement. Such linkages are not common, as the sociological literature documents (Saunders 1983).

My own talk focused on a recent article in the *New Statesman* which suggested that Croxteth Comprehensive might go the community school/free school route. I tried to emphasize a middle position between community power and the social wage, stressing that the occupation had to be viewed primarily as a holding operation to keep pressure on the state, but at the same time that the campaign for Croxteth Comprehensive wasn't significant only in party-political terms. What was happening inside the school was also very important and needed support. Pupils were getting, and could get far more, a unique experience in this school which was absent from ordinary state comprehensives. The volunteers were highly motivated to give special attention and care to the pupils, and the fact that parents were involved in the internal running of a school was important and needed appreciation and support. I also listed a number of things required by the teaching staff for our difficult job, items which teachers had requested me to list in my talk, and I called on those present to aid the staff by coming forth with more materials and financial support.

The conflict between a community and a Labour Party strategy surfaced dramatically during the open discussion which followed. Many representatives of the WRP and Cockpit group stood up from the audience and gave short speeches on the significance of the grassroots features of the struggle for Croxteth Comprehensive. Reference was made to 'common people' and 'the working class' having finally seized the initiative and the need to support this feature of the struggle. Other speakers who were not of the WRP urged a more community approach to the campaign as well. In fact, the efforts of the WRP to influence the occupation had misleadingly linked together the arguments for a community strategy with the ideology of the WRP. Implicit in the comments of all these people was the opposition of their view to Labour Party policy. One speaker, who seemed to be associated with the London Cockpit group, spoke longer than the rest:

> You should take this struggle back out to the *community*. Make these buildings serve the whole community. 'Education is the greatest social need' [a reference to a slogan on a banner hung on the wall behind the stage] but not education for examinations, education for *life*. Open the doors so that old age pensioners can have bingo sessions. Open the doors at night so that the kids getting harassed by the police have somewhere to go.

This speaker was followed by Graz Monvid, who got up onto the stage to talk. She began by asking those in the audience who actually lived in Croxteth to raise their hands. Few hands were raised, and those that were raised were the hands of Action Committee members or helpers. She then talked for some time:

> The parents of this community weren't even invited to this meeting! Discipline problems in the school are very bad and getting worse and they have been caused by the immediate reversion to an 'us versus them' situation when the teachers entered the school. The kids should be allowed to participate in the debate! It is *wrong* to exclude kids from our meetings and our demonstrations. If this occupation is just a holding operation, as Phil [Carspecken] says, then what will happen if we don't get the school back? We should have the kids and the community in here to build a strong base of resistance, to raise consciousness. The school shouldn't return to what it used to be. The discipline problems we have make that clear, they are a reflection of what the school used to be like. The speakers that we have had up here today are *useless* as leaders!

As Graz finished her talk, Phil Knibb leaned over and whispered into my ear: 'All this is WRP crap!' He then stood up to speak himself. He began by declaring that he was going to correct a number of mistakes which had been made by speakers (having Graz and some of the other impromptu speakers in mind). He said that there had been no need to invite the community because it was represented by himself and the helpers and CCAC members present. He went on to explain what had been a shift in the Action Committee's thinking and strategy:

> At first we fought to make it Croxteth Comprehensive as opposed to Ellergreen Comprehensive. Now we realize that there is a need to reorganize education throughout Liverpool. We support Ellergreen and we have been down to talk to them. We may have been politically naive, we aren't now. We are in the vanguard of the struggle against cuts.

> This meeting wasn't called by the Action Committee. It was called by the Merseyside Trade Union–Community Liaison Committee to pass resolutions for links between communities and trade unions. We want to form assemblies in different areas such as Birmingham and here in Liverpool. That is why the community wasn't invited. We represent this community, you represent the communities you have come from.

Phil also said that the reasons for discipline problems in the school were purely *technical*: problems of organization, staff shortages, the lack of previous teaching experience on the part of the volunteers.

Phil's position was thus made quite explicit. He had shifted from a community-based, horizontally competitive strategy to an identification with the local Labour Party, especially his favoured faction of the party. He had made friendships with prominent local leaders of the labour movement, and he'd come to see the purposes of the campaign in much broader terms. He saw the goals of the MTUCLC and local Labour Party as dominant; these broader and more powerful organizations could improve services to working-class areas throughout Liverpool and other cities. The Croxteth campaign was just one incident within a larger struggle. The main issues were political, party-political, and not educational. Croxteth needed its school back in much the same form as it had always existed with the same community–school relations and teacher–pupil relations. Problems in the occupied school were merely technical ones, and would be solved with a proper teaching staff.

Let me note a number of points about the development of strategy which had occurred on Phil Knibb's side:

1. There were obvious strategic reasons for drawing the campaign closer to the formal organizations of the labour movement. The Liverpool hung council was no longer an exploitable situation, the Action Com-

mittee needed the backing of a political party having an overall majority, and the Labour Party was the only party having both a real chance of soon getting such a majority (though many believed this chance was slim) and a political position which was supportive of the protest movement. Running the school also required funds of large proportions and the trade union movement was the only possible source of such financial support. It had proved itself, moreover, willing to help.

2. In drawing the movement closer to the Labour Party the interpretative theme of the social wage had become more articulated. During the second phase of the campaign the social wage theme had been present as a tacit orientation to the struggle, a way of interpreting the removal of the school and of justifying the fight to get it back in partially articulated terms calling upon the moral responsibility of the state. During this same phase the Action Committee had seen its relationship to the Croxteth community as its base of power. It was a community organization which determined its own purposes and used a political strategy aimed to exploit the situation of a hung council in Liverpool. Moreover, in addition to the view of the school as a state provision, a social wage, the Action Committee made use of a version of the community power theme, the cluster of values and norms which adhere to the term 'community', in their self-definition and their presentation of themselves to the media. But in terms of schooling practice, the Action Committee had always taken a view which deferred to the professionals of the state. In this sense the social wage theme prevailed over that of community power.

Now, however, the social wage ideology had become more than just a tacit orientation; it had become articulated policy, with the slogans of the labour movement being adopted to provide the rationale of the campaign. This meant that the goals of the campaign for the school were interpreted in terms of national goals held by the labour movement. The battle for the school was coming to be seen as an instance of the latter. This higher level of articulation was achieved by adopting formulations already present in the labour movement. At the same time that it broadened the meaning of the campaign, it limited certain possible directions that meaning might have taken. The Labour Party supported the school, as did many trade unions in Merseyside, but it didn't have a policy of political practice which could have nourished the participatory and grassroots nature of the struggle. Labour Party representatives met with Phil Knibb but they didn't visit the school on normal working days to meet the other local activists and try to get a sense of what developments were occurring inside the buildings.

3. Hence movement towards the Labour Party resulted in a more formal articulation of campaign goals in terms of the social wage. When this occurred, the views of the local activists on schooling authority, form, and purpose, which I have argued lay within a mesh of interconnecting conditions, became reinforced. It effectively backed the common-sense views of the bulk of the community activists with the political resources of a political party and a nationwide labour movement. Any tendency from within the protest movement to challenge certain features of the social wage ideology were all the less likely to become developed, simply because the labour movement itself has not formulated such challenges.

At the 20th November meeting the community power theme was also further articulated. It is significant that Graz referred to discipline problems in her talk and suggested that one reason for them lay in not involving pupils in the political activities of the campaign more, and not giving them an opportunity to discuss issues along with the other activists. Teachers had immediately adopted an informal approach with pupils, and community activists tended to focus on this as the principal reason for the disruptions. Teachers, we've seen, continued to hold to their beliefs in the desirability of informal relationships while moving in the direction of coercive sanctions, and the whole system of relationships achieved stability through the combination of teacher and adult authority relations with pupils. But teachers felt themselves vulnerable over the question of discipline because for the most part they didn't have a clearly formulated explanation of why disruptions were occurring, other than the small numbers of staff and the absence of adequate community involvement. But some teachers had begun to explain the situation in terms of curriculum and the exclusion of pupils from campaign activities. By the time of the 20th November meeting, this explanation was gaining more clarity and it was an explanation which put the goals of the occupation deeply into question.

Graz Monvid's speech, and the brief talk made by the Cockpit representative quoted above, argued that politics and education can not be separated, that the goals of the campaign ought to go beyond simply winning back a state provision. They questioned the value of restoring a school which possibly wasn't good for children and which isolated itself from adults in the neighbourhood. Both argued simultaneously for increasing the community base of the campaign, to locate power there, while putting into question the nature of schooling. Their arguments pitted the community against the state, no matter which party was in control. If the Labour Party lost the elections,

Graz argued, no community base would be left to continue with any struggle. If the Labour Party won, on the other hand, that could amount only to the restoration of an oppressive institution, one in which pupils were confronted with a 'them versus us' situation, as she expressed it.

The pro-community argument was thus becoming a challenge to, rather than a reinforcement of, the nest of conditions which I have argued tacitly connected schooling practice with a political ideology of the social wage. A number of links in this chain of conditions were on the verge of being drawn up from their opacity for critical scrutiny. Pupil disruptions were pointed to as examples, not of technical-administrative problems, but of fundamental problems of domination. School authority was linked to conditions of domination which affected all of Croxteth, domination in which state authority played a large role. The solution was to change educational practice, but exactly in what way was left unexplored. The way to change educational practice, Graz and the other speaker maintained, would involve a rejection of examinations ('Education is the greatest social need, but education for life, not for examinations') and the use of the school by all adults in the community to try to change their living conditions. Reified knowledge was thus beginning to be challenged as well, by calling for an 'education for life', an education for social change and community empowerment.

Graz's views were not confined only to herself. She was articulating the perceptions of a significant number of the teaching staff and her comments won many nods of agreement from them at this meeting. Versions of what she had to say had already been expressed, though less clearly, by teachers at previous staff meetings.

THE CONFLICTS AND INTERSUBJECTIVE STRUCTURE

The key argument in this chapter has been that two interpretative schemes held by different participants in the campaign existed in rational conflict with each other: community power and the social wage. Initially, each scheme involved a number of norms and very partially articulated theories which were in tension with those of the other scheme. As conditions in the school demanded decisions, each position became more clarified through the formulation of specific proposals. Proposals led to interpersonal conflicts and the further articulation of positions in consequence. In the case of Philip Knibb, practical considerations led to the acceptance of Labour Party political formulations which broadened his vision of the campaign for Croxteth Comprehensive and altered its meaning for him, but which did so in a way which reinforced the chains of conditions orientating him and most other residents towards the school through a social wage ideology. The congruence of the Labour Party's stance against cuts and the further congruence of policies which defended welfare provisions with traditional struggles over the wage relation on the shopfloor made it a smooth conversion for Philip Knibb. In the case of the pro-community group, further articulation began to put certain links in the chain of conditions underlying the social wage theme as held by Croxteth activists into critical discourse.

Underlying the overt conflict between specific campaign proposals generated by the pro-community group and those generated by the pro-labour movement group were a number of unexpressed conditions which were rationally in conflict but not major parts of the discourse. They were rationally in conflict because they were key components in the basic paradigms or interpretative schemes subscribed to by the two groups and hence would have to have been drawn into discourse if the groups in conflict had seriously attempted to understand each other and clearly articulate their own positions in the process. Although this never happened, these more covert conditions exerted an influence on the situation just the same. When teachers began to suggest that the campaign should alter schooling practice, for example, they were seen as being dangerously naive by their opponents in the Action Committee. They were making suggestions which threatened the 'proper' education of pupils for the sake of spurious ideals. For the teachers to have appeared other than naive, the complex relationships between local culture and school authority and practice in Croxteth would have to have become articulated in discourse at least as a first step. And if these relationships had become acknowledged as factors importantly conditioning the activities of local residents in the school, the teachers themselves would probably have developed a more realistic view of the situation: acknowledging still that traditional schooling practice is not an unqualified social good but seeing perhaps that the way to change it was not so straightforward. For the local activists' part, if the reinforcements existing between 'the proper school' and relations of domination in society working to their disadvantage had been discursively available, they may have understood better the position of the pro-community group, though the practical problems of mobilizing the community at this stage of the movement, and then organizing this mobilization, would have remained.

As the situation stood, however, the tacit conditions underlying the overt conflicts remained either totally unacknowledged or under-articulated and the two groups did not sit down together to try to reach an understanding. A major reason why these discussions did not take place was the informal organization of the local volunteers around the authority of Phil Knibb. While teachers called for greater participation and democracy, they didn't fully grasp the conditions upon which Phil's authority was constructed. These conditions included gender relationships, a local ethic of solidarity, and a host of subtle features of the Croxteth culture upon which authority is claimed and consented to. Most of the helpers and Action Committee members had as little knowledge of the 20th November meeting as did the teachers before it was held. But there was no evidence that they were particularly upset, as were the teachers, with the way it turned out. The political questions brought up at this meeting were not questions of deep concern to the bulk of the membership. They trusted Phil's leadership. For the community power ideology to have worked in practice, the organization of the Action Committee and helpers around the charismatic authority of Phil Knibb would have to have changed towards a more participatory-democratic organization. The issues would have to have been discussed by the committee in some depth. Conscious efforts would have to have been made to impart the skills and confidence required by participatory decision-making, and these efforts were not being made by the Action Committee leadership. They weren't deliberately omitted by any means, but had rather never been considered as campaign goals. Clearly, an alteration of the informal authority structure of the local residents of Croxteth would have required much time and conscious effort. The occupation of Croxteth Comprehensive had not run long enough for even the goal of such changes to arise.

Thus the conflicts over campaign strategy were embedded in interpretative schemes which covertly linked educational and political issues. The resolution of these conflicts took the form of negotiations over respective realms of legitimate decision-making. The conditions which determined the course of these negotiations were the ideology of community power, which was used to exclude the teachers in the pro-community group from decision-making about the campaign, and the conditions upon which the charismatic authority of Philip Knibb was constructed, which allowed him to act with a high degree of autonomy. The campaign course had already been virtually set, through the activities of Phil Knibb, before articulations began to be made.

However, I have several times mentioned the fact that a number of Action Committee members, in addition to teachers, were involved in the pro-community group. Amongst them were Ev Loftus, Ann Abercromby, and Anne Pines. These people could not be formally excluded from the decision-making processes which determined the course of the campaign and they did not give their consent to the charismatic authority of Philip Knibb. They were consequently seen as important allies by some of the teachers in the pro-community group. The way in which their challenge to campaign strategy ended will be described at the beginning of the next chapter. The reader will see that the manner in which campaign issues became interwoven with scandal greatly contributed to the way in which the challenge of these individuals was resolved.

THE FINAL DAYS OF TERM ONE

Before the next chapter can begin, however, I must first continue the chronology of the occupation through the final weeks of the first term.

After the 20th November MTUCLC meeting, teachers continued to discuss the need for greater community involvement and some proposals were presented to the Action Committee, though the campaign course was well established now in the direction of Labour Party affiliation. The greater articulation of the community power theme led to suggestions for altering curricular practice, but because of the commitment to teach capable students towards examinations, alternatives were proposed only for the lower streams, particularly the 3B and 4B classes. Plans for lower-stream alternatives were worked on by Barry Kushner and Tony Gannon and implemented with interesting results during the second term.

Order in the school had actually improved markedly after the first half-term break. Higher streamed classes managed fairly well and a group of boys called '4A1' demonstrated extremely high levels of motivation for learning mathematics, computer science, and physics. These boys were able to use the more informal approach of the teachers to study the subjects they liked, and they often came to the school after class hours and on weekends to take on extra mathematical and laboratory work. Sometimes the 4A1s helped to teach lower classes in computing. The first years were also well behaved and productive under the guidance of their main teacher, Pat Kellet. The fifth year offered little resistance to school authority by this time but most of these students were apathetic in comparison with the 4As. One of the most promising fifth-year students, a student who was taught individually by a tutor who volunteered to commute weekly from another city just to instruct him, finally ceased to come to the school, letting his chances for excellent examination results fall away. Two fifth-year boys named Jimmy and David, however, became extraordinarily motivated and met with individual staff for tutoring frequently after or before school hours. Both passed their examinations and one, David, got a job in the school the following year as a lab assistant. Both of these boys benefited from the occupation, receiving attention and help they had never had before in school. Discipline problems remained with the 3Bs and 4Bs, however.

The Cambridge trip went ahead on the 2nd of December and was a great success. Forty pupils and about six adults went to Cambridge by coach and were accommodated for the night by student volunteers from Selwyn and King's Colleges. Each student put up two pupils from Croxteth in their rooms. One humorous incident was reported by Yola, who had gone along on the journey. As the pupils were led about the campus by a guide to see the buildings, laboratories, computers, and the Cambridge observatory, one pupil began to marvel at the buildings and suddenly shouted out 'Let's occupy!'. The trip received nationwide coverage and did much to aid the campaign in its battle for public sympathy.

A PTA meeting held on the 8th of December didn't have as much success. Although parents did come they were small in numbers, confirming the Action Committee's contention that community support was not so easy to get (it had been well publicized). Over half of the parents who did come had familiar faces, being those active in the campaign all along.

Meanwhile, after the MTUCLC meeting of the 20th of November, Phil Knibb went ahead with his efforts to solidify links between the campaign and the Labour Party. His friends on the party agreed to bring a proposal to the district Labour Party to vote on a pledge to reopen a school in Croxteth if they won in the May elections. The beginnings of a plan to hold a national demonstration against government cuts at Croxteth School in the spring were discussed, and the efforts of the Merseyside Trade Union-Community Liaison Committee to expand continued with Phil's participation and support.

Despite continued grumbling amongst the pro-community group and the continuation of rumours about Phil in the school, no new crisis broke out until the 6th of December. The conflict over strategy had cooled a good deal due to the absence of Ev Loftus and Ann Abercromby from the premises, who had apparently taken their banishment from the office as a banishment from the campaign altogether. Ann Pines did begin to work in the school again after a brief absence, but she was no longer so vocal in her objections to the way the campaign was being run. Graz Monvid, having several writing deadlines to meet, ceased to come to the school as often as before.

Threats of bailiffs

The 6th of December was the date that a message was communicated to the school from SDP Member of Parliament Eric Ogden that plans had been laid to send bailiffs into the school over the Christmas holidays. Eric Ogden, during an interview in his surgery with myself and Cyril D'Arcy, said that he had been approached by Keith Joseph and Trevor Jones and had been told that the occupation had been tolerated long enough; plans were being laid to expel the occupiers. He was convinced that bailiffs would be sent in during the holidays when no pupils would be expected in the school, and even suggested a couple of possible dates.

This news provoked much discussion amongst the staff and Action Committee. The staff were convinced once again that the failure of the campaign to get the entire community involved in the school had left them vulnerable. They began calling for immediate steps to increase the picket numbers. Pickets had fallen in number during November and early December; some nights no pickets at all were held in the school, other nights only Jimmy and Chris, two young teenagers, were there. The staff believed the community should be made aware of the impending invasion and a phone tree was constructed to call out for extra help at the first sign of bailiffs. A small leaflet was pushed into the mailboxes of many houses on the estate:

**THERE IS STRONG RUMOUR
THAT CROXTETH SCHOOL IS TO BE
RAIDED BY POLICE
AND THE PICKET EVICTED, AND
THE SCHOOL WILL BE CLOSED.**

******* WE NEED HELP!*****
EXTRA PICKETS ARE URGENTLY NEEDED.
IF YOU WANT TO KEEP CROXTETH
COMPREHENSIVE OPEN
PLEASE GET DOWN THERE AND HELP.**

**DO NOT LET 2 YEARS' WORK
GO DOWN THE DRAIN.**

******* HELP US WIN THIS *****
YOUR BATTLE**

The problem was also taken to the Merseyside Trade Union Community Liaison Committee and the possibility of holding a large protest demonstration at the school, with community and city-wide union representation, was considered. At Philip Knibb's invitation, Reza, Kevin Stannard, and I attended this meeting and urged the demonstration idea, but in the end this possibility was dropped because the time of year wasn't favourable for a large turnout. Instead it was decided to 'blow it to the press' as soon as possible and publicly to confront Trevor Jones on whether or not he intended to force the pickets out. This was done very effectively the day after the MTUCLC meeting. During a session of the city council Dominic Brady asked Trevor Jones to comment on his intentions. Trevor Jones responded ambiguously but after the session Phil Knibb, with press reporters nearby, walked right up to Trevor Jones and demanded to be told if the rumours were true. This time Jones denied that he had any such intentions. The confrontation was reported on the radio, and several newspapers printed the story as well, quoting Philip Knibb who claimed that the Croxteth pickets would be trebled (*Daily Mirror*, 15th December 1982; *Liverpool Echo*, 16th December 1982).

As the holidays approached, the activists took defensive measures. All records and other valuable materials were removed from the school so that they wouldn't fall into the hands of the authorities. A public meeting was called at the school just after the beginning of the Christmas vacation to increase the numbers of pickets and lay plans for what steps to take if they did come. This meeting was very poorly attended, with virtually no new faces from Croxteth present, provoking the remark from Cyril that he wished more teachers had come so that they could see how little the community of Croxteth was willing to get involved in the school, even for an emergency. Just the same, picket duty was increased from the ranks of those available, and a plan was laid to contact the media immediately if bailiffs showed up.

Christmas

The Christmas celebrations held in the school on the last day of term were very successful. An anonymous donor had given a large sum of money for the meal, and staff and pupils sat together on long tables set up in the school hall while Phil Knibb and other Action Committee members served us a large, multi-course Christmas dinner. The teachers were placed as a display of respect at the head table, with pupils and helpers sitting at two rows of tables running down the hall. Phil and the other servers hustled back and forth from the kitchen in aprons, placing plates of steaming food before us. A sense of unity pervaded the room. The first term was over and everyone seemed to feel united in a sense of success and pride for what had been accomplished: teachers, pupils, and Croxteth adults.

Pat Kellet got the younger years involved in games and the youngsters ran delightedly about the hall and corridors in a number of competitions he'd arranged. Pat was our most esteemed teacher. His room was decorated beautifully for Christmas with coloured streamers, balloons, and pupil art work and essays posted on the walls.

In the evening a large party was held with a live band and food and drinks for everyone. On this occasion many new faces were seen in the school, the promise of a good time being much more successful than a call to duty in getting community involvement!

On the first Monday of vacation I joined other staff at the school to finalize first-term grades and distribute them by hand to family homes in Croxteth. First-term marks with long comments, some of letter length, were written under the co-ordination of Peter Clarke. We held some discussions as well on new ways of coming to terms with the discipline problems in the school and a group of three agreed to meet later to draw up a list of rules to be followed by all pupils from the start of second term.

It was getting cold for England, and the early dark of the English winter had fallen. I said goodbye to Croxteth and took the number 14 bus home. Lucy and Gabriel and I were going to Germany for the holidays and I left the other volunteers to secure the school without me. In Germany I often wondered whether or not the CCAC still had possession of the school. Finally, after New Year, I phoned Reza to find out what had happened. To my relief I discovered that the holidays had passed without any invasion after all. The steps taken to get the story in the press probably served as a sufficient discouragement to the city administration. The days were used by teachers and local volunteers to clean the building and plan for the coming term. I stayed in Germany an extra week, reading and enjoying the bright, affluent, and cheerful look of Hanover – such a contrast to the grey days and ubiquitous brick of England.

8
Politics and schooling

To conclude this part of the conference Phil Knibb got up to speak. He began by pulling together the themes expressed by previous speakers. He told the audience that originally the Action Committee had wanted to be non-political. But eventually this became inevitable. Like it or not, it had to turn to the Labour Party for help, as it was the Liberals and the Tories who had decided to close the school.

Similarly, it took three years to realize the nature of the struggle and the necessity for other schools to remain open, so that all communities would have a means of education. And what had happened in Croxteth must happen in other areas, where similar campaigns will be mounted. Thus he wants there to be Community Neighbourhood schools that give an understanding and easing of pressures on kids.

For this reason education has to be and always will be political.

(Report of Barry Kushner on a
spring 1983 conference and benefit
organized by the Cockpit Theatre
for Croxteth Comprehensive)

Early in the second term of the occupation the political course of the campaign for Croxteth Comprehensive became set, with absolutely no ambiguity, in the direction of Labour Party politics. A series of dramatic events took place within the first weeks of the term which eliminated all remaining opposition to the strategy worked out by Phil Knibb. During the weeks that followed, Phil and his brothers Ron and George immersed themselves in Merseyside organizations of the labour movement to maintain a steady flow of financial donations to run the school and help prepare for the coming May elections. In their experience politics and schooling had become tightly entwined through the necessity of tapping the resources of the trade union and labour movement. Involvement in such organizations changed the perceptions of these individuals as they found themselves increasingly identified with the objectives of the labour movement and integrated within its organizations.

But another sense of politics continued to operate within the school buildings – not the politics of the labour movement but the politics of control over decision-making processes affecting daily routines within Croxteth Comprehensive. For many within the school, especially for the group of teachers who had supported the community-power strategy during the first term, politics and schooling became increasingly *separated* in their daily experience, and work within the school lost its former excitement and meaning. It is these two senses of politics and their relationship to schooling that are the focus of this chapter.

FINAL VICTORY OF THE SOCIAL WAGE

On the second day of the second term (11th January 1983) Ev Loftus and Ann Abercromby reappeared in the school. They came in to discuss matters concerning their own children, who were attending Croxteth Comprehensive, but afterwards asked some of the teachers if they could be of any use. 'Gis a job,' they said. They explained that they had greatly missed being involved in the occupation and would teach art or some other subjects, or help teachers in any way needed. That evening Reza, Kevin, and I huddled about the timetable to make sure all slots were filled for the following day. As usual, some vacant slots existed which needed impromptu filling and we found we could cover all classes by slotting Ev and Ann in for art. Phil Knibb, who entered the staffroom when the assignments were being made, seemed alarmed at our decision and called Reza aside to request that Ann and Ev not be used. He told Reza that inviting them back into the school would renew some of the disputes which had plagued the occupation in November. We decided, however, that the need for extra teachers was greater than the dangers Phil alluded to and left Ann and Ev on the timetable after Phil had departed.

The next morning Phil was furious over what had been done. 'You've gone over my head!' he stormed. But Phil wasn't in a position to alter the decision: teaching and timetabling were now clearly demarcated within the staff's legitimate decision-making domain. As the day progressed, helpers could be heard heatedly discussing the presence of Ann and Ev in small groups throughout the school. In their minds, Ann and Ev were associated with the left-wing activities of the WRP and with a challenge to their trusted leader. Although I personally liked Ev and Ann very much, I sensed that their presence was controversial enough to require a discussion of the Action

Committee before allowing it to continue. I phoned up Ev that evening and asked her to wait for such a meeting before returning again.

However, Ev and Ann came in the next day just the same and spent it in Reza's laboratory preparation room. Although they weren't physically visible to most of the staff and local activists, word of their presence quickly spread around. Supporters of Ev and Ann began to give the old rumours about Phil new life. Phil was clearly very stressed by their presence in the school but said little more about it in my presence.

For a few more days Ann and Ev came to the school but spent their time in Reza's laboratory preparation room and in Yola's nearby history room, helping her sort out textbooks. Despite this low profile, their presence was fuelling fires throughout the school. On the 18th of January the fires exploded.

On this day Ev and Ann again went to Reza's preparation room but a relative of Ev's came along as well. Some time in the morning this relative met Phil Knibb in a corridor and engaged in a loud verbal confrontation with him in the sight and hearing of many helpers. Phil had been under tremendous strain because of the rumours, as his personal reputation amongst the committee was under attack. The rumours obviously were difficult for Carol Knibb as well, who continued to work each day in the kitchen. It was a matter of great worry and stress for Phil, and the confrontation in the corridors resulted in his stamping out of the school, declaring loudly that he wouldn't come back.

Immediately news of the crisis spread throughout the building and the staffroom filled with teachers and local activists talking excitedly. The school had just begun its morning break, pupils were milling about the hall and outside the building as they usually did at this time. I heard about the crisis as I left my classroom for the break and hurried up to the staffroom. There I found a large number of local activists arguing with some teachers. The teachers were insisting that Ev and Ann had been invited into the school by the staff and that Phil had no right to object. But the local residents were preparing to walk out of the school themselves, to support Phil. A number of them made slow and indecisive movements towards the door as the loud and angry arguments continued. I was personally upset and began to speak loudly to the group, while standing in front of the door, gaining the ears of most. I insisted that we retain our commitment to the pupils and continue our work. 'We will have an emergency meeting tonight, wait until then!' Suddenly, Ev and Ann appeared at the door behind me and tensions skyrocketed. I grew enormously and irrationally angry over the poor timing of their appearance when the balance between keeping or losing the campaign seemed to be so delicate. I turned on Ev and shouted at her, 'What the hell is going on!'. Ev began to explain her views, that she wanted to help in the school but that Phil had been unfair in his treatment of her. Although I liked Ev and didn't fully understand what had happened between her and Phil, I realized that this was the worst possible time to be reasonable about it and shouted again, cutting her off, calling her dispute with Phil 'extremely petty' and telling her to leave until the evening when we would hold an emergency meeting to hear all sides. Ev left accordingly and I turned to the rest of the group to vent some anger at them for being ready to leave the school at such a time: 'Get back to your posts, break is nearly over. Ring the bell! We have a school to run!' Someone went to ring the bell and, somehow, a consensus was silently formed to return to work for the rest of the day. Ev had meanwhile disappeared.

If the local activists had walked out at that point the pupils would out of necessity have been sent home, where many would have had no parent waiting, and the occupation itself may not have recovered. This was probably the worst crisis faced by the campaign for Croxteth Comprehensive. But Ev was now gone and helpers were back at work. The school continued for the rest of the day and all volunteers waited afterwards to attend the emergency meeting.

Neither Phil nor Ev attended the evening meeting but almost everyone else who had ever had anything to do with the school was there. Taking Ev's side were Graz and John Bennett who had travelled long distances to be present (they'd been phoned by someone). Yola had a letter to read written by Ev explaining her views on the conflict, and Ann Abercromby was there as well. All the regular staff and helpers were present. Cyril acted as chairman. For once there was a good deal of contribution from Action Committee members and helpers at a meeting. Very strong feelings were expressed, and a number of Action Committee members called for a ban on Ev's presence in the school. Most of them tied her to the WRP (her actual affiliation with the WRP is not known to me) and claimed that the whole problem had been caused by the efforts of the WRP, with Ev's help. Many teachers, however, argued that it wasn't fair to ban Ev just because of the personality problems between her and Phil. Their arguments were not in political terms. John Bennett used expressions like 'witch-hunt' and 'kangaroo court' in describing the proceedings. One of the helpers stood up and angrily confronted John, saying he had no right to be in the school and that people were sick of the WRP. Someone immediately suggested that all people present who were not helpers or CCAC members or teachers be forced to leave and a quick vote passed the suggestion. John and a few others left to wait outside.

Much was discussed in the hour that followed. Local residents clearly felt angry about the behaviour of the WRP. Ron Knibb, who had done much work to solicit donations from trade unions, stressed several times that the campaign must not be allowed to fail as so much had been invested for its success.

He accentuated his point with a rhetorical statement: 'This campaign belongs to the trade unions – it isn't just our campaign now.' Many teachers expressed support for Ev and emphasized all the positive work she had done for the occupation. Ev had also raised funds through her own efforts and shouldn't be banned just because of a personality dispute with Phil Knibb.

As the arguments continued it became clear that the bulk of the Action Committee saw the situation primarily as a choice between Phil or Ev, and they were determined to stand by Phil. Finally, a proposal to ban Ev from the school for two weeks until and unless the personal problems between her and Phil could be resolved was passed. This decision effectively threw the matter back into Phil's control, since it would be up to him to declare whether or their personality problems had been resolved. As it turned out, Ev never did return to the school. She pulled her son out of it and sent him to Ellergreen. Ann pulled her daughter out and never came back, in sympathy with Ev. John Bennett also ceased to come to the school, except for two appearances near the end of the campaign. Those volunteers from the community who had had some sympathy with the ideas of Ev and Ann, like Ann Pines, ceased to be vocal about their opinions.

These events were significant in many ways. First, at a time in which members of the labour movement throughout Britain were writing and talking about the campaign for Croxteth Comprehensive as an exemplary battle against cuts, a crisis precipitated by rumours and scandal had nearly destroyed the campaign from within. It demonstrates the highly contingent nature of campaigns frequently described in terms of class struggle and historical necessity on highly particular events which owe much to non-political sources, or which entwine political issues with highly contingent personal ones.

Second, although these events became an actual crisis only through the form of a personality dispute, many political issues had been tied to it. Ev and Ann had effectively led a small number of Action Committee members and helpers in opposition to the campaign strategy of Phil and Cyril. In doing so they had also had the sympathies of many from the pro-community group amongst the teachers, which had been a majority on the staff. Their banishment removed any possibility for an alternative perspective to enter Action Committee discussions. Ev and Ann had both contributed a good deal of work to help the occupation and it was a pity that some resolution other than banishment was not effected between Ev and Phil. It is not known what had really occurred between Ev and Phil on the personal level. But there is evidence that the rumours may have been deliberate distortions and magnifications of their personality conflict, perpetrated by others for political reasons. Intentionally or not, the conflict was clearly deeply tied to a power struggle over control of the course of the campaign.

Last, the way in which this crisis formed and was resolved demonstrates the intersection of many conditions of action in complex ways to produce consequences significant to the movement. Differences in the perception of campaign goals had become intermeshed with norms governing sentiments of loyalty towards the individuals involved. Ev, and with her Ann and John Bennett, were effectively excluded from any influence over decision-making through the organization of the local activists around the charismatic authority of Phil.

I questioned a number of teachers and local volunteers about their perceptions of this dispute many months after it had occurred. Most of the local activists questioned about it saw the dispute as a choice between Phil or Ev so that they felt obliged to back Phil even if they held nothing against Ev. Others blamed Ev for being spiteful and calculating in relation to Phil, for trying to impose her left-wing ideas on the campaign through an attack on Phil's character. Several claimed she was a member of Militant, which is ironic because the Militant faction of the Labour Party was one of the key sources of support Phil had managed to tap for the school. Many teachers, on the other hand, saw it as a struggle over patriarchal authority relations as well as a struggle over the nature of campaign strategy. The personal aspects of the crisis and the link to the WRP were described as a 'smokescreen' by a number of them. Yola expressed her perceptions in the following way:

> The more Ev thought, the more strongly she felt, the louder she voiced her opinions, the worse reaction she got from the people around her and the more trouble she got into. It might not have stopped her thinking, but it shut her up.

Thus teachers, by and large, saw the conflict in political and sociological terms, while helpers saw it in terms of the norm of solidarity. There is some evidence, including the quotation from Yola above based on her intimacy and frequent social contact with Ev, that the challenge presented by Ev and Ann and others on the committee to the pro-labour movement strategy of Phil and Cyril was constructed in terms of gender long before its precipitation into scandal and crisis. If local male residents on the Action Committee had used the same campaign arguments which Ev and Ann put forth, they may have been taken much more seriously and the issues probably wouldn't have become so enmeshed in scandal. At any rate, the conflict over campaign strategy was finally resolved through a process of exclusion in which the informal organization of the local activists became determinant. Phil Knibb's desperate act of walking out of the school had fully polarized the situation and turned it into one perceived by the local activists as a call for their loyalty. They responded in support of their leader.

Politics outside and inside the school

After the crisis between Phil and Ev had been resolved, little opposition remained to the strategy worked out by Philip Knibb and Cyril D'Arcy. Many external barriers to the campaign's success had been overcome by the second term as well. An invasion of bailiffs was no longer considered a real threat, the CSE and AEB examination boards had accepted our appeal to approve Croxteth Comprehensive as a centre for administering their examinations, and on the 31st of January the district Labour Party voted in favour of making a campaign pledge to reinstate Croxteth Comprehensive if they won an overall majority in the 5th May elections. The course was clear: Croxteth activists must hope for, and work towards, a Labour Party victory. For the leadership this goal soon became more than just a political one. The Liberal Liverpool city administration sent a rates bill to Phil Knibb, Cyril D'Arcy, and Croxteth resident and well-known actor Peter Kerrigan (who had served picket duties in the school) for £27,353.08. An accompanying letter indicated that this was just the first of two such bills and that the city was holding these three responsible for the school buildings' rates.

Phil Knibb and his brothers George and Ron became increasingly integrated in labour movement organizations. Phil was elected secretary of the MTUCLC and put in charge of organizing a national rally and march against cuts in welfare services. The march was to take place in Liverpool, with the Croxteth buildings its termination point and its stage for speeches. A special office was established in the school for the purpose of organizing this demonstration and for co-ordinating all other work pertaining solely to the political features of the campaign. It was called the 'campaign office' and was located in the old office formerly run by Ev and Ann. Certainly, with respect to the external features of the campaign for Croxteth Comprehensive, politics and education were fully integrated.

Yet inside the school this relationship between education and politics took an opposite course. School organization became firmer, relegating participants to more specific roles. In addition to the creation of the campaign office, a new administrative office run by Kevin Stannard, Jackie Crowley, and Mark Gough was set up to allow teachers more time to concentrate on teaching alone. But this was achieved at a price; many teachers lost touch with events taking place outside their own classrooms as they were no longer needed for many administrative decisions. Communication between the campaign office and the administration office was poor and communication between the administration office and teachers was also weak. What occurred in effect was the separation of teaching from politics and even from administration, a markedly different situation from the first term, during which all three arenas were integrated.

New conflicts emerged in a largely suppressed form, based now not over competing theories of how the campaign should be run but rather over organizational structures which excluded most activists from the decision-making process. Two senses of 'politics' were in implicit dispute: politics in the sense of state policies and party activities, and politics in the sense of participatory power over the activities and purposes of an institution. The former corresponded to the social wage theme and the latter to a form of the community power theme. The former sense of politics dominated while the latter was suppressed for many months, reaching articulation only in the spring with a series of new confrontations between teachers, helpers, and the CCAC leadership.

Several conditions underlay the new organizational structure in the school. First was the charismatic power of Phil Knibb with its proven support of the bulk of the Croxteth participants. Second were material constraints: the vast influx of information and the need for continuous decisions made on short-term notice which demanded efficient organization. Third was the victory of the social wage definition of politics. Phil Knibb stated in his London speech, 'Education has to be and always will be political', but he meant this in the sense of government policies on education. The now submerged community power theme interpreted politics in a different way. In effect, it claimed that the separation of a role like that of the teacher from decision-making processes which shape the purposes to which that role is put, is a dispossession of political rights and power. To say that politics and education are linked in this second sense is to say that the purposes of schooling ought to be placed under the control of those involved in it.

Simultaneously, the situation for many teachers during the second term worsened in other ways. The number of teachers by the second term, though stable, was still always slightly too small to fill the timetable adequately. This put teachers under a great deal of stress. Reza, for example, had to take three different groups of science students simultaneously at times. I had to teach mathematics to groups of O level and CSE candidates simultaneously. Many teachers worked long hours after school and during the weekends to tutor pupils preparing for examinations and to get ready for the next day of teaching. Discipline problems, though fewer than they had been in the first term, continued to concern everyone.

One must ask what motivated the teachers to continue under such conditions. They received no pay, of course. Many had families who were denied much of their time because of the pressing demands for planning, marking, and providing individualized tutoring. The motivation for most of the teachers during the first term had been the excitement of being involved in an empowering environment with other people sharing a common cause and with the opportunity to partake in the shaping of answers to the most fundamental questions: what the campaign was for, where it might go. I observed many expressions illustrating this concern of the teachers and present one of them below. It displays at the same time the way in which the community power theme enabled teachers to express the very personal experiences and meanings which involvement in the occupation had for them. The quotation is taken from a conversation with Neil Murtough, a biology teacher who had worked for five years in Mozambique:

P.C.: Can you describe your first impressions of the school?

Neil: The first day I felt rather at home because curiously it was rather like Mozambique because you had a dramatically different situation, a situation where people, ordinary people, had seized the initiative and then had to deal with the consequences of their action [laughter]. And not let things slip and probably more importantly, to continue believing in themselves against all the odds. So it was like that air of chaos mixed with excitement and enthusiasm which really attracted me, which I felt really at home with. I like situations which force people to respond....

I think the strongest source of inspiration that I had all along, and I got on the first day, and it's always been there, is the, how do you say, the ordinary people here, the parents and other adults who help out. The sort of [pause], the feeling that well, we're all in this shit together, we might as well make the best of it. The feeling of being together which I really miss; I miss on the street, I miss in public places. It's something which used to be prevalent in British society. It's something that we're losing as people become more and more alienated from each other or insecure....

It's the social lubrication that is really important for me and I think for a lot of other people. And to come inside the school doors is to re-enter a world which it was very difficult to find in public. And it's been, it's cheered me so often. People accept you ... and that means the world to me.

Neil had found a community of which he could be a part. The community power theme corresponded to the *personal* reasons many teacher volunteers had for involving themselves in Croxteth. Most of them had not volunteered only for the opportunity to teach children or to serve political ideals. Volunteering rather provided these teachers with social gratifications they lacked in other realms of life. For many this included participation in group decision-making on all aspects of the campaign.

By the second term, however, with the separation of internal politics from schooling and the relegation of teachers to a purely educational role, many began to feel demoralized. Some left. Others openly wondered why they continued to work 'for' the Action Committee but persisted out of a sense of duty to the pupils. As Kevin Stannard expressed it:

> The teachers didn't come here just to teach. We came because we wanted to be involved in this as a political movement. But we are cut off from the political side now. Involvement had been one of our principal sources of gratification and reward. Now we have no gratification or reward. We call this a community school, but how much of a community school is it? State schools are bad enough – we're trying to run this like a state school and we aren't even doing a good job at it.

Many of the teachers who had played the most prominent and visible roles during the first term felt that their situation had slipped by the beginning of the second. They felt they'd lost influence over campaign issues altogether and were now even outside of any discussions, ultimately influential or not, over how the campaign was going. In interviews, three factors consistently came up as explanations of what had happened:

1. The pro-community campaign they'd supported was now completely off the agenda.

2. They were now forced into the role of teaching only. This was related to their failure, in the eyes of most local activists in Croxteth, to control pupils, as explained below.

3. A new, smaller, group of teachers had 'risen' in influence to replace them.

A conversation which took place between myself, Reza, and Peter Clarke in April 1983 (and was tape-recorded) illuminates the perceptions this group of teachers had of the changes which had occurred. Some of the contributions of Reza are presented here in detail. The reader should picture an energetic man in his early thirties who is talking rapidly, varying his speed and loudness of voice frequently for emphasis, and supplementing his remarks with rapid gestures:

> Reza: Well, we were told that this whole campaign belongs to the trade unions. I heard from certain individuals that this whole thing belongs to the trade unions. That sounded to me like very bad political action, you know it was forced on the people.... It seems to me that they now are the ones who dictate the policy.

> P.C.: But who? Who's saying that this belongs to the trade unions?

> Reza: Well, I heard it first from Ronnie Knibb and although I had expected it, I'd felt the whole thing rolling away. He'd put it specifically, you know,

in so many words. I remember he said that this campaign belongs to the trade unions because of all the support they had given to it.

P.C.: I'm interested in what role teachers have played in determining campaign policy. You can come in on this too, Peter, if you like. Have you ever felt that as a teacher in the school you've had much say in the way the campaign has been conducted?

Reza: Uh, there was a time when there was more activity, more contributions made by the teachers to a certain extent, but, uhh....

P.C.: Last term?

Reza: Yeah, the time before Christmas, but then things started cooling down.

Peter: Yeah, the routine just took over. Now certain members of the Action Committee just go down to the trade unions in town, to the Transport and General, rather than discussing things here. You see, the teachers can not go to those meetings.

Reza: I mean, if you want to do anything, first of all you have to go through the channel of the Action Committee, and on the Action Committee I know one person that has got, perhaps one and a half persons, who've got the say in these things, and the rest, the rest are just sort of observers.

P.C.: Uhh, how did that come about? I mean we were saying that things got rigid after Christmas.

Reza: Well, the whole thing got rigid because certain people who wanted the campaign to be on the level of having trade union support, on that level [only], managed to organize themselves more efficiently, you know, and it was possible for them to do so. So far as our active teachers were concerned, the number of them sort of dropped. I think the other people who wanted to maintain the campaign, the people I referred to, they managed to, because they had more spare time, a lot more than me who was in here from half past nine up to five o'clock, six o'clock, sometimes up to 12 o'clock midnight. Those people had a lot more spare time to go to people to talk to members of the Action Committee, organize them, or rather develop their influence with them. I didn't have such time at all, neither did you, neither Peter or other people. Their words became the pound of the day, worth exchange anywhere, whereas our words started to [pause].

P.C.: To?

Reza: Well, also one other factor contributed. They were restricting the contribution of the teachers to the whole affairs of the campaign, I mean politically and educationally, to the mere educational work. Not directly with, 'Get on, go on and get on with your work', but rather we were told that this school is not run properly, you know, we need more discipline to be done, we need this and that to be done, and through that we were more gagged, more restricted, to the question of education.

P.C.: But why did we have to go along with these restrictions? This is an interesting question, why did we have to go along with it?

Reza: That issue was sort of connected to the issue of discipline, you know, the question of maintaining the classes and so on. I remember there was a big issue made of this matter that when parents or some members of the Action Committee go into a classroom the class goes hush-hush, they go dead quiet, and we were blamed for not being able to maintain the classes and that was another shot against us. It had by implication, 'Don't concern yourselves with the political affairs and also of the general running of the campaign'. The logic was that since we couldn't keep discipline, we couldn't do the other aspects of the work. And I raised the question to the Action Committee, 'Why don't you go into the community and ask if they would come in and help us with the running of the school? After all this is their own school. And I would hear time and time again, 'You can not mobilize any people there, you can not bring any people in,' and etcetera, etcetera, etcetera!

P.C.: Well, do you think they really believed they couldn't get the community involved or not?

Reza: They could have, they could believe it. I can not blame them for what they believe.... But that is not the point at all, that was not the point, whether, you know, we could get the people from there. What we were discussing was the fact that teachers were pushed to a corner and their contribution to the running of the general campaign was diminished. We came under quite a bit of pressure, if you remember. Every single staff meeting we were discussing the question of discipline, discipline, discipline, discipline; we could have been running a sort of a military camp here [laughs]. But behind that question of discipline was the fact that when we went to the Action Committee meetings the only question we could talk about was discipline and hence anything else mentioned by members of staff was not very much valued.

Teachers like Reza had held to their pro-community strategy partly because they felt that that was the way in which to establish better relations with pupils, both through getting more adults involved and through linking educational activity to community action and thus winning the consensus of pupils to school purposes. But local volunteers tended to locate responsibility for control with the teachers, on technical and managerial skills. Teachers felt enormous pressure on themselves in consequence. The poor performance of many teachers in maintaining control led to their loss of influence in other matters and made interactions between teachers and local activists at meetings one in which teachers felt on the defensive. Yola Jacobson gave her views on this same matter and refers to the rise of the second group of teachers into an influential position as well:

> Yola: I don't know, sometimes I get the feeling that if you can not control kids, you know, [laughing] but maybe that's just my paranoia.

> P.C.: I've heard some direct criticisms.

> Yola: I've heard parents criticize some teachers very ruthlessly, *very* ruthlessly. They don't know how lucky they are.

> P.C.: They don't appreciate us?

> Yola: No; they appreciate the ones that are in with them. I mean, that do the right things, or say the right things – I mean don't say *anything*. But if you sort of stick your neck out which I've done in some situations....

One afternoon in February I found Ann, a history teacher, crying over her lunch. She explained that she felt overworked, isolated, and unappreciated. The combination of feeling cut off from decision-making processes, overwork, pupil disruptions, poverty, and isolation was telling on many of the staff. Both Reza and Janine, an art, cookery and general subjects teacher, spent some time in the Liverpool hospital, in Reza's case for reasons explicitly related to the stress of volunteering in the school.

The situation was serious enough for several teachers to leave. As early as January several key teachers, Yola, Janine, Angela and Kevin (the administrator) amongst them, were privately declaring that they would like to leave the school and would do so if they got replacements. Graz very rarely came to the school, making only one or two visits during the second and third terms. Ian Tulip, the English teacher from Lancaster, informed the staff that he was taking a three-week break. He never returned. Paul Shackley, a regular volunteer from Lancaster during the first term, stopped coming. Volunteers from the Merseyside Arts Association, who had taught art classes in the school from the pilot summer school to the end of the first term, no longer came in the second term. The school's first-term German and French teacher Kate, who had been vocal in her support of the pro-community strategy, stopped coming as well. Yola left after Easter to move to London, saying the occupation had become stagnant for her. Janine left soon afterwards, explaining that she'd come to feel isolated, unappreciated, and cut off from the campaign.

Most of the reasons for the deteriorating morale of many of the teachers have been described but another important condition operated as well: gender.

It is important to note that most, but not all, of the teachers who left were women. Conditions of domination based on gender in the school were felt as strongly oppressive by many of the female volunteer teachers. It was more difficult for them to gain influence over the decision-making process, especially regarding the campaign as a whole than it was for the males:

> Yola: I've said it before, but I think it is rampant with sexism.

> P.C.: The staff?

> Yola: Yeah, staff and committee – you can't separate them really. I've really felt that. I've really felt that when I make a noise and when I make a persistent nuisance of myself for something like a room. You see, I haven't got a loud voice, I can not sort of lose my temper and make people physically afraid of me which in some ways is the only way things get done around here. And that's frustrating.

To summarize, teachers were thus pressed away from having control over defining their own roles in the campaign, as the roles ascribed to the position of teacher began to confine their field of possible action. Their hopes of aiding a genuine 'community struggle', and in some cases of helping to create an alternative school, had to be abandoned. But their feeling of demoralization went much deeper than that of simply finding themselves working in a campaign serving purposes to which they had ideological objections. After all, it was clear through most of the first term that the pro-community strategy probably wouldn't be implemented because it was clear from an early stage of the conflicts that the Action Committee would be very hard to sway in a new direction, for reasons discussed in the last chapter. But in the first term there was an atmosphere of hope just the same. There were many discussions and debates amongst teachers which at least had some of the Action Committee involved. There was a sense that teachers could have some influence, even if only a little. This was a goal in itself for these teachers, a participatory climate in which teacher volunteers felt themselves to be contributors to the meaning of the occupation. It was this social process which was one of the major reasons for the involvement of many of them: A chance to clarify personal values and goals and at the same time 'count' in a community of people. It was a chance to find and empower themselves.

By the second term the occupation had become objectified and external to these teachers, assigning them roles to play rather than allowing them to discover new roles for themselves. Participation became work, alienated labour if you like, a subordination of personal values to purposes determined elsewhere.

For other activists, of course, the situation was different. The small group of teachers who came to occupy more influential positions during the second term had not joined the campaign with set political ideologies and had come for the most part with the hope of trying out teaching. For several of these, participation in the school definitely opened new opportunities: friendships were created between themselves and members of the Action Committee and teaching was experienced as rewarding. Barry Kushner, Tony Gannon, Jackie Crowley, and others became integrated into high positions within the informal social structure of the Croxteth activists and found their new friendships highly rewarding. They accepted the leadership's campaign strategy, enjoyed their teaching and administrative duties, and generally found their involvement one of increasing personal power rather than the reverse. Their empowerment, however, was based on their acceptance within the informal social hierarchy of the Action Committee – their 'chosen' status, as Yola and Janine expressed it. Barry Kushner explained his experiences in this regard:

I remember having a discussion with Kevin [Stannard] when he was going through some self-examination. It was late at night and I was about to walk back to my flat and we were talking. This was just before Christmas.

I was saying that I didn't think you could be more committed than the parents. It's their decisions, it's their school. In the end you can not be more committed than the parents should be – whether they are or not is another question. It's not your struggle, it's not my struggle, it's the community's struggle. That was the way I saw it then. So, for example, with the incident with Ann and Ev it was to do with the community. I think I kept that view through, but I got closer to the community.

So I felt that I could make suggestions about how I thought the school should go to the parents, that was because I'd been there some time and got to know them. To some extent I could do no wrong in some eyes because we got on very well together, partly to do with staying there....

Croxteth consumed my social and working life. I didn't take a day off in the second term. During the first term I was coming three and then four days a week. During the second term it got to five days a week and I was picketing as well [overnight]. I mixed more socially with Phil and George.

THE RANK AND FILE: EDUCATIONAL
INNOVATIONS FROM BELOW

The meaning the campaign held for the majority of the helpers and Action Committee members during the second term, those who did not take part in decision-making to any significant extent, took its own particular forms. Although many in this group could be heard with increasing frequency to express feelings of exhaustion and being 'fed up' in the second term, most of them continued to value their participation. The occupation still provided them with social contacts, a sense of heightened purpose and meaning difficult to find in other realms of their lives, and opportunities to take on expanded identities through the new roles offered by the school. Most of these had never felt involved with the key decisions of the campaign and were content to follow the initiatives of their leaders. They enjoyed their sense of control over certain areas of the school: the kitchen, the Parkstile building, or the corridors. Moreover, and this is an important contrast with most of the teachers, they extended their new friendships outside of the school, frequently having parties and bingo sessions in the local pubs, dances, and so on. Many got to know each other's families, and the new social relationships they'd found within the school thus spilled over to relationships within the Croxteth community.

Organic pedagogy

Yet another realm of meaning the occupation held for some of the helpers was the involvement and increasing influence some began to have in educational activities. For some helpers, being able to be a part of the school which their children attended and being able to establish informal and friendly relationships with their children's teachers was highly valued. Some even became involved in teaching pupils. Margaret Gaskell regularly tutored pupils who needed extra help and took classes when teachers were absent. Kathy Donovan taught art and domestic science, Tommy Maher taught woodwork, and so on. And for at least two local activists, Mick Checkland and Joey Jacobs, a process of integration that was the reverse of Barry and Tony's took place. Mick and Joey never held high-status positions on the Action Committee; they were not close friends of either Phil or George Knibb and in fact on several occasions got into fairly serious rows with them (Mick and Joey were the teachers who had had their keys taken by Phil Knibb – Chapter 7). Mick and Joey's role in the school became that of teachers soon after the beginning of first term, when they took over the games and P.E. lessons. As time went on they became integrated into the social world of the teaching staff and became more identified as teachers than as helpers or Action Committee members.

Local resident and P.E. instructor Joey Jacobs, for example, began tutoring David, one of the second-year pupils, during lunch hours. David was having great difficulties in his classes because he was far behind in basic skills. He responded by being extremely disruptive and made teaching difficult for staff. David was frequently put on detention, sent to the office, given lines to write, but his behaviour didn't change. Joey felt that David's situation was similar to his own previous experience. He and David began to eat lunch and go over work together.

The consistent teaching provided by local volunteers in subjects like P.E., games, and crafts proved to be highly successful. These teachers were able to establish excellent rapport with their pupils, using their familiarity with the local culture to establish control and yet form warm and friendly relationships with them. Mick, Joey, Margaret, Tommy, and a few others found they could be extremely effective with the pupils and enjoyed teaching them. Pupils, for their part, listed these local residents amongst their favourite teachers when interviewed.

These activists shared the progressivist ideal of producing an environment in which pupils are self-motivated, but didn't accomplish it through what is usually understood as 'informality' or 'weak framing'. Rather, they were skilled with aspects of the local culture and could combine plenty of gruff handling with 'a laugh and a joke'. Their framing was stronger than that of many volunteer teachers from outside the estate but produced less resistance because of the style they employed, which was closer to adult–youth or even older youth–younger youth styles on the estate than to teacher–pupil styles as they had existed in Croxteth Comprehensive prior to the occupation. When the end of the occupation was approaching, several of these teachers had become confident of their abilities and expressed much resentment over the fact that their lack of formal qualifications were to bar them from continued teaching.

Another successful teacher was Paul Gerard, who, though not from Croxteth, had grown up in a similar Liverpool community (with a similar name – Toxteth). Paul was not a qualified teacher but a self-taught man and Open University student highly competent in physics, chemistry, and computing. His lessons were successful both because he could control pupils through his familiarity with local culture and because he designed lessons which involved a lot of activity on the part of the pupils. His physics laboratory was full of equipment set up into different learning centres which illustrated various principles of science. He also had a small library of physics and chemistry books which pupils were allowed to check out. In his lessons he often put the most potentially disruptive pupils immediately to work. One lesson which was observed had one of the school's most disruptive pupils swinging a huge weight suspended from the ceiling back and forth, an activity which seemed to content the pupil, while Paul explained momentum and pendular motion to the class. Many good science teachers no doubt do things in a similar way to Paul, but Paul was unique with his Liverpool gruffness and ability to speak the language of the pupils from Croxteth. When the O level examinations were held in the school Paul sat the English examination along with the fifth years, never having taken it himself.

Another innovation in the school was the awakened interest in school knowledge experienced by many of the local activists who were involved in the actual education of pupils. Keith Leatherbarrow, employed after the occupation as a laboratory technician in the school, found new interests and abilities in the sciences. 'I study more than the kids do!' he stated once during the occupation, and he obviously did spend much of his time over the laboratory equipment, computers, and textbooks in the school. His brother Frank similarly studied mathematics and physics while involved in the school. Philip Knibb, in addition to reading academic papers and articles on education, was once seen taking a German language textbook home: 'I used to work there,' he explained. After the occupation Mick and Joey both began studying for O levels in science courses and sociology. Mick went on to study A levels the next year and university afterwards. He ascribes his educational ambitions completely to his experiences of the occupation. Margaret Gaskell similarly has enrolled in adult education courses and found during the campaign that she has an interest and ability in writing poetry.

Some residents also involved themselves with alternative curricular projects which were tried out in the school with the 4Bs, one of the most difficult classes to teach. George Knibb, with Barry and Tony, managed to engage the Open Eye Gallery in Liverpool to teach the 4Bs and themselves photography during the second term. A project developed in which the 4Bs created and mounted a series of photographs comparing housing and environmental features of Croxteth with those of more affluent communities. The project was a success in so far as it captured the attention of the pupils and led them to discuss and think about their social environment and the relevance of the campaign to it. Another part of the project involved the 4Bs in designing and making posters and badges for the campaign and to write letters of invitation (a lesson in English composition) to one of the heroes of Bleasdale's *Boys from the Blackstuff*: Yosser Hughes. The 4Bs were also given their own room with a tea pot, record player and table tennis. They painted and decorated their room with posters.

These activities with the 4Bs do not differ much from some projects currently taking place in the MSC (Manpower Services Commission) training schemes for school-leavers but were the closest the teachers got to tying

educational activity with the real-life surroundings of Croxteth Comprehensive and to the campaign to save the school. The project was also unique to
Croxteth Comprehensive, which had been run much more traditionally in the
years before the occupation. The activities were enjoyed by the 4Bs and had
the advantage of involving local resident George Knibb, who shared their
interest and learned along with them. But the 4Bs continued to complain,
with justification, that they weren't treated as seriously as were the 4As, and
the contrast between them and their 'more promising' counterparts made
these projects seem less serious educationally than the examination work
they didn't take part in. Eventually the 4Bs destroyed their form room,
indicating a basic failure of the school fully to engage their commitment and
win their identification with the school.

A community headmistress

On the 3rd of March, Janine's fourth-year domestic science class cooked and
served an evening meal to the members of staff, helpers, and the Action
Committee in the Parkstile building. The meal was delicious and ended with
small speeches from Phil Knibb and myself to commend the activists and
pupils for their achievements. Afterwards Angela, a fourth-year pupil, sang
songs to the accompaniment of a piano and a party with music, drinks, and
dancing followed for several hours.

Phil Knibb commented on this occasion that the school needed a strong
figurehead, a sort of a headmaster to help control the children. I suggested to
him that one of the Action Committee might best fill this post, as that would
further symbolize the community aspect of the occupation. Phil replied that
he was in agreement with this idea and said that Margaret Gaskell would
probably be best for the job.

Soon afterwards Margaret Gaskell became the official headmistress of the
occupied school. She shared Kevin's office and served her post primarily by
talking with pupils who were involved in discipline problems, keeping
contact with parents of pupils, and assigning punishments to pupils who
violated school rules. She sometimes mediated in disputes between pupils
and teachers, and she continued with her remedial work. Margaret never took
on a full or traditional role of headmistress. Her role was very low-key,
supplementing other visible figures in the school. I continued to give the
school assemblies, probably the activity which made a teacher most visible
in a central position. Pupils felt the situation was ambiguous with respect to
who was actually the 'head teacher' of the school. Margaret, George Knibb,
and I were frequently mentioned as 'heads', and Barry Kushner also soon
became a central figure for a large number of pupils. But pupils never
consistently focused on a single figure. Margaret was soon joined in her

administrative duties by myself and the administrators Kevin and Mark in what became known as the 'core committee'. The core committee handled all discipline problems in the school, met with parents on occasion, and took decisions on day-to-day issues which didn't require the consideration of the full staff.

Thus the division of labour which was solidified by the beginning of the second term resulted in different experiences for different activists. While Phil Knibb continued to be the most powerful figure in the occupation, his daily activities kept him largely out of classrooms and corridors. Residents like Mick, Joey, Margaret, Keith, and Frank became directly involved with educational activities in the school. As the next chapter explains, these activities began to alter their interpretations of schooling, raising former assumptions for critical examination. These residents were developing their own pedagogy, an effective one organic to the culture of the pupils, and were forced to become increasingly aware of educational issues they had previously taken for granted. It was this group of activists, their daily work in the school, the unique pedagogy they were devising, and the corresponding change in their perceptions of education, which are most enlightening for the concept of community education. I will return to them in the next chapter.

SPRING THAW

Aside from some of the conversations which were stimulated by my interviews during the second term (an example, in fact, of how research and action having some effect on the occupation sometimes coincided), there was very little apparent discussion among teachers about the demoralization many were experiencing during this period. The shift in the position of the teachers took place at the same time that classroom and tutorial work had increased the demands upon them, and teachers' feelings about their political situation were entwined with the experiences of classroom isolation and hard conditions of life without adequate incomes. Demoralization had slowly crept upon teachers to be borne in silence, its causes not fully recognized for some time.

One evening in mid-April (the 14th) two teacher volunteers, Kevin and Janine, unexpectedly visited my house, saying they wanted to discuss some of their feelings. The visit had been prompted by Janine, who said she was feeling especially low and wanted to talk about it. I felt this was something new, and I welcomed it for it gave me a chance to talk about my own feelings which had also become low. This meeting was the beginning of an effort on the part of teachers to clarify their situation together and do something about it.

Janine began the discussion by saying that she wished the campaign was still the way it had been during the first term. She said she felt excluded from the campaign now and that only a few 'selected' teachers (like Barry) were allowed to have any involvement in it. She said she had the feeling that important things were constantly going on which weren't told to the staff, at least to the bulk of the staff. Kevin, also present, said that he had once felt the same as Janine but now he'd accepted that the campaign was important, even if it wasn't being conducted in the way he wished. 'Everyone has a role to play. The campaign isn't the way I'd like it to be but it is still doing some good. People should accept it or leave.' Janine replied that she was seriously thinking of leaving. She argued that it wasn't just a question of individuals having to put up with certain aspects of the campaign that they didn't like, but a question of the whole meaning of the movement. I sympathized with Janine, saying that I'd come to feel similarly about the occupation: isolated and out of touch. All three of us agreed that the situation for most of the teachers had slipped, slowly and almost unnoticeably, during the second term. It was now rigid and burdensome when it once had been exciting and gratifying.

Soon afterwards, and the day before the national demonstration organized by the campaign office, Kevin decided to try to restimulate some of the debates and discussions which teachers had taken part in during the first term by typing up a list of questions and circulating them amongst the staff. The questions were all on the meaning of the struggle: 'What will happen if the school is reinstated? Is that an end in itself?' was one of them.

These questions not only stimulated the interest of many teachers; they appealed to a number of local residents as well – in particular, those who had been involved in the educational activities. The staff, joined by these residents, met later in the day and discussed them. It was immediately obvious that the feeling of demoralization was widespread. Some of the discussion was recorded in my notebooks and it is worth presenting here:

Paul G. (teacher): I'm only here to teach. Teaching is part of the campaign.

Mick (teacher and former resident): I feel left out! When I first came to the school it was like a big family here. Everybody talked about everything together. But it declined. Now I don't know anything, we don't know anything, and this is affecting us. Lots of us are becoming despondent.

Pat B. (helper): The pickets in the Parkstile building have the same feelings.

Paul G. (teacher): We should only teach – that's our job. I trust the way the campaign is being led. There is a division of labour here: they let me teach and I let them run the campaign.

Reza (teacher): I didn't come here just to teach. The question of education has only one meaning to me – political. We have been put on the defensive. We should become offensive. We could go on like this for years now and no bailiffs would be sent in because we are actually no threat, no challenge. I'm not here just to teach kids.

Mick (teacher): We're not told anything any more.

Margaret (helper and headmistress): Yes, this has happened. But it wasn't deliberate. We got really involved in running the school, it's so demanding. The people running the campaign really got involved in that. The communication got cut off but it got cut off unintentionally.

Henry M. (teacher): The national campaign is disconnected from teachers and parents. Parents should get into the classrooms again and the running of the school needs to be tied more to the campaign against cuts.

Pat B. (helper): We tried that but it didn't work.

Margaret (helper and headmistress): More information should be sent home to make parents more aware and interested in what's happening here.

Henry M. (teacher): Actual visits should be made to the homes.

Mick (teacher and former resident): Public meetings used to keep the community involved. These have dried up, they should be reinstated.

At this point one teacher came in with a copy of a leaflet about the march and rally to be held the next day – the nationwide demonstration against cuts which had been organized from the campaign office. The leaflet listed speakers to talk at the rally which was to be held outside the Parkstile building. All the names listed were Labour Party figures not directly involved in the occupation except for Phil Knibb and Collette D'Arcy. But Phil was now himself seen as a Labour Party figure and Collette had not been active in the running of the school at all. She was possibly better known citywide for her activities in the Young Socialists. No teacher or helper was on the list to speak. The staff became upset as a result:

Joey (teacher and local resident): We're being used! This is outrageous, I'll boycott the march!

Kevin (administrator): This campaign isn't about the school, it is about cuts in general.

Teacher (name missed): But 'Croxteth' is written in big letters on the top of the leaflet. The name of Croxteth is being used by other organizations!

The consensus reached was to approach Phil Knibb immediately and insist that a representative of the staff and of the helpers be put on the list of speakers. I was voted to represent the teachers and Margaret was voted to represent the helpers. Barry agreed to take the message to Phil Knibb that evening.

At this point the meeting was officially ended but Kevin invited all who wished to stay to participate in a further discussion. No one left. Again, the record of the discussion throws yet more light on the conflicts which had persisted under the surface between staff and the campaign leadership:

Pat B. (helper): You keep hearing that we're just hanging on until May because if Labour loses, it's all over. If Labour wins, it's on. What happens if Labour loses – are we going to just give it all up?

Margaret (helper and headmistress): Ultimately it is up to Keith Joseph, not the Labour Party, whether or not the school opens. People are kidding themselves.

Barry (teacher): If Labour doesn't win, we could make this a free school. That should be discussed.

Pat B. (helper): We should be discussing these things, but at Action Committee meetings only the chair makes the decisions, no one else.

Margaret (helper and headmistress): That's right, only the chair.

Pat B. (female helper): It's mostly women on the committee. They want to be led, they don't understand anything.

Margaret (helper and headmistress): That's true. They can not make decisions because they just don't understand the issues.

Teacher: We have got to push for more involvement.

Joey (teacher and local resident): We are being used by the Labour Party. This demonstration should be only for Croxteth, not all the other cuts and things.

Kathy (teacher): But this struggle is related to other cuts.

Joey (teacher and local resident): But those other cuts should be fought against away from this school, not by using the school. The Labour Party just wants to get votes by using this school. They're not the ones here fighting for it every day.

Paul G. (teacher): The Labour Party has a lot to do with the way England is these days [many nods of agreement].

Thomas (teacher): After the May elections this struggle shouldn't end. It should go on in new directions.

P.C: The possibility of it going in new directions certainly exists, but whether or not it will is another question. There would have to be a lot of pushing to make it do so, and that pushing would have to take place on the Action Committee.

Again these comments were recorded rapidly during the actual discussion and much has been left out. Although the comments are verbatim they are truncated; participants talked longer than the above passages suggest. But the issues of concern are clear: many teachers and some helpers were feeling 'left out' and isolated. The expression of these feelings tended to draw upon the community power theme, just as this theme had been heard so frequently during the first term. Community power was again put forward as an alternative to dependence on the Labour Party; the possibility of broadening the occupation into other issues in Croxteth was put forth.

However, something more than just a return to articulations of political views prevalent amongst the teachers was going on in these meetings as well. In assessing what had been most of value to teachers during the first term, and most missed during the second term, teachers and residents were becoming conscious of various investments they had in the campaign. Mick's term 'family', and his complaint of 'feeling left out', expressed feelings held at personal levels which were disassociated from the goals of the campaign. They were now being brought forward as legitimate concerns, explicit goals, which teachers like Mick now felt the campaign ought to have. The community power theme was again coming into open articulation, this time more closely tied to personal experiences.

Kevin Stannard was especially aware of this and tried to make it yet more explicit by continuing to write his question sheets and to call non-business meetings over the goals of the campaign and the feelings held by teachers. He was concerned to do something about the complaints of many female members of staff that they were isolated and had difficulty in speaking at meetings. His efforts were applauded by many members of staff but were found to be irritating by others.

On the 16th of April a procession of about 550 people marched from the Clubmore playing fields in Liverpool to the Parkstile building of Croxteth school. It was led by Tony Mulhearn, the president of the district Labour Party in Liverpool and a well-known supporter of Militant, and Phil Knibb. Many banners were carried, the T&G union banner, a banner of the Young Socialists and others, and the Labour Party and Militant newspapers were sold by hawkers to people watching. Very few residents of Croxteth other than the usual group who worked in the school were present in the march although the Young Socialists had reportedly distributed 7,000 leaflets to houses in the area.

The speeches for the most part called on those listening to vote Labour in the coming elections, and the closure of Croxteth Comprehensive was pointed to as an example of the policies of the national Conservative government. Collette D'Arcy gave a particularly effective speech along these lines, drawing much applause and a positive review in the *Daily Echo* of the following day. I gave a short speech on what was taking place inside the school buildings, stressing the importance of taking alterations in traditional educational practice as essential features of this campaign: 'Schools aren't always such nice places for our children; we've been trying to change some of that.' Margaret didn't speak, having received insufficient encouragement from the Action Committee.

The following Monday many teachers complained of the obvious party-political orientation of the rally, that it was primarily a Labour Party affair, not a rally for the school. This occurred at another of Kevin's organized discussions on political and personal aspects of the campaign. The combination of Kevin's efforts and the shock to teachers and many residents of the nature of the demonstration had reawakened discussion and debate in the school. These meetings continued for some time. The staff decided to start an internal newsletter to break down some of the communication barriers which had developed during the second term, and this newsletter came out continuously every two weeks for the rest of the school year. It often included humorous sections to take the mickey out of some of the helpers and staff and definitely served its intended function of drawing staff back together. The staff also decided to pressure the Action Committee (Phil Knibb, actually) to hold fortnightly meetings again so that communication about the campaign would be more widely distributed. The Action Committee agreed to this during the joint CCAC-staff meeting of the 19th of April, described below.

During the 19th April staff and Action Committee meeting, the first held in several months, several teachers complained to Phil about the nature of the demonstration. Once again the conflict between charismatic authority, the ideal of community power, and the strategy of affiliation with the Labour Party came up. Some portions of the meeting follow:

Kev: Can some representatives from the Labour Party come to talk to the teaching staff? We want to know what will happen if this school is reinstated – will the community retain any involvement? What will happen to the teachers? That sort of thing.

Phil K.: I doubt it, they are too busy with their campaign.

Barry: Some could come – those who aren't running.

Phil K.: They would represent the Labour Party. We can not make demands to the Labour Party.

Jackie: The district Labour Party ought to be in communication with the school.

Barry: Someone must come.

(A vote was taken in favour of requesting a representative to come.)

Reza: That demonstration was a Labour Party demonstration.

Harry (AC member): We accept help from whoever will offer it.

Phil K.: It was the Merseyside Trade Union-Community Liaison Committee who organized that demonstration.

Reza: We weren't even invited – the teachers, the helpers, even the Action Committee!

Phil K.: I represent the Action Committee on the Merseyside Trade Union-Community Liaison Committee.

Kev: The Action Committee wasn't involved in any of it.

Phil K.: I know what the Committee thinks.

This brief revival of vocal opposition by teachers to the campaign policies of the Action Committee didn't constitute as much of a genuine challenge to the Action Committee as it had during the first term. By this time it was obvious that the campaign absolutely depended on the victory of the local Labour Party in the May elections. Efforts to get the community further involved in the school through circulars put out in the second term had failed, and a real alternative didn't seem to exist. The staff complaints had more to do with their own experiences in the school and with doubts about the school's future. The new discussions did, however, lighten the mood on the staff a good deal. Although Yola had already left by this time and Janine left shortly after the demonstration, those who remained began to feel less isolated and more involved in discussions about the campaign. The discussions themselves were more structured than those of the autumn had been through the efforts of Kevin, and more of the tacit issues involved began to be articulated than before. The internal newsletter kept staff informed of developments in the campaign as well as in the school.

The new discussion sessions began to include educational as well as political issues: streaming, methods of discipline, remedial extractions, and so on were repeatedly discussed, with the teachers favouring policy of more progressive than traditional form. With the increased stability of the school, and the months of teaching experience in it, teachers felt less constrained than they had during the first term and openly regretted their inability to implement more progressive educational methods, such as mixed ability teaching, now that the basic organization of the school had been set.

The 5th May elections were a success for Labour, the party winning an overall majority on Liverpool city council. The Action Committee held a celebration in one of the local pubs. Two eyewitnesses reported that at other celebrations in the city during election night deputy leader Derek Hatton and leader John Hamilton independently stood up, at two different celebrations, and announced that the first thing they would do in office would be to reinstate Croxteth Comprehensive. The next day John Hamilton gave an interview on television in which he was asked about the policies the new Liverpool government intended to implement, and the first thing he commented on was education: 'We are going to staff schools by curriculum, not by pupil numbers,' he declared, providing an immediate indication and justification of the party's policy towards Croxteth. Members of the Action Committee most intimately involved in the campaigning claimed in interview that the success of the Labour Party undoubtedly owed much to the inclusion of Croxteth in their campaign pledges, and several prominent members of the party agreed in interviews that taking on Croxteth definitely helped their campaign a great deal.

The victory was announced in a special assembly in the school the next morning, an assembly which was filmed for nationwide television, making Croxteth a symbol of the local Labour Party victory. As usual, I stood in front of the assembled ranks of pupils, teachers, helpers, and CCAC members to deliver a talk, but this time faced several television cameras as well. My first sentence had more meaning to me than my audience realized:

Politics and education are necessarily, inextricably, linked.

9
Community education and the Croxteth occupation

This concluding chapter completes the story of the battle for Croxteth Comprehensive and reconsiders several theoretical questions raised in Chapter 1. The theoretical analysis is sandwiched between narratives which finish the history of the campaign and give the reader a brief description of what Croxteth Comprehensive is like today.

AFTER THE VICTORY

Reinstating Croxteth Comprehensive as a state-funded school proved not to be as straightforward as many of the activists had anticipated. The Labour Party could not immediately declare that a new state school existed in Croxteth. It could have pushed a council resolution to this effect through, but realized that Sir Keith Joseph would simply block such a proposal, just as he had done one and a half years before. It was expected that Keith Joseph would allow a new school to be opened in Croxteth only as part of an overall reorganization plan affecting the entire city. But a citywide plan would take time to refine and vote into policy. It was thought, in fact, that the reorganization should go into effect in the autumn of 1984 rather than the autumn of 1983, leaving a year of uncertainty for Croxteth Comprehensive.

The only immediate changes which the victory of the Liverpool Labour Party brought to Croxteth were the return of free school meals and the employment of caretakers for both the Parkstile and Stonebridge buildings. Repairs in the buildings and maintenance of the grounds were also begun by paid city staff; one could hear lawn mowers and the hammers of window repair work only a few days after the election. Also, importantly, the rate bills were written off by the new government.

Phil and George Knibb, sometimes accompanied by Jackie Crowley (the administrator) and sometimes by myself, met frequently with the Labour Party's chairman of education Dominic Brady and the director of education Kenneth Antcliffe to try to find a way to finance the school for the upcoming year. Different possibilities were considered with care, much research going into the legal and financial implications of each one. The goal was to fund Croxteth Comprehensive as much as possible with local government resources, but to do it in a way which precluded the rights of the Department of Education and Science to intervene. For a time it appeared that the school could be funded as a 'public facility', but research soon revealed problems with this approach. Eventually it was agreed that Croxteth Comprehensive could get state support in 1983–84 only by declaring itself an independent school, which would allow it 50 per cent government funding. The remaining 50 per cent would have to be raised by the Action Committee.

While discussions with Dominic Brady and Kenneth Antcliffe proceeded, most members of the teaching staff grew concerned about their personal futures with the school and about the nature of the new Croxteth Comprehensive which would soon emerge. They now had absolutely no power over either area. I acted as the teacher representative at a number of meetings between Phil Knibb, Jackie Crowley, and government officials in town. Both Phil and Dominic Brady expressed the desire to aid volunteers in the school in some way, but Phil made it clear that only those volunteers who were 'appropriately qualified' would get jobs in the school for the 1983–84 school year. I was invited to collect the résumés of those who wished to teach. Kenneth Antcliffe agreed to help those unqualified get into teacher training courses if they wished.

Of course, the insistence on qualifications was really a way of screening out volunteers who hadn't proven themselves able to handle Croxteth pupils in the judgment of the Action Committee leadership. The governors of an independent school are legally free to hire anyone they like as teachers, qualifications or no qualifications. There were many volunteer teachers the Action Committee did not want to come back. Phil Knibb expressed his gratitude for the work the volunteers had done during the year of occupation but explained to me his worries about the quality of education they had been providing. In his judgment, pupils in Croxteth would need more experienced and competent teachers in the future. Phil addressed several staff meetings to prepare volunteers for possible disappointments when hiring decisions would be made: 'Some of you will have to become disassociated with the school,' he said. Meanwhile, George Knibb began observing classrooms to help the Action Committee decide whom they wished to retain. His main criterion for judging the competence of teachers was the state of discipline they maintained in the classroom.

Phil was also determined to have as many helpers hired for the school's ancillary staff as possible. But the helpers, like the teachers, were basically powerless in the matter, and they too began to voice worries in informal conversations. The great majority of the activists wished to retain some kind of involvement in the new independent school.

COMMUNITY SCHOOLING AND CROXTETH: AN ANALYSIS

The nature of the new school was also in doubt. Campaign speeches of the Labour Party and reports and articles in the media frequently referred to the occupied school buildings in Croxteth as a 'community school', a 'school taken over by its community', and to the campaign as a fight 'of the community' against the government. As the Labour Party in Liverpool formulated its citywide educational reorganization programme, moreover, it based its policy on the concept of 'community comprehensives', closing down 26 secondary schools in Liverpool officially and opening 17 new 'community comprehensives' in the buildings of some of them, the Croxteth and Ellergreen buildings included. In media and campaign reports after the May elections, it was not uncommon to hear Croxteth mentioned as 'a community school already' or as 'a community school in the real sense'.

At a meeting with the staff during mid-May Phil Knibb explained his determination to make Croxteth Comprehensive a 'community school':

> When we got started we just wanted our school back. Now we want a community comprehensive. What we've tried to achieve, we've achieved. Now the priority is to plan what we want to have in the school, to carry out the ideals we've struggled for.

Yet it was by no means clear what Phil or the Labour Party meant by 'community comprehensive'. Phil was now a highly respected member of the Labour Party's Education Group which was planning the citywide reorganization programme. One thing the term certainly referred to was the ideal of ensuring a school for all areas of the city, making the distribution of schools geographically even. An indication of the extent to which Phil had become identified with the goals of the local Labour Party was a comment he made just after the one quoted above. In response to a question Phil said he wouldn't support re-establishing a school in Croxteth if that meant that another nearby community would lose theirs. Thus Phil was presenting arguments from a citywide perspective, 180 degrees from the horizontally competitive arguments used during the first phase of the campaign. From Phil Knibb's perspective, phase three of the battle for Croxteth Comprehensive had shifted its basic goals and rationale from an effort to win back a single school to an identification with local Labour Party policies supporting community education throughout Liverpool.

However, 'community school' implies more than an even distribution of educational resources. It implies community involvement and decision-making rights, and, in some interpretations of the term, profound alterations in traditional curricular and pedagogic practice (Chapter 1). I have shown that the issue of community involvement was continuously in dispute during the campaign and occupation, and this dispute continued into the summer term. To what extent was Croxteth a community school, and in what sense? What policies could make it more of a community school? These were some of the questions debated in the staff meetings of the third term, at the same time that the Labour Party Education Group, with Phil Knibb and George Knibb actively contributing, considered the future of the Croxteth school and the policy for all schools in Liverpool.

The situation of the school by the third term can be summarized as follows:

1. The occupied school had reproduced traditional forms of schooling in a number of ways described in Chapters 4 to 8. Four points will summarize the traditional aspects of education in the occupied school which had developed very quickly during the first term and had remained largely unchanged for the rest of the year:

   a) the implementation of a traditional curriculum for most pupils;

   b) the division of pupils into classes based primarily on ability;

   c) the creation of authority relations which, although uniquely involving two forms of adult–youth relationships, reproduced traditional school authority;

   d) the failure to involve other adults from the estate, despite the participation of approximately 30 adults in the school during the year.

2. However, the daily presence in the school of over 30 adults from Croxteth led to some unintended consequences which deviated from traditional schooling, especially traditional schooling in Croxteth Comprehensive. Four general areas of such innovations can be listed. The first two were discussed in previous chapters and the last two will be elaborated below:

   a) The dual system of authority in the school had led to very warm relationships between some of the teachers, adults, and pupils. School authority was still imposed as a principle upon pupils, but it was done in a way which opened new spaces for social relationships with pupils to develop. Some of the teachers established very close relationships with pupils at the expense of a certain amount of control, but control was maintained through regular interventions by local adults (Chapter 6).

b) Many of the local adults were becoming interested in school knowledge themselves and learned alongside the pupils. Moreover, a number of residents were actually teaching pupils and using a successful pedagogy organic to the culture of Croxteth (Chapter 8). These local activists were successful partially because they were perceived by pupils as being on 'their side', as being 'not-teachers' (Chapter 6), and partially because of their familiarity with the adult–youth relations of the local culture.

c) Almost all of the Croxteth adults who worked regularly in the school had begun to develop critical awareness of traditional schooling practices by the third term (see below).

d) Most of the local activists had a much greater political awareness by the third term than they had had before their involvement in the campaign, and their perception of the schooling process itself was beginning to become framed within a new political orientation (see below).

In the rest of this section I shall look at changes in political and educational outlooks experienced by the local activists as a result of the campaign. I will then consider the significance of such changes in light of community education theory (Chapter 1). This will involve a discussion of the relationship of schooling to broadly drawn social relations of inequality and the extent to which community involvement can and cannot alter it.

Attitudes towards education in the third term

After the election victory, when the end of the occupation was clearly in sight and the reabsorption of the school into the hands of the Local Education Authority was imminent, helpers and Action Committee members began to express a changed perspective on schooling:

> When I first came in, I just was interested in a school, and being involved during those 12 months, that's when I started to (pause), I mean, you were trying to decide if you should have exams, you should have that many O levels, CSEs. And the kids would turn around and say, 'Well, why?' And I started to think about it, you know, and then I said to myself, 'Well, why!?' You know, they're leaving school, the kids with O levels, A levels and what have you, and they're still on the dole.
>
> (Margaret Gaskell)

In the passage above, Margaret is questioning the primary purpose of education which she and most volunteers in the school, both teachers and residents, had assumed at the beginning: employability. Margaret had observed both the small number of pupils who had been able to take the examinations in Croxteth and the effects which an emphasis on examination syllabuses had had on those who had not been able to. Unemployment rates for the 16 to 19 age group in Croxteth, the reader will recall, had been estimated at 90 per cent (see Chapter 2). Yet in Croxteth examinations had been made a priority and limited educational resources were deployed to their end, creating a number of 'sink' classes. For many activists, critical awareness of schooling began with the observation of the plight of the non-examination groups during the first term.

Ann Pines, for example, became closely associated with the 4Bs during the school year and was well aware that they were getting less teacher time, fewer resources, and less relevant education until the special projects were tried out with them. She began to feel bitter about it, expressing her thoughts on the matter at several staff meetings and personally to several teachers. Phil Knibb joined her in this, as did George Knibb and Pat Brennen. Margaret saw it as a general problem, existing not only in Croxteth but in all schools: 'That's very unfair! And I found out it wasn't just going on in this school, it is happening in other schools!'

When enough time and stability had been achieved in the second term to try out more appropriate educational activities with the non-examination groups, the non-examination pupils still felt themselves in a second-class position and greatly resented it. The value of the special projects tried out with the 4Bs, for example, was subjectively diminished through the fact that it wasn't leading towards examinations, and the 4Bs continued to be disruptive and to express resentment towards the preferred treatment of the 4As.

By the middle of the third term, activists like Margaret had come to think that a form of schooling ought to exist which wasn't linked so tightly to examinations and jobs, and which had relevance to the social situation of pupils:

> I think we should be offering something. Maybe there are no jobs, but there must be something else they could be doing worthwhile, that'd make them feel as though they're not a burden on society, which is what a lot of the kids feel they are. *What* I don't know. I know there should be something.

Thus critical awareness was growing with respect to the purposes of education. Margaret Gaskell was one of the most articulate activists with respect to this, but she was joined by a number of others as well. As shown below, during the third term a discourse of criticism was just beginning amongst the local activists demonstrating growing discontent with traditional schooling and an interest in exploring alternatives.

As well as a growing critical awareness of what is taught to whom in schools, most local activists in the occupied school had altered their views on discipline by the third term as well. Almost all of these activists had appreciated the warmth of most teacher–pupil relations in the school, and by the third term few still believed that the cane ought to be used. The belief that a fundamental purpose of schooling is to discipline and control pupils had not been dropped because, as argued in Chapter 5, there are reasons for this view rooted in conditions of life on the Croxteth estate. But helpers and Action Committee members came to believe equally that warm and informal relationships between teachers and pupils were good and thus questioned the *form* in which discipline ought to be imposed. Marty McArdle explained his view of this:

> I think the teachers are great, like. I've never had teachers like these. You know if I was at school and I'd had teachers like these I'd never have been in trouble. Because they seem to fit in with you. You know you get some of these teachers 'cause they got a bit of knous [i.e., knowledge] at the top here. They think, they tell you where to go, push you about, you know you're dirt to them. That's what I looked at in school. You know [they think that] all you've got to have is discipline in school. You have discipline. You have discipline and discipline. You know, like they're pushing you about left, right, and centre. That's the thing that's wrong....

> But being honest, if we'd had these teachers what we have today I'd been a lot happier. They seem to have more understanding. They seem to, like, understand more and there was, like, some lads down there and some of the lasses, they are slow, some of these right. And, like, Tony and Barry and yourself, you spend time with them, talking to them, don't you? Know what I mean? Where in another school you wouldn't. They'd say, 'Back to your lesson and listen, sit up and listen,' like.

Growing political awareness and involvement

The local activists were questioning their original, taken-for-granted assumptions about the purposes of schooling: employability and discipline. They were also, as a result of their involvement, perceiving linkages between schooling and political activity. They were more aware of political issues on their estate and nationally as well. While very few of the community activists had taken part in political activities or belonged to political organizations before the campaign to save Croxteth Comprehensive, most had become involved in some form of political or community activity, outside of the occupation, by the third term.

I've already noted the involvement of Phil Knibb in the local Labour Party and the efforts of the MTUCLC to establish official channels between community movements and the labour movement. These activities were new for Phil. Similarly, George Knibb, Margaret Gaskell, and Jackie Crowley all became supporters of the reforming factions of the local Liverpool Labour Party. Collette D'Arcy, having had no previous political interest or involvement at all, became a very prominent and publicly visible member of the Young Socialists. These people were all either part of the leadership of the Action Committee or socially close to it. The experience of the campaign started them thinking in politically new ways and recruitment into the Labour Party seemed the best way to make sense of their campaign within a broader political ideology.

For many of the rest of the Croxteth activists an increase in political interest and awareness took place but didn't lead to affiliation with any political organizations. The need to justify illegal action, to answer the questions of their neighbours and family members as to why they were involved, forced these volunteers to construct a rational account of their activities which necessarily meant thinking about politics:

P.C.: Had you been involved in any struggles before, or any political organizations?

Jackie Madden: No [laughs], I actually, uhh, I thought politics was really really boring like, didn't want no part of it. And then when we took over the school, well no, it was before when we first started fighting for the school, we'd go down when there was a council meeting or something, you know, someone would be going past and they'd say, 'What's going on?' And you'd say, 'I don't know, they're voting on something to do with Crocky School, I haven't got a clue really, I'm just standing here demonstrating.' And like, you know, you sounded stupid. The people didn't know what we were talking about so you had to know what you were going down there for and you had to know the ins and outs of it.

Most of the activists also stated that they had become more aware of political issues as a result of their experiences in the campaign. A large number of them joined the Croxteth Tenants' Association and began attending other community meetings. The occupation had given them more confidence in their ability to do something about the conditions in which they live. As Kathy Donovan expressed it:

You know, normally when you pick up a paper and read out, 'so many jobs going here', you think like, 'Oh my God, it would have to be on Merseyside as well.' But then that's it, you just put it down. But then being here I've learnt, umm, just how important it is, just everyday things that you've always read about but never sort of cared about and never cared to do anything about it. And then being and fighting for the school and we've won it now for 12 months, hopefully for ever. It makes you want to go on, not just let things drop here, carry on in life. You know things in life, you've got to fight for them.

And Mary Kane:

I got involved in a lot of things, through this school, that I'd never even talked about before.... Now I can talk to these people about different things. If I hadn't joined this committee I [garbled] not knowing what was going on, not being involved. But now I seem to get involved in things because I get involved in committees I don't know anything about, till I go to the meetings.

With the large number of women volunteering in the school, the experience of participation also put traditional gender roles more into question. In the summer of 1984, a year after the end of the occupation, Henry Stewart and I interviewed a number of the former activists in the occupation and found most of them involved in a large number of community activities:

Pat Brennen: The thing is, I don't think you could ever go back to being an ordinary housewife again. I mean, when you're stuck at home there are all these jobs and you get them all done, and there's nothing to do then. Now you go home and you try to get bits done, you know, every bit of the time, because we've got meetings nearly every night now as well. The tenants' group, the women's health group and all that.

Henry Stewart: You know, the women's health group, would you have gotten involved in something like that before?

Margaret Gaskell: I don't think I would have. I was never involved in many things before, but this [pause], this sort of trained me. Just going back to being a housewife when you know you are capable of doing more. It makes you want to use what you're capable of.

Thus in many ways the campaign for Croxteth Comprehensive led to increased social awareness and activity on the part of those who were involved in it. For some this included a break with the social-wage orientation, which placed the internal features of education and other social services unquestioningly into the hands of experts and professionals. Cyril D'Arcy commented three years after the campaign on some of the long-term effects which this alteration produced in Croxteth residents elected to the school's board of governors:

Without going at length, I see the tremendous spin-off that the campaign was responsible for. People became more educationally aware, socially and politically as well. The strength of character that people acquired was enormous, being able and willing to fight and speak up for themselves and others.... They [resident governors of the new school] understand education and its jargon. Making decisions that they think and agree are best for pupils, staff, and the school in general. They are not easily persuaded by educationalists to do what is 'best' for them and the system. The governors have the confidence and respect of most of the staff and parents for what they know, through experience and through what they are prepared to do.

There was a rise in the confidence of the participants in the campaign for Croxteth Comprehensive, the feeling that by being involved they could do something about the circumstances of their lives. This translated into a trust of their own perceptions of educational processes so that some could challenge the experts. This growth in the desire for political and community activity alongside the growth in a critical awareness of schooling is precisely what advocates of community schooling have called for but have found so difficult to create through the policies of education authorities and educationalists.

Community education, power, and the Croxteth occupation

In Chapter 1, I reviewed the literature on community schools and noted that the so-called 'radical' version of the concept calls for an alteration of the curriculum to make it more community-based and socially empowering, an alteration of pedagogy along progressivist lines, and the involvement of local adults so that schooling and community action may be integrated. Actual community schools, however, have usually attempted to implement changes in pedagogy and curriculum without the support of local residents. Local residents have consistently been found to have little desire to become involved in schooling or have become involved through insisting on traditional forms of education and thus by hindering the objectives of the teaching staff. A radical community school calls for the devolution of decision-making power to the community but this has either not been possible to carry out in practice or has resulted in the mere reproduction of traditional educational forms.

The story of Croxteth Comprehensive differs from attempts to create community schools through government policy because the activists from Croxteth took possession of their school and thus put themselves in formal control of its internal policies and practices. Not only did they have formal control of their school, but their organization, the Croxteth Community Action Committee, had by the third term gained a good deal of influence over both political and economic resources, the first through friendships with local government Labour leaders and the second through connections with the trade union movement.

However, at the start of the 1982–83 school year, as previous chapters document, it became clear in Croxteth that educational power resides in deeper realms than that of formal decision-making rights. Schools are involved in power relations which extend beyond their boundaries. These relations of power are mediated in different ways, through sets of constraints and through interpretative schemes embedded in culture. Initially, the interpretative schemes of the local activists ruled out any educational innovations from their side. Schooling was perceived to be mainly about jobs and discipline. Jobs meant examinations. Discipline was to be imposed as deference to the symbolic authority of the school which only certified individuals in possession of school knowledge could represent. I have argued at length that these components of the interpretative frameworks of the local activists were tightly related to systems of social practice existing between home, school, and work and that they featured in the intersubjective supports of class reproduction. Formal control of school buildings therefore did not amount to genuine power over education.

Setting constraints aside for the moment, let us further consider what happened to the power relations transmitted through cultural interpretative schemes by term three. As argued in the section above, formerly tacit interpretations of schooling had come under the critical gaze of the local activists, particularly of those activists whose daily work in the school had involved them in educational activity. In late May efforts were made by some of the teacher volunteers to begin dialogues with local activists on the form of education which would be best for pupils in the new independent school about to be created.

At the suggestion of Henry Miller, a lecturer at Aston University who volunteered to teach history regularly in Croxteth during the occupation, two meetings were held for staff and local activists at which the theory of community education and some examples of contemporary community schools were presented for discussion. The second of these produced the most discussion as it was held as an informal affair during a lunch break at the school and not during a formal Action Committee meeting. At this meeting Henry Miller gave a brief history of community education in Britain and described a few contemporary community schools such as the Sutton Centre. Henry then indicated some of the unique features of the Croxteth school which gave it an advantage over other efforts to create community schools. Instead of having a school run by educationalists who try to get the community to accept their ideas and become involved, community activists were presently in possession of some power over their school and were in a position to negotiate for what they wanted. It would be important to take advantage of this situation now, he said, before the opportunity is lost, by becoming clear about what the helpers and Action Committee wanted and putting it forth to the Education Group. Comments by helpers present at this meeting included the following:

Margaret: I know what I want but I don't know how to put it into words. Schools are frightening. They are academic and some kids aren't academic, are they?

Mary Kane: In the system as it is now, kids who aren't academic feel like failures. That's wrong.

Charlie Irving: Some kids aren't good at academics but they're good with their hands. We should bring them around to another system so that they aren't left to feel inferior, and when they leave they have a qualification [nods of agreement].

Pat Brennen: I think they should continue with the O level qualifications.

Mary Kane: But I don't want this school going back to reading, writing, and arithmetic!

These remarks were just beginnings, yet they were significant. They were expressions of discontent with traditional schooling – some of the first made publicly by Croxteth residents, in dialogue with other residents and teachers. The difficulties of coming up with alternative ideas were obvious, but that would be expected in a community school. New ideas could be tried out, discussed, and altered over time. What was beginning in Croxteth, and it took eight months of intensive involvement in the school for it to begin, was the growth of critical awareness or, in Boyd's terms, 'conscious dissatisfaction', in the school (Boyd 1977: 21). Boyd points out, no doubt correctly, that this necessary ingredient for 'community education' to really be community education is hard to come by. It cannot be imposed from above, and the unique and delicate feature of the Croxteth occupation by the third term was precisely that this dissatisfaction and desire for involvement had arisen from below.

Moreover, conscious dissatisfaction, or critical awareness, was manifested in a dialogue between residents and teachers. The innovations which had occurred in the school consisted in part of mutual learning processes taking place between local activists and teachers. Many of the former had developed educational activities with pupils which were successful in winning student enthusiasm because of their close relation to local culture. This familiarity was naturally lacking on the side of the teachers. Community activists had much to teach the teachers in this way. The teachers for their part were familiar with aspects of school knowledge which many local activists now wished to learn too. If these two groups had been able to continue to work together, new ideas and practices would undoubtedly have evolved over time.

Croxteth Comprehensive thus had several of the ingredients prescribed in the literature for the radical version of the community school. It had involvement, a degree of community power, political awareness, and the beginnings of a dialogue in which teachers and local residents were together starting to discuss alternative educational practice. A number of the reproductive features of the occupation in which systematic linkages between features of local culture and traditional schooling practice became reconstituted during the first term were now coming into critical discursive awareness: school authority, schooling purposes, and the traditional curriculum were all just beginning to come into question.

Moreover, the local residents who had been involved in the occupation did not wish to leave it when their most overt objective, winning back a state-funded school, had been achieved. All those interviewed (17) on this matter expressed a strong desire to stay. Three representative comments follow:

P.C.: Think you'd like to continue as a teacher?

Kathy Donovan: Well, I was really considering it in cookery or art. But anything like this, I think it's really great. Even all the kids today have long faces and they say, 'We won't be seeing you any more, will we?' And I say, 'You know, you should be made up with winning the school and all.' And they say, 'Well, you know, we are made up, we just thought we might be in with the people who have won it for us.' A lot of kids have said this.

P.C.: Would you like to still be involved in the school if you could be, you know, in the autumn?

Kathy: Oh yeah! Definitely!

P.C.: Do you think you will be?

Kathy: Well, I don't know. A few weeks ago somebody said to me, 'Well, would you stay in the school, would you work here for pay, in the kitchen or whatever?' And I said, 'Well, I've done it for 12 months for no pay, I'd still do it voluntary, just to be here, just to be part of it.' We tell the kids we'll be here for the first day at least.

P.C.: What will you do if the school closes? [interviewed before the election victory]

Keith Leatherbarrow: For 80 per cent of us working here, it would be like having most of your teeth removed – a big gap in your life. Most of the helpers would probably go back to being like sheep around here: sleeping until 12:00 and then moping around looking for something to do.

P.C.: What do you think you'll be doing after this term? Would you like to still be involved in the school?

Marty McArdle: Like what school has helpers? When this goes I know I'm going to go with it. I'm really going to miss it. But like people've said, it's going to be a community school, you can come in and see them. But you're going to put them off [the new staff]. And getting up every morning and coming into the school, that's going to be done [finished].

Other forms of power: constraints

The reader will soon find that none of the local activists were able to retain the same level and type of involvement they had had in Croxteth Comprehensive during 1982–83, and will learn why. But here I should state that even if this involvement had been retained, fundamental constraints still prevailed which would have limited innovations in the school. Local activists had come to question the curricular, organizational, and pedagogic practices which had existed in the school before the occupation. Yet all three of these practices were related to examinations. The case of Croxteth Comprehensive demonstrates the power of standard national examinations on internal school arrangements, which compel teachers and pupils to structure pedagogic and curricular features of schooling around the standard syllabuses. Unless the organization of knowledge in a school is changed the experience of the pupils will not be fundamentally altered, and other innovations will be limited in both form and effect (see also Keddie 1971a; Salter and Tapper 1981: 71). In Croxteth it was clear that school knowledge was organized in a way which ensured an experience of failure for the majority of pupils in the school and the organization of knowledge was controlled from far outside the school –2doors of Croxteth Comprehensive – primarily through the examination system.

Hence the location of the school in society is not one in which the mere transfer of formal power over one school to parents and other community members will result in an educational practice more suited to the needs of the community, even if neighbourhood adults manage to develop critical awareness of their common-sense perceptions of education. At the time of the occupation, all schooling in Britain was tightly bound to the job market through the national examination boards. The link between schooling and jobs is necessary in one form or another, but the subsumption of all possible educational goals to this single one has adverse effects in a working-class community like Croxteth. Moreover, the connection could be made in a number of different ways; it needn't depend on national examinations. There are many sociological studies that document the spurious connection between the skills learned in schools for passing examinations and the skills actually required by many jobs which require qualifications (Collins 1979). The terms which pupils must meet to become eligible for types of jobs are not beyond alteration, and the terms set by the O level examinations acted as mechanisms which selected some cultural groups over others. The connection between schooling and jobs could be made much looser with the substitution of alternative forms of assessment, flexible to local conditions and more in line with actual job requirements. Let me note once again that the new British GCSE examinations, which have replaced O levels and CSEs, have not yet been implemented long enough for us to be certain of their effects.

This study indicated another area of constraint on educational innovation: the lack of precedents for alternatives in the labour movement, and the lack of interest on the part of the labour movement in forms of educational experience as opposed to educational provision. It was the labour movement which supported the campaign for Croxteth Comprehensive and enabled it to succeed. The local activists of Croxteth looked towards the labour movement for support in its struggle and eventually for the struggle's very rationale. The Liverpool Labour Party was thus in a position to encourage at least some *explorations* of how such involvement could be utilized for the benefit of Croxteth pupils. But such encouragement was not forthcoming, no doubt because alterations in educational practice are not clear parts of Labour Party educational policy. Hence teachers and parents were constrained from the beginning of the occupation to the end through the lack of clearly formulated alternatives to traditional forms of schooling.

Thus the campaign for Croxteth Comprehensive was both a great achievement, attained only through labour movement support, and a lesson for educational policy-makers. I believe its lessons should be noted and absorbed. Community involvement in the schools of our working-class communities is rare and should be treated gently and supportively when it does occur. Educationalists concerned with the low achievement rates of our urban schools should welcome such involvement and investigate it whenever it is found. By the third term of the occupation of Croxteth Comprehensive, the presence of local residents in the school and their developing relationship with the teaching staff was a delicate situation which would have required nurturing and support for its potential to grow. But educational experience, issues of assessment, curriculum, and pedagogy, have not been prominent features of the labour movement's educational agenda. The story of Croxteth Comprehensive suggests that they ought to become so.

To summarize, the battle for Croxteth Comprehensive demonstrated the ways in which broadly drawn power relations characterizing society as a whole take certain expressions within the intersubjective frameworks through which working-class parents view the schooling process. These frameworks are related to systems of practice, which have developed and been maintained over many decades, between the working-class home, school, and work site. The occupation of a secondary school by residents of Croxteth for an entire school year eventually led to important alterations in these interpretative schemes, but the positive innovations which may have developed in consequence were limited by fundamental constraints which only national policies could alter. These constraints included the national system of examinations and the lack of clearly formulated policies on alternative educational practice. The organizations most capable of encouraging such alterations in the case of Croxteth failed to note their need.

THE LAST HALF-TERM

Sunshine

To return to the chronology, Croxteth Comprehensive was being run during the final term with a light and almost joyous atmosphere. The weather was brilliant, day after day of sunshine and warmth. Classes were often held outdoors and many trips were arranged for the pupils. Pat Kellet took the first and second years on several field trips. Margaret Gaskell, Pat Brennen, Tony Gannon, Barry Kushner, Keith Leatherbarrow, and others took a group of pupils on a trip to the Isle of Man in June. The Liverpool Graphical Society and the Open Eye Gallery both provided donations for the trip. Another group of pupils were taken caving with Barry and Tony. Henry Miller took his 4A2 history pupils to the Maritime Museum on the Mersey River and to visit Janine's art gallery in town, and a group of teachers and pupils spent a couple of days on the beaches of Freshfields and the swimming baths of New Brighton. On the 7th of July, all pupils, staff, and local volunteers went to Alton Towers for the day.

The atmosphere was generally light and informal. Pupils seemed to share the sense of having won a long battle and relations between teachers, parents, and pupils had never been better in the school. A record from my diary describes scenes from a not uncommon day in late June:

29th June: I walked around the school grounds at lunch-time. A beautiful, sunny day. Many of the staff were playing rounders with pupils on the front lawn. Laughter and cries of excitement. Margaret was sitting on the front steps reading a book of Trakl's poetry, several pupils sitting next to her.

Later in the day I noticed a number of infants and babies in the school as usual. Margaret was holding one while she directed pupils moving for class changes through the corridors. Others were near their parents or friends of their parents by the front door, people talking and drinking tea as they kept an eye on the kids.

I saw Mick [Checkland] playfully enacting a street fight with two pupils in the corridor. Mock kicks and karate chops, jabs to the stomach followed by smiles and laughter.

The change in the status of the school from an illegally occupied one to a legally recognized one resulted in new interest from outsiders. Many pupils who had left the school for Ellergreen during or just after the first term began requesting admittance to the school for the last term. Most of these were initially accepted, but as the requests continued pupils and parents were told to wait until the autumn. Representatives from the Liverpool Education Authority occasionally visited the school to examine the buildings. The kitchen was inspected and all kitchen staff required to wear uniforms according to government regulation. Former teachers at Croxteth before the closure returned to explore possibilities for a job in the autumn. Many community groups and service organizations also asked for interviews with the Action Committee. They were met at the school by Phil Knibb or George Knibb and the latter began to request the helpers and staff to stop drinking tea in the corridors during school hours so that the school would look more official and presentable. This was an early sign of the effect which official status would ultimately have: Croxteth Comprehensive was becoming less and less a community school and more an institution of the state.

Closing rituals

As the last week of term approached most teachers gave final examinations to their non-fifth-year pupils. Year reports with many comments from each teacher were written out to be delivered to the homes. At several staff meetings the last day was planned. It was decided initially to have an awards ceremony in which certain pupils would be given certificates of honour for outstanding contributions to the campaign. Staff members decided that very broad criteria would be used to determine which pupils were worthy of awards – effort as well as achievement in school work, helpful behaviour in classrooms, original contributions made by some pupils to the campaign through writing songs or making posters and badges, were all to be included. A certificate was actually ordered, paid for, and collected from the printers which had a large area left free for personalized comments. But at a staff meeting only days away from the final day of school, teachers changed their minds. Largely through arguments made by Barry and Tony it was decided that certificates of merit, no matter how broad and non-traditional the criteria of selection used, would leave many pupils out. The criteria were bound to be both somewhat arbitrary and expressive of certain values of which the staff members weren't perhaps fully aware. As Tony put it, 'I wouldn't want to be responsible for the damage done to the pupils left out.' The idea was dropped, though it was agreed to give a trophy to the fifth-year pupils David Edwards and Jimmy Kane for the very hard work both had put in on their examinations.

On the last day of school an assembly was held at which David and Jimmy were given their awards and a final commendation was expressed for all pupils, staff, and helpers for the year of hard work which had led to a victory for Croxteth.

This campaign and your parts in it are part of history now. Many eyes from all over England and eyes from areas of Europe have been on you throughout this year. Some hoped we would fail, others were very anxious that we succeed. We have won this struggle, and we've won it together. We've proved something that will not be forgotten in this community or in this country. We've done something together which all of you should always remember with pride.

After the assembly pupils, helpers, and staff gathered together outside the school for a photograph: Croxteth Comprehensive, year of 1983 (see frontispiece). Both the arrangements made to produce the photo and the visual result itself well symbolized what had taken place in Croxteth Comprehensive during 1982 and 1983. Pupils scrambled and struggled with each other for places most visibly in view of the camera. The photographers, volunteers from Liverpool's Open Eye Gallery, made several suggestions in vain as to how pupils could align themselves orderly for an effective shot. Different groups moved about as various individuals shouted out new suggestions. The helpful comments of a few teachers fell on deaf ears. It was chaotic and noisy. Finally George Knibb, the school authoritarian, had all pupils line up by year groups just as in traditional school photographs: the first years at the bottom sitting down, the second years behind, and so on up to the fourth and fifth years at the back. Teachers stood to the side and behind. Then George took his place in the middle next to one of the school's most disruptive 3B pupils.

Three members of the kitchen staff, one with her baby in arms, took a position to the right and back, and a couple of the younger helpers got on top of a ledge of the building. A banner hung from this ledge prepared for the school by the Cockpit Theatre Group:

CROXTETH COMMUNITY SCHOOL
GIS' OUR SCHOOL!

The photographers took their shots and a week later there appeared, in frozen form, a representation of the year for all pupils and activists. Like the school itself had been, the picture is organized in very traditional form; the class of 1983 lined up by age groups at the front of their school building. And yet there is George Knibb sitting with the third year in the middle, there are the kitchen staff standing in between groups of teachers. Pickets and maintenance crew are scattered amongst the rest, and two young pickets sitting on the roof next to a political banner. Phil Knibb and Cyril D'Arcy, as often during the campaign, are not visually present, but it was their skilful work which made the picture, and the occupation and campaign themselves, possible.

That evening a party was held in a local church hall, St. Pauls' Hall, for all teachers and local volunteers. Education Group chairman Dominic Brady arrived to give a short informal talk, and activists danced, listened to music, talked, and shared food and drink late into the night. John Bennett showed up, reportedly uninvited, for part of the evening. This party had been planned separately from a party held a week before in Netherley for 350 trade unionists who had supported the campaign. Helpers and teaching staff had not been invited to the earlier party though some helpers attended to serve food and drink to the trade unionists present. It had been intended as a thank-you party for those who had provided the absolutely essential financial support for the struggle. But the separation of these two events was resented by many helpers who thought there should have been a single victory party in which all who had been involved would participate together. This idea was strongly resisted by Phil Knibb, who insisted that they be separate affairs.

The two parties, two separate closing ceremonies for the protest movement, provided another indication of the old community power versus labour movement conflict which had appeared many times during the occupation. The labour movement and the grassroots of Croxteth never really met during the year of protest. Despite their mutual acknowledgement of each other's importance, they were linked together only through the campaign's leaders.

Just before this final party the teaching staff handed back their school keys. After the party they went home, most never to return to Croxteth. The teachers' last day had ended without any clarification of whether or not they could expect employment in the autumn or get into training courses. Nor were there yet any answers to the questions of how the community would continue to be involved in the school and what type of schooling was to be provided.

'CROXTETH COMMUNITY COMPREHENSIVE SCHOOL'

In August of 1983 I returned to Croxteth to find that plans had gone ahead for running the school during the 1983–84 school year. The missing 50 per cent of the funding for the school was to be supplied primarily by having the new teaching staff donate half of their salaries back to the school but also by getting grants here and there, some from the Labour-controlled Merseyside county council to run the adult education portions of the school. Phil and George Knibb worked hard to make the necessary financial arrangements. The Action Committee had been anxious to get a head teacher of their choice and an informal invitation was made to Henry Miller, who was on sabbatical for that year, to fill this post. Henry refused for various reasons and the job was given to Dr Allen Kaye, a former teacher in Croxteth with a Ph.D. in chemistry who had left teaching at Ellergreen to volunteer in the occupied school during the final two months of the occupation. Jackie Crowley was hired as school administrator to act as a go-between for the staff and the Action Committee, and Phil Knibb intended to remain in close contact with the school to make sure community input wasn't lost, although Phil was actually employed on a NACRO project in Netherley. Margaret Gaskell, Pat Brennen, and Debbie Johnson, all from Croxteth and all former activists in the occupation, were to work in the school as volunteer secretaries. Many of the former helpers got part-time work in the school kitchen and as cleaners. Jimmy Coza, a young former pupil and budding Croxteth poet who had served many overnight picket duties throughout the occupation, was hired as caretaker for the Parkstile building. Caretakers for the Stonebridge building were local residents as well, though not former helpers or Action Committee members.

The assessment made by George and Phil Knibb on the abilities of the volunteer staff resulted in only three choices from their number: Tony Gannon, Reza, and myself. Reza, Dr Kaye, Jackie, and I formed a hiring committee and added a fourth former volunteer to the staff: Hugh Sanderson, who had served as substitute teacher during the second and third terms. Keith Leatherbarrow and the former fifth-year pupil David Edwards were hired as laboratory assistants. All the rest of the teaching staff were new to the school.

A few things may be said about the 1983–84 school year of relevance to this study. No community curriculum was introduced into the school and the involvement of parents was now minimal, despite the hiring of many onto the ancillary staff. I constructed the timetable for the new school year and based it entirely on traditional subject divisions with examination and non-examination streams. The lack of a policy for involving parents and the absence of a highly motivated faculty made this curricular policy inevitable. The same constraints we'd faced the year before remained, while community involvement had been forced away.

On the first day of school Phil Knibb addressed an assembly of pupils. His beginning line was revealing: 'I hope that this is the last time that a parent addresses you from up here.' The policy was to keep the community and the teaching of secondary pupils as separate as possible. Phil was convinced that this was in the best interests of the pupils. Of all the activists involved in the battle for Croxteth Comprehensive, Phil's position as unchallenged leader made him feel most responsible for the education which future Croxteth pupils would have. The many problems which had occurred during the year of occupation, problems of discipline, timetabling, and staff organization, discouraged Phil from considering any experiments in community education. The presence of local adults in the school for the previous year had had both advantages and disadvantages and Phil believed that the safest and most responsible course to take now was to return Croxteth Comprehensive to educational professionals. The school was expected by many now to be run 'properly', its former disorganization and discipline problems to be eliminated by the removal of the local adults and the hiring of a properly trained and experienced staff.

Despite the fact that many of the former helpers and Action Committee members had been hired as ancillary staff of the school, the impression given in interviews was that they had felt pushed out of the school's other functions with the argument that their presence would interfere with the proper teaching of the pupils. Moreover, there weren't enough jobs for all the local activists; choices had to be made, and a fair number of old activists were pushed out altogether which caused some bitterness.

Within a few months of the 1983–84 school year it became obvious that the school had at least as many discipline problems as it had had during the year of occupation. By my own observations, discipline problems took place on a scale roughly equivalent to that of the most stable periods of the previous year. Reza claimed that they were possibly even worse. Phil Knibb, who retained close involvement in the school, very quickly realized that simply having a more trained and qualified staff without local adults to 'get in the way' didn't improve matters for the pupils. Within a month and a half of the new school year he expressed his belief that 'some mistakes were made' and that perhaps the old activists shouldn't have been discouraged from continuing to be involved in the school. At the end of the year, when Henry Stewart and I carried out some follow-up interviews, those former activists who had remained in the school, like Phil, Margaret and Pat, expressed further regrets over what had occurred. Following are some comments made by Margaret and Pat:

> Pat: See, what I think happened, because the school was getting taken over you know, getting a proper headmaster, proper staff you know, so we thought it was going to be run like a normal school, that's the idea we got. I mean, we thought the kids were just going to change overnight, you know. It just didn't work like that. Well, they said it would be better to let the teachers on their own. Really like, we were like the others, weren't we? [looking at Margaret]. We were getting thrown out [Margaret nods agreement].

> P.C.: Who was doing that?

> Pat: Nobody really, because everyone was getting told, like, not to come back. The only reason we were still here was, there were bringing Debbie and me because if we stayed we could show the new people the ropes in the office, that sort of thing.

> Margaret: I think we could have got over that with a little more communication. And I don't think it was deliberately done. I think what it was, people just assumed everyone knew what was going on and I think that if there'd been a bit more communication and letting everybody know what was happening.

> Pat: But they're still doing it now, aren't they?

> Margaret: It still goes on now and as I said, I don't think it's deliberate. I know that quick decisions have to be made, but at the same time, everybody involved should be brought together to let them know what is going on, because otherwise it makes the people not want to know any more. It all boils down to communication.

But it boiled down to more than communication, to the *reasons* why communication was poor between the leadership of the Action Committee and the local activists in the school. The loss of the community volunteers from the school was a result of their informal organization which had consisted of many passive and only a few active individuals (see also *Schooling and Culture*, summer 1984 issue for a discussion of the loss of community involvement after the occupation).

But in the autumn of 1984 Croxteth Independent Community Comprehensive School was about to become Croxteth Community Comprehensive with yet another new staff and a new head, Mr Blair, who had former experience as head of Netherley Community Comprehensive in Liverpool. Phil's hope was that improvements in the school would occur with its full funding and permanent staff, and Phil now wished to increase community involvement and power over the internal features of the school through the creation of a strong, active, local board of governors.

I left teaching at Croxteth School at the end of the 1984 school year but visited it one year later, towards the end of its first year as a county secondary school. Tony and Reza had remained as teachers for this year but Hugh and Jackie had left. Allen Kaye had remained for the year, this time as deputy head. In a talk with Tony it was discovered that, to his mind, much of the original spirit which had characterized the school during the year of occupation was gone. Disruption was still a constant problem and now little of the former unity existed between the staff and ancillary workers, partly due to differences in pay, partly due to the lack of a common purpose beyond that of working a job in the same buildings. Tony was due to leave teaching for a year of training but he expressed doubts as to whether or not he would in the end choose teaching as his career. One of our most successful and liked teachers, Tony had come to feel discouraged about the amount of good a teacher can do and noted his frustration with pupils who were so disruptive and who showed so little enthusiasm for schoolwork. Needless to say, Croxteth Community Comprehensive still had not made any explorations of a curricular policy in line with 'radical' community education theory. Neither were local residents and parents involved in the formulation of school curricular policy. Reza left Croxteth School the next year to take a job at another Liverpool secondary school.

Croxteth Community Comprehensive has, at the present time, a board of governors with strong representation from the old Action Committee, now disbanded. Phil Knibb is the chairman of the board of governors and Cyril and Collette D'Arcy are members. The physical aspects of the two school buildings have been greatly altered and improved and a paid member of staff has a full-time job as school–community liaison officer. Many adult education classes are being held within the building and plans for more of them exist. Phil and Margaret hold community jobs with offices in the Parkstile building and both feel positive about continued changes in the school towards greater community involvement. Phil Knibb has been working hard to increase community involvement. Cyril D'Arcy wrote of events since my departure:

> It is now becoming a true community school and linking with others in the area. Phil is doing an excellent job as full-time liaison officer. H.M. Inspectors of Schools came and were most impressed and full of praise.... School governors are very active in controlling what goes on in the school, probably more than any other governors countrywide.

Cyril added that those residents who are active on the board of governors (most of whom were formerly close to the leadership of the Action Committee) have taken an interest in curricular and pedagogic policies and are no longer daunted by the opinions of professional educators. The extent to which their activities have influenced school practices could only be determined through a new study, but on the whole it seems that some of the lessons of the occupation took time to become assimilated by residents. Ten of the old activists are on the school's board of governors; several others are also on the board of governors of Croxteth Infants' School and Croxteth Junior School. Hence a community school in the moderate sense discussed in Chapter 1 certainly does exist in Croxteth at the moment, and it may be developing towards greater community involvement.

A letter from Margaret Gaskell provides another perspective on Croxteth Community Comprehensive. It also comments on the effects of low educational budgets in Britain during the 1980s:

> I am still working in the school. It is very different than it was when we were running it. A lot of things are better, but the atmosphere and comradeship just isn't there as it was before.

> I don't think we can ever recapture that feeling again. Most of the teachers are very caring and really put themselves into the work with the kids. But not all have that dedication that we felt when you were here, Phil.

> We haven't had enough requisitions and some departments are really short on materials. It is very disappointing when you think how hard we fought for this school, and we can't even get some very basic things. A lot of money has been spent on the buildings, but without materials that is not much use, is it?

FINAL COMMENTS

The evidence of this study suggests that a more effective community school could have been developed in Croxteth after the year of occupation if certain policies of the Labour Party and/or the Liverpool Local Education Authority had been different. If, for example, it had been recognized by these groups that the presence of local residents in the school having the desire to remain involved in some capacity was educationally advantageous, they could have encouraged them to remain there, perhaps offering suggestions as to how their presence alongside teachers could be organized. It is not unlikely that the Action Committee leadership would have been responsive to such encouragement. If the Local Education Authority and Labour Party had had a policy which encouraged the development of a community curriculum, they could have supplied advisers to the staff with recommendations not only on educational content and practice but also on some of the organizational difficulties involved in keeping a continuous dialogue between parents and teachers – a dialogue which had certainly begun in the school during the occupation. Precedents exist for such arrangements (Poster 1982; Moon 1983a) of which the LEA could have made use.

The occupation of Croxteth Comprehensive resulted in a dependency on the Labour Party which was linked to the Action Committee solely through its leaders. Communication barriers existed between the leadership and the rest of the activists in a way which limited the influence the latter could have had on the crucial decisions made after the electoral victory of May 1983. Such barriers plus the passivity and lack of confidence on the part of most local participants may be expected conditions in a social movement of any kind. They should serve as lessons to those organizations supportive of grassroots movements: participation is itself a positive feature of community movements, a feature which must not be taken for granted but rather nurtured when it arises.

These lessons, however, have been absorbed in some form by Phil Knibb and other former members of the Croxteth Community Action Committee in the years which have followed. All in all, the battle for Croxteth Comprehensive was a great success which has charted new ground for other community movements. It generated rare links between the grassroots and the traditional organizations of the British labour movement. It has taught us that such links should be made with great care, however, so as not to rob the grassroots of its initiative and power. It demonstrated that alliances may be made as well between middle-class activists and the working class, though such alliances may be expected initially to impose problems of communication between their diverse cultures and perspectives. Finally, it demonstrates the advantages which grassroots participation in service institutions may yield. The British working class fought for many decades to win such state-funded services as free education. In Croxteth residents demonstrated that they could additionally win greater control over the logic and purposes of such services to free themselves from a dependency upon experts and professionals who don't always understand their needs.

The battle for Croxteth Comprehensive continues to this day as local residents involve themselves more and more in the internal features of the school. Let us hope that the battle may continue on other fronts as well: that the battle for Croxteth Comprehensive may serve as a precedent for other communities, and that its lessons may be noted and incorporated by those nationally based organizations concerned with the plight of urban communities like Croxteth.

Appendix: notes
on theory and method

THEORY

Broadly speaking, this book addresses itself to three areas of theoretical concern: the sociology of education, social movements, and social theory. The narrative is explicitly framed, from Chapter 1 on, as an investigation of issues pertaining to community education. In particular, a literature review of theory on community education is used to generate a focus upon the concept of power in the first chapter which the rest of the text returns to again and again. Chapters 2 through 4 weave the historical narrative about power relations built upon resources and constraints on action. In Chapter 5 the intersubjective structure of the occupied school is described as the basis for understanding a range of power relations which are then described and further analysed in the final chapters of the book. These include class relations, relations between leaders and led, and the continuously contested relations between teachers and local residents – pupils and adults. I use the term 'intersubjective structure', rather than 'culture', because my account emphasizes the active construction of interpretative schemes within the school by groups activists in interaction with each other, and thus their shifting and non-homogeneous nature. It is a feature of what has come to be called 'lived culture' (Thompson, E.P. 1963, 1978).

The contributions of this study to social theory and the analysis of social movements generally, however, are much more implicit than are its contributions to educational theory. Yet I wrote this book partially as an empirically embedded consideration of a number of broad issues within these two bodies of literature, and did so in a very conscious manner. I have so far published two papers in which I take explicit positions on the nature of social structure, interests, action and a broader consideration of power, through logical analysis alone (Carspecken 1988a, 1988b – see also 1989). These positions were worked out rather independently from my study of Croxteth Comprehensive and yet are illustrated in the pages of this book, though in unstated

ways. I lacked the space to make many points explicit and properly referenced to fine points in the relevant literature. My object in the following
paragraphs is to provide a very condensed summary of the theory I had in
mind when writing the previous pages. They are intended largely for the
reader familiar with these theoretical schools.

With respect to social theory, the entire account works from an integration
of perspectives developed by Anthony Giddens (1976, 1979, 1984), Jurgen
Habermas (esp. 1981), and the Birmingham school of cultural studies
(Johnson 1983, Willis 1977, 1981, 1983 – for an excellent American contribution to the Birmingham paradigm see Apple 1986). From Giddens I have
taken, and developed, two main ideas: his stratified model of action and his
important distinction between social system and social structure (these are
both more formalized versions of insights independently set forth in Willis's
classic study, 1977). From Habermas I have made use of the theory of
communicative action, adding some of his ideas on rationality to my study
of intersubjectivity and conflict resolution. From the Birmingham school I
have given attention to the modes in which tacit conditions of action may
become articulated by actors in ideological ways. These modes are partially
produced on social sites other than the specific ones under study, distributed
through complex processes to the sites in question, and drawn upon in both
transformative and reproductive ways by people who daily produce and
maintain their local culture.

Thus my concepts of ideological theme, reinforcing intersubjective relationships, and relationships of tension, while fitting immediately into
Giddens's concept of 'virtual structure', also directly involve Habermas's
theory of rationality. They are features of virtual structure, rather than social
system, for they are sets of generative rules, connected in various ways to
each other, which are implicated together in individual actions. As an
illustration of the structure of these rule sets I specify two sorts of relationship
which may exist between themes: relationships of tension and relationships
of reinforcement. In the case of reinforcement I indicate, but do not elaborate,
that reinforcing relationships may be either those of logical implication or of
homology. Each type of reinforcing relationship has different implications
for conflict resolution because each differ in the ways they may meet
rationality requirements. Homologous relationships are fairly loose with
respect to rationality requirements and consist primarily of normative linkages alone, or of linkages forged within the identity complexes of specific
activists. They chain themes associated with action on distinctive social sites:
the home, community, school, and occupational sites of the Croxteth residents in this particular study. Linkages of logical implication, on the other
hand, are much tighter and chain themes which come into play on a single
site – in this case the occupied school of Croxteth. Following another

distinction elaborated by Giddens, I can say that homologous themes within the virtual structure of the activists owe their existence, as a structure, to processes of system integration developing over long stretches of time. This is the particular way in which intersubjectivity is related to routine social action in the case of homologous relationships. Themes linked through logical implication, on the other hand, are related to social action through the stronger requirements of social integration – the development of consistent routines between actors over shorter periods of time within the same social site in face-to-face interactions.

I draw upon Habermas's theory of rationality when I describe the conflicts which arose between actors. My discussion of the disputes between the pro-community and social-wage groups in Chapter 7, for example, demonstrates the progressive articulation of formerly tacit intersubjective themes into discursive arguments and refers to the types of rational claim made by activists as debates between these competing groups escalated. Arguments moved towards Habermas' original concept of 'discourse' (see McCarthy 1982) as background assumptions took on verbal representations in the heated debates of November 1982. Debates involved intersecting sets of rational claims: from empirically referenced claims (which policies would work best to achieve agreed upon goals), through claims of which policy was normatively right and why (what the real purposes of education and political struggle ought to be), to positions tied tightly to the identities which the activists struggled to maintain for themselves (culturally embedded concepts of 'adult', 'male', 'female', 'teacher', and so on). Each of these types of claims was related to the practices which came into dispute between activists via Habermas' three dimensions of action: goal-rational, normative and dramaturgical (where identities became threatened). When verbal disputes developed about these practices the three sorts of rational claim were made, always in complex and intersecting ways. I present the movement towards discourse as only a partial development, skewed at all times by uncontested relations of power existing between the competing groups. This may correctly be interpreted as a delineation of factors preventing the formation of Habermas' 'ideal speech' situation. Consistent with Giddens's theory of stratified action, I seek at all times to explicate the unarticulated conditions which shaped the outcome of these debates. I also indicate that relationships of tension between themes may be tolerated by those who hold to them simultaneously as long as social interactions do not require their articulation and thus rational justification.

When I speak of the origins of intersubjective structure and the basis for their relationships in either homologous or logical forms I have Giddens' concept of social system in mind. Ideological themes, especially in the case of those themes held by the local residents of Croxteth, are developed and maintained in social routines linking the home, school and work site through the life-cycle of the individuals concerned. A social system is precisely an empirically observable set of social routines on a series of sites which maintain and reinforce each other over time, often through unintended consequences. Intersubjectivity, or virtual structure, corresponds to these routines by directing the volition of the agents in limited directions. I believe that Giddens has best formalized the distinction between intersubjectivity and patterned social activity in his differentiation between structure and system, but the same idea has been expressed by Willis whose specification of locking processes (system integration) and isomorphic relations (homologous intersubjective linkages) directly parallel several of my own categories (see Willis 1983).

Lastly, consistent with Giddens' stratified model of action, I emphasize both the extent to which ideological themes are discursively available to activists in this story and how empowerment accompanies a growth in the articulation of themes. Not only articulation, but the mode or the particular discourse used in the articulation, are noted as having important implications for power relations between groups of people.

The literature on social movements also informed my construction of this narrative though its presence is even less explicit than is the literature on social theory. The campaign for Croxteth Comprehensive was in every way an example of an urban protest movement structured by the relationship of a residential population to a state-funded service. During the 1970s a school of neo-Marxist theorists interested in such movements developed a fairly consistent analysis of the post-World War II West European State which predicted events such as the Croxteth closure (Castells 1977, 1978; Pickvance 1976; Saunders 1981, 1983; Offe 1974a, b). In Chapter 2 I trace out the structural determinations of the school closure which agree broadly with the analysis of this particular school of social movement theorists. However, I also show that the closure of Croxteth Comprehensive was not inevitable given this structural context, but rather only made possible by it. It was the coincidence of many factors, both structural and contingent in nature, which closed the school. In Chapter 3 I shift the level of analysis downwards from considerations of broad economic relations and the state to a look at the protest group which formed to protest the closure within Croxteth. This chapter would be most interesting to social movement theorists who use the resource mobilization school in their work (Oberschall 1973, Gamson 1975, Tilly and Tilly 1981, Zald and McCarthy 1979). This is primarily because I have found their categories most useful for the study of group behaviour: the horizontal bonds which help to unify communities about single issues like a school closure, the basis of leadership formation, and the field of possible strategies and tactics which available resources delineate.

The chapters following Chapter 3, however, shift the analysis down further, from the protest group to the individuals within a protest group – the interpersonal conflicts they engage in, the real reasons they have for joining and remaining within a movement, the cultural schemes they make use of to understand and justify their involvement. The social movement theory which best informs this analysis is that of the work on new social movements. This literature has taken issue with both of the other schools mentioned above by insisting on the importance of culture and identity in social movements (Melucci 1989, Cohen 1983, 1985). Social movements according to this view alter the possible identities actors may take on by shifting the cultural codes through which identities are constructed and maintained. In Chapter 8, especially, I discuss the personal importance of the Croxteth occupation for a number of distinct groups of participants. In each case the issue of identity is shown to be overwhelmingly important. The occupation resulted in new possibilities for taking on expanded roles and identities for many, but not all, of the participants. The implicit theory addressed is concerned with the nature of interests. Interests are not merely economic or material in nature but cultural and intersubjective as well. In general, people need to maintain acceptable identities, feel empowered, and experience dignity, as much as they need state funded services like schools. The possibilities for meeting such interests are structured by cultural and ultimately structural conditions, just as the possibilities for meeting material needs are. However, unlike many from the new social movement camp, I don't think a sharp dichotomy between resource mobilization or structural approaches and the identity-oriented school is either helpful or valid. I think the differences between these schools have more to do with differences in the objects they have taken for study than to purely analytical concerns. The more analysis reaches downwards to the individuals constructing relationships within movements, the more the issues of identity, subjectivity, and culture will have to be addressed to explain what is occurring. The more broad structural issues, such as the fiscal difficulties faced by the state in periods of economic recession, are taken as the object of study the less will identity come directly into the analysis and the more the concept of interests will take a purely material appearance. Thus this narrative is built partially about an integration of three schools on social movements through a descending analysis begun in Chapter 2 and reaching its final descent in Chapter 5. A certain primacy is accorded to economic conditions, an implicit but qualified agreement with the economics in the last instance position, by the way I've integrated the three schools.

Yet social movement theory is nowhere directly discussed or referenced in the text itself and, in fact, my use of the frameworks of Giddens, Habermas, and Birmingham cultural studies basically supersedes the specific issues raised in social movement theory anyway. The theory of structuration, in particular, points the way towards redefining and integrating key concepts in each of these approaches to social movements by specifying the different levels of abstraction used to frame objects of study (rather like Giddens' distinction between institutional and action analysis; see Giddens 1979). In a recent paper (1989) I compare four schools of work on social movements according to their respective understandings of action, structure, interests, and power, and indicate grounds for their integration partially through applications of some of Giddens' work.

What does this particular study add, if anything, to the social theory of Giddens, Habermas, and Birmingham? Most obviously it demonstrates the usefulness of these theoretical models by taking them out of their abstract and formalized realms and integrating them into a historical account. In most places they are so integrated into the story as to be almost unnoticeable. In addition, I have in a number of respects filled these theories out a bit by introducing the concept of types of linkage in intersubjective structure and by demonstrating the existence of a large realm of conflict resolution falling between Habermas's discourse and coercion. I hope to make these theoretical contributions more explicit in future publications. Meanwhile they are carried by the narrative of Croxteth Comprehensive, awaiting notice and further interpretation by its readers.

METHOD

My basic method of collecting information on the Croxteth Campaign was historical and ethnographic. Chapters 2 and 3 are historical reconstructions of events which took place before my arrival at the school. They are based on a vast amount of material. It includes long interviews with many people who had been active from the campaign's beginning, with the education spokesmen from each of Liverpool's three political parties (David Alton for the Liberal Party), the Liverpool director of education, Liverpool city planners, the former head and deputy head of Croxteth Comprehensive, and others. I also unearthed a good deal of documents pertaining to the school's closure: city reports, minutes of council meetings, newspaper articles, reports prepared by the former teaching staff at the school, school records, and a large quantity of letters exchanged between the Action Committee and various officials between 1981 and 1983.

My ethnographic methods included constant observations, recorded on the spot, of school meetings, Action Committee meetings, demonstrations, corridor behaviour, classroom activities, behaviour on school grounds, comments overheard in local shops, the tenants' group, the Croxteth Labour Club, the Lobster Pub, and various homes of activists and non-active residents. I also interviewed people constantly throughout the year of occupation. Interviews included a programme of administering semi-structured question domains to most teachers, residents and pupils as well as many spontaneous, issue-oriented conversations. These were all tape-recorded and transcribed.

Because I was so highly involved myself in the campaign I often found myself either caught between the competing groups described in this study or actively on one particular side (usually, but not always, the teachers' side). Naturally this affected the sort of information to which I had access, and the types of comments people would provide. Thus some of the events referred to in the narrative are of a disputed nature (e.g. the conflict between Phil Knibb and Ev Loftus). However, in all such cases I sought to elicit a variety of reports on the events in dispute and my narrative focuses upon these reports, upon what they tell us of the interpretative schemes of those who provided them, rather than upon objective claims of what really occurred. Where I describe events as actually occurring, I had the consensus of the majority of activists on them. I constantly used triangulation, checking my own perceptions against those of other activists. Early drafts of several of the chapters were sent out to other participants to solicit their comments and the narrative has been amended where conflicting views were discovered.

Finally, a good deal of this narrative concerns itself with interpretations of behaviour leading to the construction of intersubjective frameworks, some of which I claim lay outside the discursive consciousness of those drawing upon them. My method of interpretation in this case consisted of something akin to strip analysis (Agar 1986) – the examination of consistencies in my ethnographic notes and the construction of tacit cultural frameworks in order to explain them. My conclusions (eg. that many of the teachers viewed the occupation through what I call the theme of community power) were checked by looking for consistencies in the field notebooks and through interviews with the relevant activists which elicited their own interpretation of events. Strips of action and discourse could be consistently predicted once I had formulated the tacit schemes. Moreover, I found that activists themselves formulated versions of the schemes when conditions within the school altered and debates forced them to articulate what had formerly been unnoticed and taken for granted.

Bibliography

Agar, Michael H. (1986) *Speaking of Ethnography*, Newbury Park, CA: Sage.
Apple, Michael (1979) *Ideology and Curriculum*, London: Routledge and Kegan Paul.
Apple, Michael (ed.) (1982) *Cultural and Economic Reproduction in Education*, London: Routledge and Kegan Paul.
Apple, Michael (1983) *Education and Power*, London: Routledge and Kegan Paul.
Apple, Michael (1986) *Teacher and Texts*, London: Routledge and Kegan Paul.
Bachrach, P. and Baratz, M. (1970) *Power and Poverty*, New York: Oxford University Press.
Barton, L. and Meighan, R. (eds) (1979) *Schools, Pupils, and Deviance*, Driffield: Nafferton Books.
Bell, Colin and Newby, Howard (1971) *Community Studies*, London: Allen and Unwin.
Berg, Leila (1968) *Risinghill: Death of a Comprehensive School*, Harmondsworth: Pelican Books.
Bernstein, Basil (1977a); 'Pedagogies, Visible and Invisible', in J. Karabel and A. H. Halsey (eds), *Power and Ideology in Education*, New York: Oxford University Press.
Bernstein, Basil (1977b) 'Social Class, Language, and Socialisation', in J. Karabel and A. H. Halsey (eds), *Power and Ideology in Education*, New York: Oxford University Press.
Beynon, Huw (1973) *Working for Ford*, London: Penguin.
Bourdieu, Pierre and Passeron, Jean-Claude (1977) *Reproduction in Education, Society, and Culture*, London: Sage Publications.
Bowles, S. and Gintis, H. (1976) *Schooling in Capitalist America*, London: Routledge and Kegan Paul.
Boyd, John (1977) *Community Education and Urban Schools*, London: Longman.
Broadfoot, Patricia (1979) *Assessment, Schools, and Society*, London: Methuen.
Buhr, W. and Frederick, P. (eds) (1982) *Planning in Stagnating Regions*, Baden Baden: Nomos Verlagsgesellschaft.
Carspecken, Phil (1983) 'What kind of education?', *Schooling and Culture*, 13, Summer.
Carspecken, Phil (1985) 'Community action and community schooling: the campaign to save Croxteth Comprehensive' in Geoff Walford, *School Knowledge and Social Control*, London: Methuen.
Carspecken, Phil (1987a) 'The campaign to save Croxteth Comprehensive: an ethno-

graphic study of a protest movement', unpublished Ph. D. thesis.

Carspecken, Phil (1987b) 'Schooling and working-class culture: an analysis of power, structure, and secondary schooling', Aston Doctoral Working Papers, 119, Birmingham, United Kingdom.

Carspecken, Phil (1988a) 'Social theory and social movements I: theoretical approaches', Aston Doctoral Working Papers, no. 123, Birmingham, United Kingdom.

Carspecken, Phil (1988b) 'Social theory and social movements II: concepts and paradigms', Aston Doctoral Working Papers, no. 124, Birmingham, United Kingdom.

Carspecken, Phil (1988c) 'The theory of community education: a social theoretical critique', Aston Doctoral Working Papers, no. 125, Birmingham, United Kingdom.

Carspecken, Phil (1989) 'Uniting the general and particular in the study of social movements', Unpublished conference paper presented to the Southwestern Sociological Association, March 1989.

Carspecken, Phil (in press) 'Education limited', in CCCS, *Education Still Possible, Schooling and Training in England Since 1979*, London: Unwin Hyman.

Carspecken, Phil and Miller, Henry (1983) 'Parental choice and community control: the case of Croxteth Comprehensive', in Anne Marie Wolpe and James Donalds 1983.

Carspecken, Phil and Miller, Henry (1984a) 'Community education in Croxteth', *Forum*, Autumn 1984.

Carspecken, Phil and Miller, Henry (1984b) 'Croxteth Comprehensive: curriculum and social relationships in an occupied school', *Socialism and Education*, 11, no.1.

Castells, Manuel (1977) *The Urban Question*, London: Edward Arnold.

Castells, Manuel (1978) *City, Class and Power*, London: Macmillan Press.

Central Advisory Council for Education (1963) *Half Our Future: A Report of the Central Advisory Council for Education* (Newsome report), London: HMSO.

Centre for Contemporary Cultural Studies (CCCS) (1981) *Unpopular Education, Schooling and Social Democracy in England since 1944*, London: Hutchinson and Company.

Centre for Contemporary Cultural Studies (CCCS) (in press) *Education Still Possible, Schooling and Training in England Since 1979*, London: Unwin Hyman.

Clarke, John, Critcher, Chas, and Johnson, Richard (1979) *Working Class Culture: Studies in History and Theory*, London: Hutchinson and Co.

Clegg, S. (1974) *The Theory of Power and Organization*, Henley-on-Thames, Oxon: Routledge and Kegan Paul.

Clegg, S. (1975) *Power, Rule and Domination*, London: Routledge and Kegan Paul.

Coates, K. and Silburn, R. (1970) 'Education in poverty', in Rubenstein, D. and Stoneman, C. (eds), *Education for Democracy*, Harmondsworth: Penguin.

Cohen, Jean (1983) 'Rethinking social movements', in *Berkeley Journal of Sociology*, 28, 97–113.

Cohen, Jean (1985) 'Strategy or identity: new theoretical paradigms and contemporary social movements', *Social Research*, 52, no. 4, Winter.

Collins, Randall (1979) *The Credential Society: An Historical Sociology of Education and Stratification*, New York: Academic Press.

Connell, R. W., Ashenden, D. J., Kesslerl, S. (1982) *Making the Difference*, Sydney: Allen and Unwin.

Cormack, Margaret (1980) *Liverpool Housing: Facts and Figures*, Liverpool: Liverpool Council for Voluntary Service.

Crick, Michael (1984) *Militant*, London: Faber and Faber.

Croxteth Area Working Party (1983) *Croxteth Area: Report of the Working Party Appointed to Consider the Needs of the Area*, Liverpool City Council.

Dale, R. (1979) 'Control, accountability, and William Tyndale', in L. Barton and R. Meighan (eds), *Schools, Pupils, and Deviance*, Driffield: Nafferton Books.

Department of Education and Science (1982) *Report by HM Inspectors on Educational Provision by Liverpool Education Authority in the Toxteth Area*, London: DES.

Evans, Bob (1983) 'The Countesthrope team system: towards the mini school' in Bob Moon, *Comprehensive Schools: Challenge and Change*, Windsor: NFER-Nelson Publishing Co., Ltd.

Everhart, Robert B. (1983) *Reading, Writing and Resistance: Adolescence and Labor in a Junior High School*, Routledge and Kegan Paul.

Ferguson, Steven and Brown, Peter (1982) 'Issues relating to decision making in the planning of inner city primary school provision', in W. Buhr and P. Frederick (eds), op cit.

Flecknoe, Mervyn (1983) 'The Sutton Centre, Mansfield, Nottinghamshire: a philosophy of assessment', in Bob Moon (ed.), *Comprehensive Schools: Challenge and Change*, Windsor: NFER-Nelson Publishing Co., Ltd.

Fletcher, Colin (1980) 'Developments in Community Education: A Current Account', in C. Fletcher and N. Thompson (eds), *Issues in Community Education*, Barcombe (Sussex): Falmer Press.

Fletcher, Colin and Thompson, Neil (eds) (1980) *Issues in Community Education*, Barcombe (Sussex): Falmer Press.

Friend, Andrew (1981) *Failed Strategies, Falling Investment: Liverpool's Housing Programme and Government Policy*, London: The Catholic Housing Aid Society.

Galton, Maurice and Moon, Bob (1983) *Changing Schools, Changing Curriculum*, Harper and Row.

Gamson, William A. (1975) *The Strategy of Social Protest*, Homewood, Ill.: Dorsey Press.

Giddens, Anthony (1976) *New Rules of Sociological Method*, London: Hutchinson and Co.

Giddens, Anthony (1979) *Central Problems in Social Theory*, London: Macmillan Press.

Giddens, Anthony (1984) *The Constitution of Society*, Cambridge: Polity Press.

Giroux, Henry (1981) *Ideology, Culture and the Process of Schooling*, Philadelphia: Temple University Press.

Giroux, Henry (1983) *Theory and Resistance in Education: A Pedagogy for the Opposition*, London: Heinemann Educational Books.

Habermas, Jurgen (1981a) 'New social movements', *Telos*, 49, Autumn.

Habermas, Jurgen (1981b) *The Theory of Communicative Action, Vol. 1: Reason and the Rationalisation of Society*, Boston: Beacon Press.

Halsey, A. M. (ed.) (1972) *Educational Priority*, London: HMSO.

Hargreaves, David (1982) *The Challenge of the Comprehensive School: Culture, Curriculum, and Community*, London: Routledge and Kegan Paul.

Hatch, S. and Moyland, S. (1972) 'The role of the community school', in J. Raynor and J. Harden (eds), *Equality and City Schools, Readings in Urban Education*, vol. 2, London: Routledge and Kegan Paul.

Hyde, Francis E. (1971) *Liverpool and the Mersey: The Development of a Port, 1700–1970*, Newton Abbot: David and Charles.

Johnson, Richard (1979) 'Three problematics: elements of a theory of working-class culture', in J. Clarke, C. Critcher, and R. Johnson (eds), *Working Class Culture: Studies in History and Theory*, London: Hutchinson and Co.

Johnson, Richard (1983) *What is Cultural Studies Anyway?* , CCCS Stenciled Occasional Paper, 74.

Karabel, J. and Halsey, A. H. (eds) (1977) *Power and Ideology in Education*, New York: Oxford University Press.

Keddie, N. (1971a) 'Classroom knowledge', in M. F. D. Young (ed), *Knowledge and Control: New Directions for the Sociology of Education*, London: Collier-Macmillan.

Keddie, N. (1971b) *Tinker, Tailor... The Myth of Cultural Deprivation* (Introduction). Harmondsworth: Penguin.

Liverpool City Council (1983a) *Bulletin of the Joint Steward's Committee*, Liverpool: LCC.

Liverpool City Council (1983b) *Policy and Finance Report: A14*, Liverpool: LCC.

Liverpool City Council (1984) *Campaign Bulletin*, 1, January.

Liverpool City Planning Department (1982) *Planning Information Digest: Economy 1982*, Liverpool: LCC.

Liverpool Education Committee (1965–77) *Statistics of Education*, Liverpool: LCC.

Liverpool Education Committee (1978) *Reorganisation of Non-Roman Catholic Secondary Schools*, Liverpool: LCC.

Liverpool Education Committee (1978–84) *Form 7 Statistics*, Liverpool: LCC.

Liverpool Education Committee (1983) *Proposals for County Secondary Reorganisation: A Consultative Document*, Liverpool: LCC.

Liverpool Policy and Finance Committee (1973) *Provision of Amenities on the Croxteth Estate: Report of the Chief Executive and Town Clerk*, Liverpool: LCC, TC/181/73.

Lukes, Steven (1974) *Power, A Radical View*, London: Macmillan.

Marriner, Sheila (1982) *The Economic and Social Development of Merseyside*, London: Croom Helm Ltd.

McCarthy, Thomas (1982) *The Critical Theory of Jurgen Habermas*, Cambridge, MA: MIT Press.

McLaren, Peter (1989) *Life in Schools: An Introduction to Critical Pedagogy in the Foundations of Education*, New York: Longman.

Melucci, Alberto (1985) 'The symbolic challenge of contemporary movements', *Social Research*, 52, No. 4, Winter, 789–816.

Melucci, Alberto (1989) *Nomads of the Present, Social Movements and Individual Needs in Contemporary Society*, Philadelphia: Temple University Press.

Merson, M. and Campbell, R. (1974) 'Community education: instruction for inequality', *Education for Teaching*, 93, Spring.

Midwinter, Eric (1972) *Priority Education*, Harmondsworth: Penguin.

Midwinter, Eric (1973) *Patterns of Community Education*, London: Ward Lock Educational.

Midwinter, Eric (1975) *Education and the Community*, London: Allen and Unwin.

Moon, Bob (ed) (1983a) *Comprehensive Schools: Challenge and Change*, Windsor: NFER-Nelson Publishing Co.

Moon, Bob (1983b) 'Stantonbury Campus, Milton Keynes, Buckinghamshire: A study in teacher responses to innovation', in Bob Moon (ed.), *Comprehensive Schools: Challenge and Change*, Windsor: NFER-Nelson Publishing Co.

Oberschall, Anthony (1973) *Social Conflict and Social Movements*, Englewood

Cliffs, NJ: Prentice-Hall.

Offe, Claus (1974a) *Contradictions of the Welfare State*, edited by J. Keane, London: Hutchinson.

Pickvance, Chris (ed) (1976) *Urban Sociology: Critical Essays*, London: Methuen and Co.

Poster, Cyril (1982) *Community Education, Its Development and Management*, London: Heinemann Educational Books.

Raynor, J. and Harden, J. (eds) (1972) *Equality and City Schools, Readings in Urban Education*, vol. 2, London: Routledge and Kegan Paul.

Salter, Brian and Tapper, Ted (1981) *Education, Politics and the State: The Theory and Practice of Educational Change*, London: Grant McIntyre.

Saunders, Peter (1981) *Social Theory and the Urban Question*, London: Hutchinson.

Saunders, Peter (1983) *Urban Politics, A Sociological Interpretation*, London: Hutchinson.

Thompson, E. P. (1963) *The Making of the English Working Class*, London: Victor Gollancz.

Thompson, E. P. (1978) *The Poverty of Theory and Other Essays*, London: Merlin Press.

Thompson, Neil (1983) 'Abraham Moss Centre, Manchester: the experience of continuing education', in Bob Moon (ed.), *Comprehensive Schools: Challenge and Change*, Windsor: NFER-Nelson Publishing Co., Ltd.

Tilly, Charles, Tilly, Louise, and Tilly, Richard (1975) *The Rebellious Century, 1830–1930*, London: J. M. Dent and Sons.

Tilly, Louise, and Tilly, Charles (1981) *Class Conflict and Collective Action*, Beverly Hills, CA: Sage Publications.

Topping, Phil and Smith, George (1977) *Government Against Poverty?* Liverpool Community Development Project, 1970–75, Home Office.

Vigier, François (1970) *Change and Apathy, Liverpool and Manchester During the Industrial Revolution*, Cambridge, MA: MIT Press.

Walford, Geoff (1985) *Schooling in Turmoil*, Beckenham: Croom Helm Ltd.

Whitty, Geoff (1977) *School Knowledge and Social Control*, Milton Keynes: Open University, Units 14/15 of Schooling and Society.

Whitty, Geoff (1985) *School Knowledge and Social Control: Curricular Theory, Research and Politics*, London: Methuen and Co.

Whitty, Geoff and Young, M. (eds) (1976) *Explorations in the Politics of School Knowledge*, Driffield: Nafferton Books.

Williams, Michael R. (1989) *Neighborhood Organizing for School Reform*, New York: Teachers' College Press.

Williams, Wyn and Robins, Wayne (1980) 'Observations on the California Case', in C. Fletcher and N. Thompson (eds) *Issues in Community Education*, Barcombe (Sussex): Falmer Press.

Willis, Paul (1977) *Learning to Labour: How Working-Class Kids Get Working-Class Jobs*, London: Gower.

Willis, Paul (1981) 'Cultural production is different from cultural reproduction is different from social reproduction is different from reproduction', *Interchange*, 12 (2/3).

Willis, Paul (1983) 'Cultural production and theories of reproduction', in L. Barton and Walker.

Wrong, Dennis (1988) *Power, Its Forms, Bases, and Uses*, Chicago: University of Chicago Press.

Zald, Mayer N. and McCarthy, John D. (1979) 'Utilitarian logic in the resource management perspective', in M. Zald and J. McCarthy, *The Dynamics of Social Movements*, Cambridge: Winthrop.

Index